OCR RELIGIOUS STUDIES

A2

Philosophy and Ethics

OCR and Heinemann are working together to provide better support for you

Chris Eyre
Richard Knight
Graeme Rowe
Series Editor: Ina Taylor

Official Publisher Partnership

Heinemann is an imprint of Pearson Education Limited, a company incorporated in England and Wales, having its registered office at Edinburgh Gate, Harlow, Essex, CM20 2JE. Registered company number: 872828

www.heinemann.co.uk

Heinemann is a registered trademark of Pearson Education Limited

First published 2009

13 12 11 10 09
10 9 8 7 6 5 4 3 2 1

British Library Cataloguing in Publication Data
A catalogue record for this book is available from the British Library

ISBN 978 0 43530 358 7

Edited by Beeline Publishing Partnerships Ltd
Typeset by Phoenix Photosetting, Chatham, Kent
Original illustrations © Pearson Education Limited 2008
Cover design by Dickidot Ltd
Picture research by Suzi Paz
Cover photo/illustration © Duncan Walker/iStockphoto
Printed in Scotland by Scotprint

Websites
There are links to relevant websites in this book. In order to ensure that the links are up to date, that the links work, and that the sites are not inadvertently linked to sites that could be considered offensive, we have made the links available on the Heinemann website at www.heinemann.co.uk/hotlinks. When you access the site, the express code is 3587P.

Contents

Teacher Introduction

Notes for teachers

This book is designed to support units G581 (A2 Philosophy of Religion) and G582 (A2 Religious Ethics) of OCR's new A2 Religious Studies specification. The specification builds on the knowledge, understanding and skills that candidates may have developed through the study of GCSE Religious Studies or Religious Education at AS level.

Structure of the book

OCR A2 Philosophy and Ethics is divided into 11 chapters. Chapters 1–5 cover the A2 Philosophy of Religion element of the specification (G581) as follows:

- Chapter 1: Religious language
- Chapter 2: Religious experience
- Chapter 3: Miracle
- Chapter 4: Attributes of God
- Chapter 5: Life and death: the soul

Chapters 6–11 cover the A2 Religious Ethics element of the specification (G852) as follows:

- Chapter 6: Meta-ethics
- Chapter 7: Free will and determinism
- Chapter 8: Conscience
- Chapter 9: Virtue ethics
- Chapter 10: Environmental and business ethics
- Chapter 11: Sexual ethics.

The chapters themselves are typically arranged as follows:

- Chapter openers – contain the learning objectives, a 'what do you think?' question based on the chapter content and an introduction to the chapter.
- Content organised by topic in double-page spreads, with accompanying activities.
- A visual spread linking the main ideas, issues and thinkers covered in the chapter.
- An Exam Café section, providing revision tips and exam preparation.

How to use this book

Engagement with, and understanding of, the key philosophical and ethical concepts needs to run throughout teaching and learning for OCR Philosophy and Ethics. *OCR A2 Philosophy and Ethics* has been specifically written to provide comprehensive coverage of these concepts, thinkers and movements. The accompanying Activities, Fact Box, For Debate, Further Research, Making Links and Stretch & Challenge features are designed to test and consolidate student's understanding and skills.

The content of this book is further supported by extra resources in the Planning and Delivery Resource (PDR) and Resource Browser CD-ROM. These resources vary from worksheets, to original extracts from key thinkers to audio, video and PowerPoint® resources. Where the student book content is supported by extra material in the PDR, this is indicated on the page with the following icon . Similarly, where extra resources are available on the CD-ROM, this is signified by the following icon .

Methods of assessment

The A2 GCE is made up of two mandatory units chosen from nine options. This book supports two of these nine units: G581 (A2 Philosophy of Religion) and G582 (A2 Religious Ethics). At A2, units are externally assessed and each unit forms 50% of the corresponding four-unit Advanced GCE.

Philosophy of Religion is assessed by a written paper, 1.5 hours for 70 marks. Candidates are required to answer two essay questions from a choice of four.

Religious Ethics is also assessed by a written paper, 1.5 hours for 70 marks. Again, candidates are required to answer two essay questions from a choice of four.

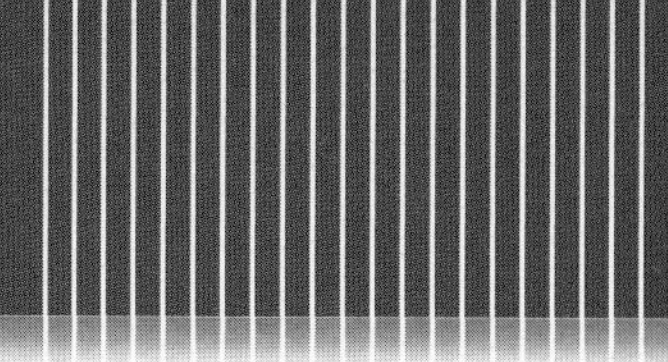

Student introduction

How to use this book

OCR A2 Philosophy and Ethics has been specifically written to support you through the study of the OCR A2 Philosophy of Religion and A2 Religious Ethics units. This book will help you to understand the thinkers, theories and concepts that underlie the topics you are studying. You should refer back to this book during your revision. The Exam Café sections at the end of each chapter will be particularly helpful as you prepare for your exam.

Each chapter in the book makes use of the following features:

Activities

The activities have been designed to help you understand the specification content.

For Debate

Each chapter will include some For Debate activities, made up of statements, quotes or concepts for you to discuss in pairs, as a group or as a whole class. The For Debate activities have been designed to promote the sharing of ideas, to improve your speaking and listening skills, and also to challenge you to argue from viewpoints that you may not necessarily agree with.

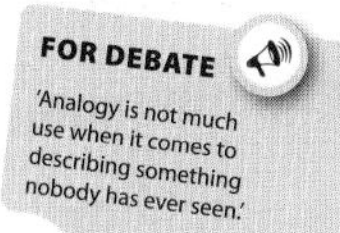

Stretch and Challenge

This feature is designed to stretch your knowledge and understanding. Sometimes this means going beyond the requirements of the specification to further inform your understanding of a concept. Or it could be more probing questions about the topic studied requiring you to think and respond at a higher level.

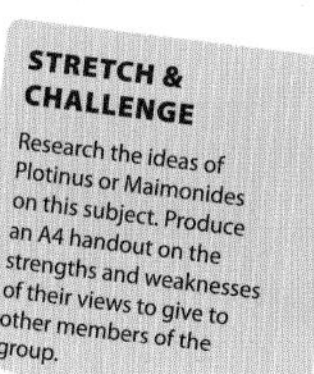

Further research

Ideas for further research into particular topics. Completing the Further Research activities will extend your knowledge of the specification content.

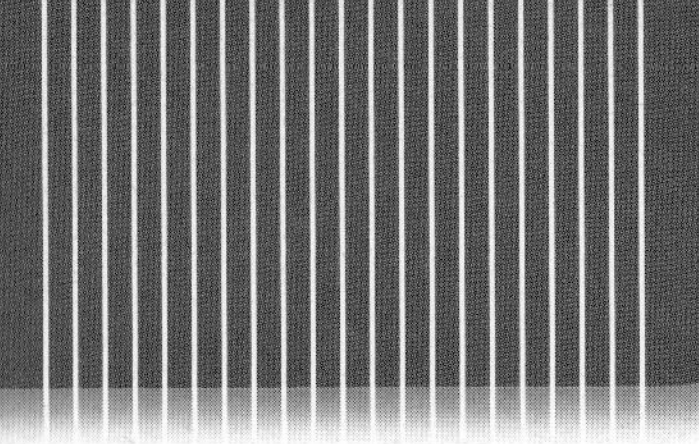

Key words

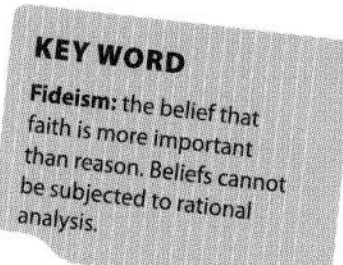

Definitions of new words can be found in the margin next to where the word appears in the text to help put the word in context.

Making Links

This shows the links that exist between units and encourages you to explore them.

Fact Box

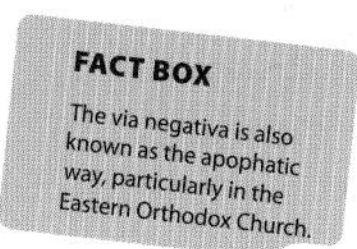

Occasional fact boxes provide additional information you may find useful.

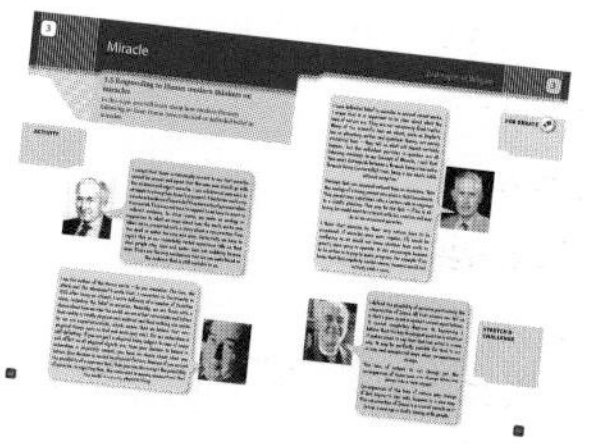

Each chapter also contains a visual spread, where the key topics, ideas or thinkers studied in that chapter are brought together and compared visually.

Exam Café

The Exam Café is the ideal place to be if you are revising content, practising exam questions or if you need some advice about how to be successful at A2 Religious Studies.

Here you'll find lots of ideas to help you prepare for your exams. So **Relax**, because there's handy advice from fellow students, **Refresh** yourself with summaries of the key ideas, and Get That **Result** with lots of hints and tips direct from the examiners.

Acknowledgements

Photo acknowledgements

2007 Stefan Jeremiah/WireImage/Getty Images – 163; Aldo Murillo/iStockphoto – 118; Alfred Eisenstaedt/Time & Life Pictures/Getty Images – 137 (Niebuhr); Andrew Butterton/Alamy – 146; Basque Country: Mark Baynes/Alamy – 76; Bettmann/CORBIS – 136 (Darrow); Bettmann/CORBIS – 62 (bottom); bonnie jacobs/iStockPhoto – 165; Christian Liewig/Corbis – 167; Classic Image/Alamy – 137 (Hume); Classic Image/Alamy – 137 (Locke); Corbis RF/Alamy – 107; David McGlynn/Getty Images – 124–25; Dorling Kindersley/Getty – 16; EMPICS – 117; G Stock/Alamy – 122; GoGo Images Corporation/Alamy – 216; Graça Victoria/iStockPhoto – 12; Heide Benser/zefa/Corbis – 206; Ian Berry/Magnum Photos – 114; imagebroker/Alamy – 202; INTERFOTO Pressebildagentur/Alamy – 150; Iofoto/Dreamstime.com – 40; iStockPhoto – 108; iStockPhoto – 168; iStockPhoto – 180; iStockPhoto – 210; iStockPhoto – 218; James Andanson/Apis/ Sygma/ Corbis – 137 (Sartre); Janice Richard/iStockPhoto – 21; Jeff Morgan education/Alamy – 136 (Honderich); Joe Gough/iStockPhoto – 54; John Robertson/Alamy – 120; Karina Tischlinger/iStockphoto – 200; Kathy deWitt/Alamy – 187; Kenneth C. Zirkel/iStockPhoto – 132; Leabrooks Photography/Alamy – 103; Lebrecht Music and Arts Photo Library/Alamy – 136 (Kant); Liz Leyden/iStockPhoto – 195; LOOK Die Bildagentur der Fotografen GmbH/Alamy – 72; Marco Secchi/Alamy – 89; Marko Georgiev/Getty Images – 141; Mary Evans Picture Library/Alamy – 100; Mary Evans Picture Library/Alamy – 137 (D'Holbach); Michael Ventura/Alamy – 135; Mike Goldwater/Alamy – 157; moodboard/Alamy – 96; Nasa – 182; Nejron/Dreamstime.com – 15; Nick Turner/Alamy – 197; North Wind Picture Archives/Alamy – 136 (Leibniz); Pakhnyushchyy/Dreamstime.com – 10; Paul Glendell/Alamy – 191; Paul Rapson/Alamy – 93; Paula Solloway/Alamy – 162; Paula Solloway/Alamy – 204; Photofusion Picture Library/Alamy – 209; Pictorial Press Ltd/Alamy – 170; Pictorial Press Ltd/Alamy – 170; Rob Howard/CORBIS – 143; Robert Dodge/iStockPhoto – 88; Ronald Martinez/GettyImages – 51; Solarseven/Dreamstime.com – 130; Steve McCurry/Magnum Photos – 32; SuperStock/Alamy – 40; Tammy Peluso/iStockPhoto – 178; The Print Collector/Alamy – 89; Thomas Hoepker/Magnum Photos – 115; Tom Wald / iStockPhoto – 74; Travis Manley/Dreamstime.com – 40; Trevor Smith/Alamy – 22; V&A Images/Alamy – 89; Visual Arts Library (London)/Alamy – 184; Willie B. Thomas/iStockPhoto – 40

Text acknowledgements

BBC News for abridged article – page 55; Juniper TV, for the extract from Richard Dawkins' interview with Sheena McDonald, Channel 4 News – page 93; Nelson Thornes, for the table adapted from Robert Bowie, *Ethical Studies* (2nd edition) – page 169

This resource uses the New International Version of the Bible for quotations from the Bible. Any OCR A2 examination questions containing quotations from the Bible will use the New Revised Standard Version of the Bible, but students can quote any version in their exam answers.

Examination questions, lesson plans and mark schemes are reproduced with permission of OCR.

Religious language

What is the purpose of religious language? Is talk about God meaningful?

In this chapter you will learn about:

- the uses and purpose of religious language
- the verification principle as developed by the Vienna Circle and A.J. Ayer
- the falsification principle of Anthony Flew
- the via negativa as a means of describing God
- the use of analogy, symbol and myth to describe God
- the thinking of Ludwig Wittgenstein.

Religious language

1.1 Mind your language! 

In this topic you will learn why the issue of religious language is considered important by philosophers.

Philosophy of language

In the 20th century, many philosophers focused on issues relating to language. They realised that language is the way that we communicate concepts and make ourselves understood. In the philosophy of religion we are trying to describe concepts that no one physically sees and hears, such as God.

Two problems in the use of religious language

How can words be used to accurately describe God?

The discussion point in the 'For Debate' feature illustrates the first major problem in religious language. Religious believers have to use language to make statements about God. How accurate can these statements be, given that God is unlike anything or anyone that we can actually experience? How do the meanings of words change when they are applied to God?

Same meaning: Do words mean exactly the same when applied to God as they do when applied to human beings? This is to use language **univocally**. This raises a problem. God can be described as faithful, but so can a cat or dog! We could argue that God is good and loving. I would use the same words to describe my wife (and she is not God despite what she thinks!) Hence, if language applied to God is univocal, it has the effect of bringing God down to a human level.

Different meaning: Do words mean completely different things when applied to God? This is to use language **equivocally**. The problem raised here is obvious. If I say that God is holy, it means something completely different to what it means when I apply it to a person or object. So I can never know what a word means when it is applied to God.

Is religious language meaningless? 

The second difficulty is more serious. The above discussion has assumed that when we speak of God we are speaking **cognitively**; in other words we are assuming that our statement is something that is either true or false and that it is able to describe an existent being, God. Some philosophers dispute this. They suggest that statements about God are **non-cognitive**; in other words they are not statements that are true or false. For example if I stub my toe and say 'ouch', it would be strange if you asked if I was sure about my ouch. However it would make sense if I made a statement such as 'the cat is black', a cognitive statement. This has led to a strong challenge to religious faith. Some philosophers claim that religious belief is literally meaningless; religious statements are nonsense and should not be the basis of philosophical discussion. It is this debate that is the subject of the next few pages.

ACTIVITY

'Great is our God, the creator, whose work is perfect, for all his ways are just, a faithful God who does no wrong; how righteous and true is he!' (Deuteronomy 32:3–4)

Great, creator, just, faithful, righteous and true are all words used to describe God. They can also be used to describe people. Draw a diagram to show what we mean when we use these words to describe people and again when the words are used to describe God.

KEY WORDS

Univocal: the word has exactly the same meaning at all times. For example, the word 'boy' or 'girl'.

Equivocal: the same word is used with two completely different meanings. The word 'cricket' could describe an insect or a game.

Cognitive: a statement that is subject to being true or false. For example, 'the cat is asleep on the chair'.

Non-cognitive: a statement that is not subject to truth or falsity. For example 'hurray' or 'ouch'.

Religious language

1.2 The Vienna Circle and the verification principle

In this topic you will learn about the verification principle and its implications for religious statements.

KEY WORDS

Logical positivism: a movement in philosophy that believed that the aim of philosophers should be the analysis of language, particularly the language of science.

Vienna Circle: the group of philosophers including Schlick (1882–1936) and Neurath (1882–1945) who gave rise to the logical positivist movement.

Verification principle: the belief that statements are only meaningful if they can be verified by the senses. There are strong and weak forms of the principle generally associated with the Vienna Circle and A.J. Ayer (1910–89) respectively.

Tautology: a logical statement that we can know to be true by definition.

The views of the Vienna Circle

How many times have you heard the phrase 'you can't prove it!' during a religious or ethical debate? It is frustrating and often quite difficult to respond to. You may find yourself saying 'you can't prove it either'. That usually ends the discussion! One group of philosophers in the 1920s and 1930s would have suggested that the discussion might as well have not taken place. They believed that any statement that cannot be proved or verified is literally nonsense.

These philosophers were the **logical positivists** and they have their origins in a group called the **Vienna Circle**. They believed that some statements were meaningful and others were not. In order to distinguish between what is meaningful and what is not, the logical positivists came up with the **verification principle**; a statement is only meaningful if it is able to be verified by an actual experience or is a **tautology**. A tautology is a logical statement that we can know to be true by definition. If someone were to say that 'triangles have three sides' or that 'all widows have been married', we understand that these statements have to be the case without the need for any sensory experiences.

'It is meaningful to talk about the boiling point of water but not the existence of God.' Why would a verificationist say, 'It is meaningful'?

So if I were to say that behind you is a tiny hobbit that becomes invisible whenever anyone looks at it, never makes a sound and can move faster than any human being can poke it, you might wonder how you could verify this claim. Clearly you can't, so the claim is meaningless nonsense. Crucially the philosophers of the Vienna Circle state that this is the problem that religious claims face.

Was this a new idea?

The thinkers of the Vienna Circle built upon a philosophical tradition stretching back several hundred years. Empiricists such as Locke (1632–1704) and Hume (1711–76) had argued that truth and knowledge were to be found in that which was observable via our senses. The Vienna Circle shared the view that science would provide knowledge and that areas such as metaphysics, religion and ethics should be avoided.

What is different here is that we are dealing with language. It is no longer a matter of saying that we cannot know whether God exists because we cannot have an experience that would confirm it. The Vienna Circle thinkers were claiming that the existence of God is a meaningless issue; it is nonsense and cannot be discussed in any meaningful way. In fact it is not only the religious believer that has problems here. The atheist and agnostic are making equally meaningless statements

Difficulties with the verification principle

The verification principle adopted by the Vienna Circle became known by later thinkers as the strong verification principle. This was because of its insistence that statements had to be verifiable in practice. In other words there was something that you were able to do to verify the statement. This led to a number of difficulties:

- The strong form of the verification principle is too rigid. It suggests that we cannot make statements about history. For instance there are no empirical observations that you can make that can verify facts about the life of Julius Caesar.
- Scientific laws are also meaningless. To say that gravity is constant at all places on earth is impossible to verify as I can only be in one place at once.
- Richard Swinburne (1934–) has pointed out that universal statements cannot be verified. If we were to say that 'all ravens are black' or 'all humans are mortal', these do seem to be meaningful yet they are statements that are excluded as nonsense by the verification principle.
- Any statement about works of art, such as expressing the view that Leonardo da Vinci's 'Last Supper' is more beautiful than the picture drawn by your five-year-old cousin, is also nonsense.

Later logical positivists such as Ayer recognised the difficulties and were forced to adopt a modified version of the principle.

MAKING LINKS

The empiricism of Locke and Hume is influential for the Vienna Circle. Remind yourself of the terms ***empiricism*** and ***a posteriori*** (covered at AS).

ACTIVITY

'Salt is made up of Sodium and Chlorine'

'Triangles have 3 sides'

'God is all powerful'

'Henry VIII had 6 wives'

'Van Gogh was a good painter'

Think about the statements that we might make in science, maths, religion, history and art. How does the verification principle apply to these areas?

FOR DEBATE

'Only things that can be proven are worth discussing; the rest is a lot of hot air.'

1.3 A.J. Ayer and the weak verification principle

In this topic you will learn about the ideas of A.J. Ayer and consider how he developed the verification principle.

ACTIVITY

Make up an example of a statement that is tautological, one that is false by definition, one that is verifiable and true, one that is verifiable and false and another that is meaningless. Challenge the rest of your group to identify them correctly.

MAKING LINKS

Look back at the arguments for the existence of God you considered at AS. Which are ***a priori*** and which are ***a posteriori***?

KEY WORD

Metaphysics: literally meaning 'above or beyond physics', metaphysics involves questions concerning being and ultimate reality.

ACTIVITY

Look back at weaknesses of the verification principle on page 13. Which criticism of the verification principle would still apply to Ayer's version?

Arguably the most famous advocate of the verification principle was the 20th-century British philosopher, A.J. Ayer. Ayer's most famous book *Language, Truth and Logic* was published when Ayer was only 25 and served to establish his reputation as a brilliant philosopher. Ayer had visited the Vienna Circle two years previously whilst on honeymoon. Whether his wife thought this romantic is not certain but Ayer went on to marry three more times!

Language, truth and logic

In *Language, Truth and Logic* Ayer has several motivations:

- He accepts the *a priori/a posteriori* division emphasised by thinkers such as Hume and Kant.
- He wishes to follow both Hume and the thinkers of the Vienna Circle in rejecting **metaphysics** as meaningless. Chapter 1 of *Language, Truth and Logic* is entitled 'the elimination of metaphysics'.

Ayer argues that for a statement to be meaningful it must be either a tautology (*a priori*) or verifiable in principle (*a posteriori*). However, it is the criteria of statements that are verifiable in principle that is perhaps most closely associated with Ayer.

Verification principle

> *The criterion which we use to test the genuineness of apparent statements of fact is the criterion of verifiability. We say that a sentence is factually significant to any given person, if, and only if, he knows...what observations would lead him, under certain conditions, to accept the proposition as being true, or reject it as being false.*
>
> *Language, Truth and Logic*

The above quote shows the key difference between the verification principle as taught by Ayer and that of the Vienna Circle. Ayer states that we do not have to conclusively prove something by a direct observation. Verification in principle means that in order for a statement to be meaningful, we need to suggest how it could possibly be verified.

Ayer's own example of this is the statement, 'there are mountains on the far side of the moon', which at the time of his writing could not be conclusively verified. This was not a meaningless statement as we can suggest that if we were to orbit the moon we would be able to check the truthfulness of the statement.

Where Ayer differs from the Vienna Circle

A.J. Ayer's version of the verification principle is thought by many thinkers to be an improvement upon the strict criteria imposed by members of the Vienna Circle.

Applying the principle only to cases that we can directly verify by experience would be limiting. Ayer is extending the principle by suggesting that we specify what might be required for the statement to be considered factually true.

Ayer's principle is known as weak verification. The principle states that in order to be meaningful, a statement may not be provable: however it may be possible to show that it is probably true beyond any reasonable doubt.

Ayer's version of the verification principle enables us to make statements about the past and other people's emotions, and to make predictions in science. Hence history and science are now meaningful, religion and ethics are not.

FURTHER RESEARCH

Find out about Hick's story of 'The Road to the Celestial City' and his idea of eschatological verification.

MAKING LINKS

What links are there between Ayer's view on religious language and the topic of meta-ethics?

ACTIVITY

This couple seem to be in love. Can it be proved that they love each other? 'If you can't prove you are in love, then it's not true.' How would the Vienna Circle and Ayer respond to this assertion?

Criticisms of the weak verification principle

The following criticisms are also relevant to Ayer's version of the verification principle.

The philosopher John Hick (1922–) has questioned whether the verification principle renders religious statements meaningless. He gives the example of two travellers walking down a long road and arguing about whether the road leads to the celestial city. Hick draws the analogy between this and the statements made by the believer about God and heaven. Like the traveller, the believer's statements can be verified at the end of the journey. Hick calls this **eschatological** verification.

Some thinkers argue that a number of religious statements are verifiable in principle, for instance statements relating to the life of Jesus.

Many thinkers have objected to the verification principle as it is itself unverifiable. It is not a tautology and no amount of evidence can establish whether it is true that only things experienced are meaningful. Ayer's response to this was to argue that the verification principle only applied to statements or propositions, not to whole theories.

KEY WORD

Eschatology: literally the study of 'the last things' or end times.

STRETCH & CHALLENGE

'The verification principle cannot be verified.'
Write a couple of paragraphs explaining this point and considering whether Ayer's response to the criticism is sufficient.

1 Religious language

1.4 The falsification principle

In this topic you will learn about the falsification principle and consider its effect upon religious language.

KEY WORD

Falsification principle: a principle for assessing whether statements are genuine scientific assertions by considering whether any evidence could ever disprove them.

The **falsification principle** aims to improve upon the apparently limited verification principle by suggesting that the difficulty with religious statements is that there is no possible state of affairs that could ever lead to a religious statement being proven false.

If the gardener was invisible, intangible (and liked weeds!), would we be able to tell the difference between the work of this gardener and there being no gardener at all?

Stu and Lou's garden

Lou: That gardener you hired hasn't showed up colleague.

Stu: He started work 3 days ago, my friend.

Lou: I haven't seen him. I don't believe you.

Stu: You won't see him, he's invisible.

Lou: I knew you'd say that. That's why I had a trip wire installed. If he existed, he would have set it off by now.

Stu: You misunderstand the nature of the gardener, he is also intangible. We cannot detect him via our senses. Look how well the flowers are doing!

Lou: Maybe, but wouldn't they have grown anyway? In any case, the weeds are still there and there is no sign of the gardener.

Stu: As I said, there is a gardener who is invisible, intangible and not detectable by human senses. He comes to the garden secretly and works here.

Lou: Well I'm guessing that he likes weeds too.

We are left to wonder how to persuade Stu that there is no garden.

ACTIVITY

Script a TV chat show, along the lines of the dialogue on this page, between an atheist presenter and her guest, a believer.

ACTIVITY 

Explain how Stu and Lou's dialogue links in with the topic of religious language.

The falsification principle and religious language 

The falsification principle has its origins in Karl Popper's (1902–94) philosophy of science. Science works by providing theories about the world that are able to be tested and possibly falsified. Eventually theories are superseded by better theories as more observations take place. For instance, the work of Einstein has come to be seen as an improvement on the ideas of Newton. For Popper this is what marks out scientific ideas from non-science. Any theory that it is impossible to disprove is no valid theory at all. (Popper was famously critical of Freudian psychology with its appeal to sub-conscious explanation.)

Antony Flew (1923–) applied this principle to the use of religious language. The problem with religious language is that it cannot be falsified and it is not a genuine statement at all. Flew used a scenario similar to the one in the dialogue. Two explorers come across a clearing in a jungle and debate whether there is a gardener. After a series of tests have been proposed and carried out, the believer asserts that there is an invisible, intangible gardener who works secretly. This prompts the following response from the sceptic:

> *But what remains of your original assertion? Just how does what you call an invisible, intangible, eternally elusive gardener differ from an imaginary gardener or even from no gardener at all?*

Flew's analogy effectively claims that religious believers shift the goalposts so much that the claims they make are so 'watered down' that they are barely statements at all. Flew calls this the 'death of a thousand qualifications'. No matter what disaster strikes, a believer will continue to argue that God loves them, is testing them or 'moving in mysterious ways'.

Flew's point is to ask what would have to happen in order for the existence of God to be disproved. Although Flew himself does not raise the issue of meaninglessness, some thinkers have used the falsification principle to show that religious language is meaningless. However it is important to be aware that this is not Flew's point.

Falsification: criticisms and responses

Flew's article 'Theology and Falsification' provoked some interesting responses.

R.M. Hare (1919–2002) suggested that Flew did not understand the nature of religious belief. He used the example of a lunatic who believed that all professors were trying to kill him. Nothing would alter the belief. When faced with an incredibly nice professor, the lunatic merely remarked that this illustrated how cunning professors were. Hare calls basic beliefs such as these '**bliks**'. They are not verifiable or falsifiable. However we all have 'bliks', our beliefs about the world. Religious ideas are just some of our bliks.

Basil Mitchell (1917–) disagreed with Flew's analysis. Religious believers are not blind to the problems of faith. They recognise that certain evidence can count against belief in God but they do not allow it to count decisively against. Mitchell uses the story of the stranger to illustrate this point. In wartime, a resistance fighter meets a stranger who claims to be the secret leader of the resistance. He makes a good impression. The stranger's subsequent actions are ambiguous but, on the strength of the original meeting, the resistance fighter continues to trust him. This illustrates Mitchell's other main point. Unlike Flew and Hare, Mitchell argues that religious belief does have some grounding in reason.

As already noted on page 15, Hick argues for eschatological verification. Verification and falsification are not opposites. Hick argues that religious beliefs can be verified in principle *if true* but never falsified *if false*.

ACTIVITY

Role play a telephone conversation to the emergency services placed by the lunatic in Hare's story.

FURTHER RESEARCH

Look up the original sources for Flew, Mitchell and Hare's contributions to the debate.

KEY WORD

Blik: Hare's term for a basic belief that is not altered despite empirical evidence.

ACTIVITY

Consider the death of Princess Diana in 1997. Do those who believe she was murdered just have a 'blik'? Can their hypothesis be falsified?

1

Religious language

1.5 The via negativa

In this topic you will learn how some thinkers have solved the problem of speaking meaningfully about God by making negative statements of what God is not.

'The via negativa is not always useful in everyday life!'

FACT BOX

The via negativa is also known as the apophatic way, particularly in the Eastern Orthodox Church.

ACTIVITY 

Think of a famous person and attempt to describe them to a friend using only negative statements, e.g. the person is not tall. How easy is the process? Would it be more or less difficult to describe God?

MAKING LINKS

Remind yourself of Plato's ideas of the Form of the Good from your AS work.

The benefits of saying nothing

The idea behind the via negativa is both simple and ingenious. First it accepts that statements about God cannot be accurately made as God is utterly different and greater than anything that we can comprehend. To say that 'God is good' means something completely different from saying that 'John is good'. However this is not the end of the story. Rather than having no possible knowledge of God, it is argued that negative statements can be made; in other words, we can say what God is not. Hence the name via negativa (The way of the Negative).

The supporters of the via negativa argue that language when applied to God is equivocal. Although it is quite easy to say that God is good or merciful, it is another thing to know what that phrase could mean when applied to God. It would mean something completely different to the meaning when applied to a human being. However we can make some statements about what God is not: God is not wicked, not mean, not a bully, not hateful, etc. By making a number of such statements we may arrive at a knowledge, albeit limited, of what God is.

Where did the idea come from?

The idea of the via negativa has been influential in both Christianity and Judaism. However it came initially from followers of Plato.

In the 3rd century CE, the neo-Platonist philosopher Plotinus (c.205–270) used this method to describe the Form of the Good. Unlike the **gnostic** groups of his day who claimed that the Good (or in some cases God) could be known through secret knowledge, Plotinus argued that the good is separate to the world and is unknowable.

In the 5th century CE, a Christian writer known as Pseudo-Dionysius (or Dionysius the Areopagite) used this method. He speaks of God as being 'beyond assertion'. God is beyond our ability to describe. Making positive statements about God results in an anthropomorphic idea of God. To say that God is good limits his goodness because it puts a human idea of goodness into our minds.

In the Jewish tradition, the philosopher Moses Maimonides (1135–1204) emphasised the importance of the via negativa in his 'Guide for the Perplexed'. To make positive statements about God is improper and disrespectful as it brings God down to human level. The only positive statement that can be made is that he exists. Description of God then comes via the negative.

STRETCH & CHALLENGE

Research the ideas of Plotinus or Maimonides on this subject. Produce an A4 handout on the strengths and weaknesses of their views to give to other members of the group.

ACTIVITY

Attempt to write a description of God in negative statements. Do you think it works?

KEY WORD

Gnostic: religious groups in the 1st and 2nd centuries after Jesus who claimed to have secret knowledge of God and salvation.

Strengths of the via negativa

The via negativa has a number of possible strengths:

- It prevents anthropomorphic statements being made about God. We are not left with an inadequate idea of God formed using our limited language.
- It can be seen as more respectful. Maimonides argued that positive statements about God are improper as they do not fully convey the idea we require.
- It supports the view of many thinkers, especially mystics, that God is beyond description and that experience of him is ineffable (see chapter 2) that limit God from being made. Thus we do not speak of God in an improper way.
- Related to this it can be argued that only the via negativa adequately conveys the transcendence of God.

Weaknesses of the via negativa

However there are a number of weaknesses too:

- It could be argued that the result is a very limited understanding of God at best. The method does not even work for everyday objects, let alone an all-powerful, transcendent God.
- The via negativa is not a true reflection of how religious people speak of God. They do not talk in the negative but rather seek positive knowledge of what God is.
- The via negativa claims that no positive statement about God can be made. However if we are saying something negative, we are surely implying the positive statement as well.

1.6 Using analogy to understand God

In this topic we will be looking at how using language analogically may help us to express an understanding of God.

KEY WORD

Analogy: an approach to religious language that compares the normal use of a word to its religious use. To say God is good means a similar thing as saying that John is good.

ACTIVITY

Someone emails you asking what it is like to visit a cinema. Reply to the email, but only use analogies in your answer.

ACTIVITY

Look back at page 11. Write a paragraph explaining the difficulties of suggesting that language used of God is univocal or equivocal.

What is analogy?

Analogies are something that we use frequently in everyday speech. To describe strawberry ice cream to someone who had never tasted it, you might say something like this, 'It's like vanilla ice cream but it tastes like strawberries'. An **analogy** is describing something that is unfamiliar to us by making a comparison with something that we already know.

Sometimes the analogy drawn may seem odd when we reflect on the language literally. Yet a phrase such as 'her face was like thunder' does communicate something to us. Hopefully low rumbling sounds are not coming from her face but nevertheless the phrase conveys something of the 'storminess' of the anger she has.

Why analogy?

Hence analogies are comparisons that are helpful to a point. We find ourselves saying, 'It is like…but…'. Religiously, analogies are the only option available given the difficulties of making univocal or equivocal statements about God.

> *It seems that no word can be used literally of God.*
>
> Aquinas *Summa Theologica*

Types of analogy  

Thomas Aquinas (1224–74) argued that language cannot be used literally of God. The writers of scripture certainly do use analogies (the Lord is my shepherd) but thinkers such as Aquinas suggest that even terms such as 'God is good' should be understood analogically. When I say that 'God is good' I cannot mean exactly the same as when I say that 'Gemma is good'. God's goodness must be on a different scale. Aquinas uses analogy in two different ways:

- analogy of attribution, and
- analogy of proportion.

Analogy of attribution

The qualities that we ascribe to each other are a reflection of the qualities of God. Brian Davies (1951–) uses the example of the baker and bread. If we say that the bread is good and the baker is good, there is a relationship between the statements. The bread is the product of the baker and his goodness or skill at baking 'spreads' to the bread.

Aquinas' own example comes from medieval medicine. It was believed that if a bull's urine is healthy then they are healthy. Their urine is a reflection of them.

What does this have to do with God? Essentially properties such as wisdom, love and goodness that we see in others are reflections of the properties of the creator God. Hence when we see these attributes in others, we are able to make analogies with the attributes of God.

Analogy of proportion

The type of properties that something has depends on the nature of the being that possesses the properties. An example might be musical ability. To say that your younger sister is a good guitarist means that she is good for her age. If you went to see a band where a professional musician played to your sister's standard, you would be disappointed. You would expect the guitarist to be good according to the standard of a professional musician.

Again what does this have to do with God? When we use words to describe God, we are describing an infinite being. When we use words of each other, we are describing finite beings. The meaning cannot be the same, it changes in proportion to the nature of the being that is described. The modern philosopher John Hick (1922–) uses Baron von Hugel's example of the term 'faithfulness'. This is a word that we might use of a dog, a human or God. If we compare the faithfulness that humans have (at least potentially!) to that of a dog, the dog's faithfulness is limited. Yet when we assert that God is faithful, we are using the word in a way that makes our faithfulness seem quite tiny by comparison.

Assessing analogy

The idea of analogy has several strengths and weaknesses.

Analogy seems to show that religious language is not absurd and can provide some understanding of God. It may avoid the twin pitfalls of agnosticism and **anthropomorphism**. However some thinkers such as Duns Scotus (1266–1308) argued that analogy is too vague and leaves us unable to understand God and his actions.

Hick comments that analogy enables us to make some statements about God yet still preserve the degree of mystery present in Judaeo-Christian theology. Hick also offers the Christian idea of the incarnation as a possible solution to the problem of meaning. God's attitudes and character are seen in the stories of Christ and this enables us to make some statements about God.

One difficulty with the use of analogy is that it assumes some similarity between God and humans. However if God is completely different to humans then it is difficult to see how words can be used in a similar way.

ACTIVITY

List six words that are used to describe God, e.g. judge, shepherd, king. What is the meaning of each in ordinary use? How is each different when applied to God?

FOR DEBATE

How is the word 'father' helpful for us when we try to understand God? What would the differences be between a human father and God as a father?

KEY WORD

Anthropomorphism: conception of God as having the form, personality or attributes of man.

FOR DEBATE

'Analogy is not much use when it comes to describing something nobody has ever seen.'

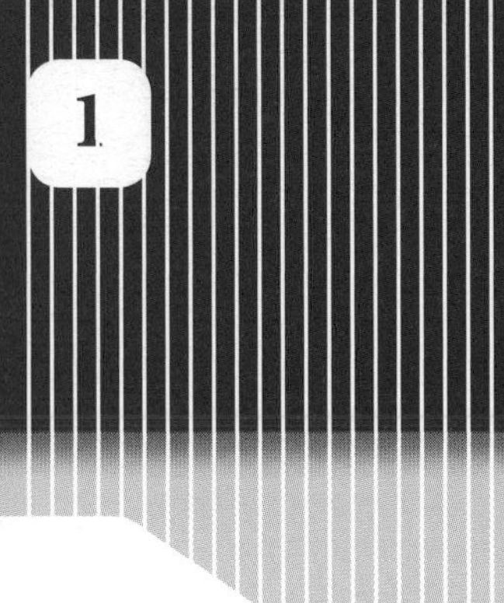

Religious language

1.7 Symbol and myth

In this topic you will learn how an understanding of God might be conveyed via symbol and myth.

Religious language as symbolic

The poppy functions as a powerful **symbol**. The poppy is not just something to remind us of the horrors of past conflicts, in the way that a road **sign** reminds us which town is ahead. The poppy has become part of Remembrance Day. It has come to represent it in a deep way.

The poppy gives a powerful reminder of the sacrifice made by so many British soldiers in 20th-century conflicts. What emotions are aroused when you see poppies?

Paul Tillich (1886–1965) argued that religious language ought to be understood in a similar way. Religious statements are symbolic but are nevertheless cognitive statements. A symbol 'participates in that to which it points'. For example a flag is symbolic of the nation it represents and in a way it participates in the power and dignity of the nation it represents.

So we are able to learn something of God, but our words become symbolic rather than literal. We are familiar with religious symbols such as the cross or the bread and wine of communion. What Tillich is suggesting is that even statements such as 'God is good' are symbolic rather than literal. Tillich suggests that symbols in religion function a little like our appreciation of the arts. A good piece of music or a painting may in Tillich's words 'create symbols for a reality which cannot be reached in any other way. Symbols like the arts work on a deep and powerful level. A symbol unlocks something within our soul and expresses something about the ultimate'. Tillich refers to God as 'the ground of being', and suggests that this is the only non-symbolic statement that can be made about God.

Tillich views symbols as having both positive and negative aspects. Because words cannot adequately describe God, their meaning is always 'partially negated by that to which they point'. However there is a positive aspect of the symbol participating in that to which it points which makes Tillich's view a credible alternative to analogy.

ACTIVITY

Draw ten symbols people might choose as tattoos. What emotions could be linked with them and why?

KEY WORDS

Signs point us towards something else whereas a **symbol** 'participates' in that to which it points.

STRETCH & CHALLENGE

Find out more about Tillich's view of religious language. Write two or three paragraphs explaining and assessing his views.

ACTIVITY

Select four songs, paintings, TV programmes, films or sculptures that have moved you emotionally. Is Tillich right to claim that the arts can function on a deep level?

There have been a number of criticisms of Tillich's views:

- Tillich's ideas can be seen as a little vague prompting some thinkers such as J. H. Randall to agree that language is symbolic but is non-cognitive. Randall argues that religious symbols function in a similar way to art. They do not tell us anything about external reality; they do however tell us much about our own human experience.
- Some thinkers have argued that if religious statements are not literally true, then it is difficult to see what content they may have.
- It is difficult to be clear on what is meant by the idea of a symbol participating in something.

Myth

Some thinkers argue that religious ideas conveyed through myths can give cognitive knowledge of God. For many people the idea of myth is the same as the idea of legends, ancient stories that are unlikely to be true. However myths are stories that convey the values and beliefs of the communities that tell them. All cultures and societies have myths and many of them are similar. As well as giving insight into the world view of the community in question, religious myths may provide a way of making meaningful statements about God. One example of myth would be the creation stories in the Bible. These teach believers that God created everything and that he cares for his people.

One thinker who is particularly associated with the idea of myth is Rudolf Bultmann (1884–1976). Bultmann defines a myth as the use of imagery to express the other worldly in the terms of this world. A myth effectively draws readers in and requires a response. What is presented in myths is not literal truth but a deep truth that requires an existential response. It inspires action and calls the hearers to respond. Bultmann attempted to demythologise the New Testament. This involved the removal of the supernatural 'mythical' element to arrive at what he considered the essential message of Christianity to be, the teachings of Jesus. Bultmann suggested that the gospels show little more than the fact that Jesus lived, taught about the Kingdom of God, called others to follow him and was crucified. The miracle stories added later should be regarded as statements of faith, stories told in the early Church. This is not a problem for Bultmann as the literal truth of these accounts is unimportant to the teaching (or kerygma) of Jesus. Some scholars have disputed Bultmann's approach and questioned the assumption that the mythical elements were later additions to the story of Jesus. This has recently been disputed. Some scholars have suggested that the supernatural elements of the story were not later additions but were part of the original tradition.

A difficulty

Although viewing stories given by religion as myths can be liberating for some believers who struggle to accept them as literally true, it is difficult to see how the interpretation of myths can be straightforward. Theologians often disagree on the meaning of passages, and how something is interpreted may also depend on the culture of the interpreters.

ACTIVITY

What truths about God are conveyed in the creation story? Examine other myths from the Bible or from other cultures. Explain why myths can convey religious truths effectively.

STRETCH AND CHALLENGE

Clear summaries of the work of both Tillich and Randall are found in chapter 6 of John Hick's *Philosophy of Religion*. Read this chapter to extend your knowledge of the area.

Religious language

1.8 Wittgenstein 

In this topic you will learn about Wittgenstein's views on religious language.

The Tractatus

The Austrian-born philosopher Ludwig Wittgenstein (1889–1951) published only one major book during his lifetime. *The Tractatus Logico Philosophicus*, commonly known as the *Tractatus*, was published early in Wittgenstein's life. In it he developed the picture theory of language and argued that the purpose of language is to enable us to represent the world. This book proved highly influential. In particular philosophers drew on his enigmatic concluding sentence: 'Whereof one cannot speak, thereof one must remain silent.' The logical positivists interpreted this as suggesting that religious language is meaningless. However it is unlikely that this is what Wittgenstein himself intended.

Do you see a duck or a rabbit? Wittgenstein suggests that the way we see and describe the world is a matter of perspective.

Later Wittgenstein

After some time away from philosophy (working as a gardener amongst other things!), Wittgenstein came to see his earlier writings as exemplifying the language and method of science. He became interested in analysing how words were used in various forms of life or settings. In his later work *Philosophical Investigations* (published after his death) Wittgenstein argues that his role is to let the fly out of the fly bottle. In other words, philosophers resemble flies trapped in the jar of language, buzzing around and not really getting anywhere due to misunderstanding what words do. Wittgenstein notes that the meanings of words are not something that are mystically fixed. What is more important is how a word is used. Consider how you might use the word 'wicked' in a positive sense. We might also note how the meaning of the word 'gay' has changed as a result of its use in the later 20th century.

- The main task of philosophers is to analyse the use of language. The meaning of a word is really its use. This use of language helps to create our perspective of the world.
- Wittgenstein saw words as tools. The question 'what is a word really?' is analogous to 'what is a chess piece?'. Our words are moves that we make playing various language games.

Language games 

Wittgenstein argues that language use is like playing a game with rules. Within our groups, we have agreed rules about how words are used. If I point to a table and say the word 'cabbage', someone will correct me just as if I had moved a chess piece incorrectly. Different settings and situations each have their own language games. Religious language and the statements of different religious groups are in themselves different language games.

If we were to say that 'God allows suffering to develop our character and we will be rewarded in heaven'. The statement may meet with approval amongst Christians as it fits in with a Christian interpretation of the world. It is not a statement that fits within the atheistic or Hindu language games for instance.

To suggest that the best explanation of evil is that God does not exist would not fit within the rules of their game. It would be rather like an athlete choosing to cycle the Olympic marathon. It is not within the rules of that particular game.

Wittgenstein and religion

Although Wittgenstein did not seem to be in any sense a religious believer, he respected religion and realised that it could not be analysed via the narrow criteria of the verificationists. Religion cannot be spoken of and analysed in a scientific way as it is not the same sort of thing. Nevertheless it gives a profound and important interpretation of human life to those who are religious. Some thinkers have suggested that Wittgenstein's ideas resemble **Fideism**; the beliefs of religion do not have rational foundations and are removed from criticism.

One thinker who opposes this direction is D. Z. Phillips (1934–2006). He argues that it prevents philosophy of religion as it suggests that no one who is outside the game can criticise belief. Phillips develops Wittgenstein's approach by arguing that some of the problems caused by religious language exist because we take the language literally. The concept of 'soul' for instance is problematic if we are looking for an actual non-physical thing at the core of our being that will survive death. However if we pay attention to how the word soul is used in phrases such 'selling his soul' and 'saving her soul', then the word 'soul' seems to be a way of speaking about what is most important in life. Hence Phillips agrees with Wittgenstein's idea, which seems to be that religious statements cannot be understood in a literal way but still have a profound meaning for those who make them.

ACTIVITY

List ten words that you might use differently depending on who you were speaking to, for example your parents, your friends, your teacher, at a job interview.

ACTIVITY

Write a short conversation between two friends who are using language in a way many people would not understand.

KEY WORD

Fideism: the belief that faith is more important than reason. Beliefs cannot be subjected to rational analysis.

STRETCH & CHALLENGE

Produce a PowerPoint® presentation explaining the difference between Wittgenstein's early and later philosophy.

Religious language

1.9 Religious language: putting the map together

In this topic you will revise your knowledge of religious language.

ACTIVITY

Look at the diagram and trace a couple of possible routes through. Write a paragraph for each route justifying the conclusions of a person who chooses that route.

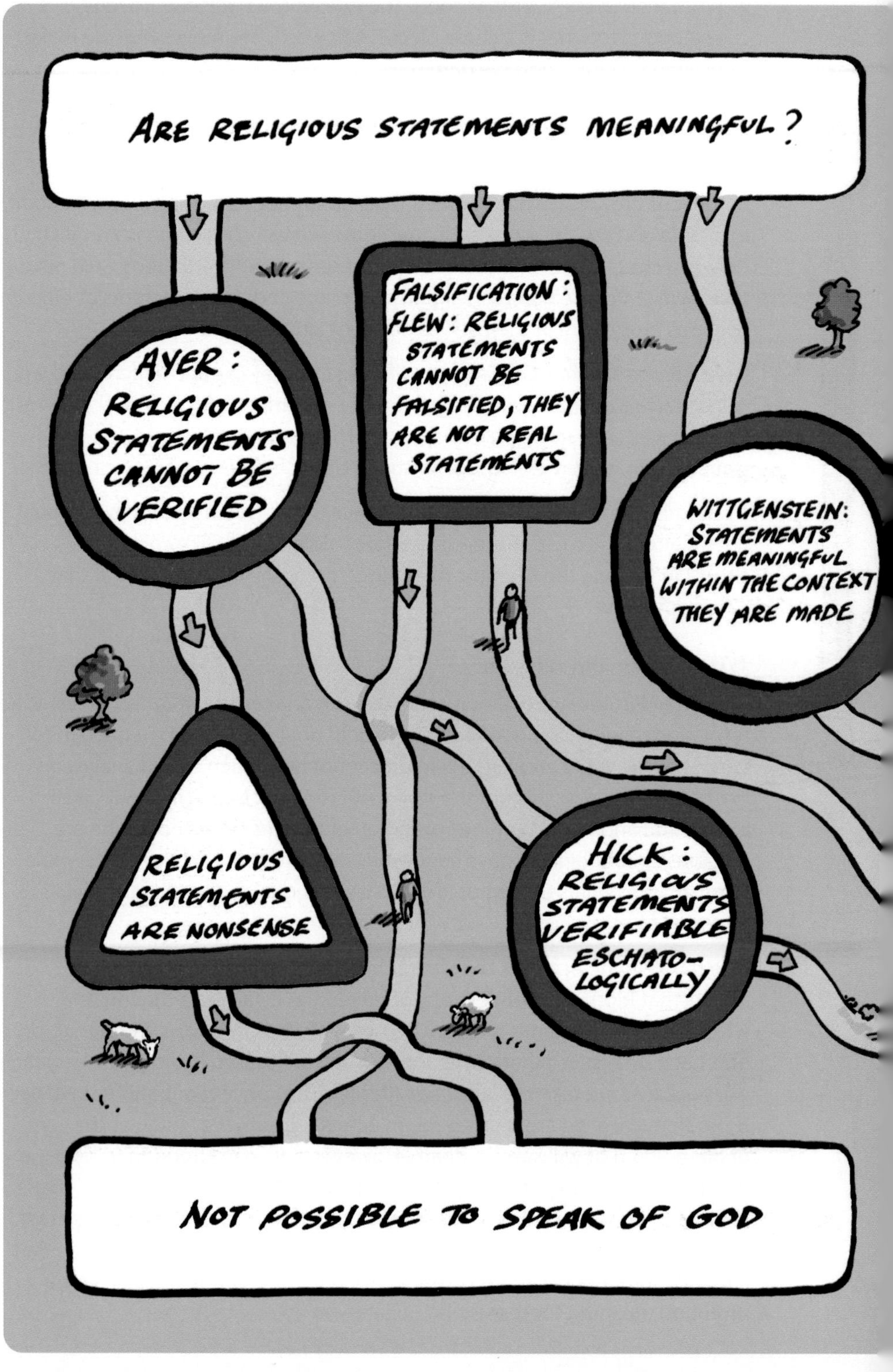

ARE RELIGIOUS STATEMENTS MEANINGFUL?

AYER: RELIGIOUS STATEMENTS CANNOT BE VERIFIED

FALSIFICATION: FLEW: RELIGIOUS STATEMENTS CANNOT BE FALSIFIED, THEY ARE NOT REAL STATEMENTS

WITTGENSTEIN: STATEMENTS ARE MEANINGFUL WITHIN THE CONTEXT THEY ARE MADE

RELIGIOUS STATEMENTS ARE NONSENSE

HICK: RELIGIOUS STATEMENTS VERIFIABLE ESCHATOLOGICALLY

NOT POSSIBLE TO SPEAK OF GOD

WHAT DOES LANGUAGE MEAN WHEN APPLIED TO GOD?

VIA NEGATIVA: LANGUAGE IS EQUIVOCAL WHEN USED OF GOD.

KNOWLEDGE VIA STATEMENTS OF WHAT GOD IS NOT.

TILLICH: NO LITERAL LANGUAGE, WORDS USED SYMBOLICALLY OF GOD.

AQUINAS: LANGUAGE USED ANALOGICALLY, WORDS ARE SIMILAR WHEN APPLIED TO GOD

HARE & MITCHELL: RESPONSES TO FALSIFICATION

STATEMENTS ABOUT GOD CAN BE MADE

Exam Café

Relax, refresh, result!

Relax and prepare

Lauren

I really struggled with religious language as a topic. I just didn't get what everyone was going on about and I got confused about who said what. I think I'll drop it and answer other questions in the exam. What do you think?

Jodie

Lauren, I know what you mean about this topic! I had to go back through the textbook. As soon as I sussed out what the key issue was, the pieces of the jigsaw fitted in. I found the diagram on pages 24–25 really helped. My teacher also gave me a copy of the original university debate between Flew, Mitchell and Hare. That helped me to see what they were saying. In my mock exam I could only remember the stories, not the point of them.

Ali

Remember when you revise a topic, a good way of presenting the information is to use concept maps or spider diagrams. An outline of one of these diagrams is below. You could copy and complete the diagram, then do others for the other bits of the religious language topic.

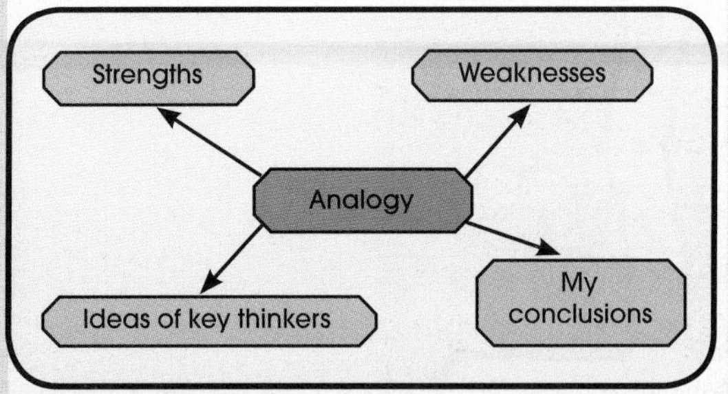

Hot tips

Jason

Lauren, you need to be careful. That sounds like a risky strategy. You've got to answer two questions in the exam from a choice of four. What if two of the questions were on this topic? You'd have to answer whatever else came up whether you liked it or not.

Getting started...

'If I've done AS, I'll be fine with the A2 won't I?'

Students who have passed the AS should cope with the step up to the A2. However it is important to note that there is a step up in standard. So it is important not to get complacent. You will need to work just as hard, if not harder, in your A2 year.

'So, what exactly is the difference?'

There are several differences. At A2 you will have the opportunity to study issues in a more in-depth way than you did at AS. It's even more important to read around the subject to extend your knowledge. Another difference is in how you are assessed. There are no part a)'s and part b)'s. Each question is an essay question testing both assessment objectives.

'How does that work, I can't picture that?'

Well at AS you had part a) 'Explain how Descartes developed Anselm's argument that God's existence is necessary' followed by part b) 'Evaluate the claim that God's existence is necessary.' An A2 question on this topic might

Getting started. . .contd

be 'Assess the view that neither Anselm nor Descartes succeed in proving God's existence to be necessary.' In answering the question you have to present an argument and, in doing so, show your knowledge and understanding of the theories and ideas in question. In other words you are doing AO1 and AO2 together. You have 45 minutes to answer it, so there's a real opportunity to show what you can do!

'Have you just given me next year's question?'

Afraid not, you will be assessed on A2 content and topics, not AS!

Refresh your memory

Revision checklist for religious language

In order to do well on this area of the course you will need to:

- Explain different ways of understanding religious language.
- Be able to understand terms such as univocal, equivocal, analogical, cognitive and non-cognitive.
- Understand the verification principle as used by the Vienna Circle and A.J. Ayer.
- Assess whether these thinkers succeed in demonstrating the meaninglessness of religious language.
- Explain the falsification principle of Anthony Flew and how other thinkers have applied this to religious language.
- Assess the implications of the falsification principle for our understanding of religious language.
- Explain how the via negativa attempts to deal with the problem of religious language.
- Assess whether the via negativa is successful in providing an understanding of God.
- Explain how different understanding of analogy may help believers to understand God.
- Assess whether analogy solves the problems of religious language.
- Explain Tillich's view that religious language is symbolic.
- Assess whether symbol enables human understanding of God.
- Explain and assess whether myth enables understanding of God.
- Assess Wittgenstein's contribution to the area of religious language.
- Assess whether any approach to religious language is successful in providing an understanding of God.

Get the result!

The language of the exam

Critically compare: The following question is a 'critically compare' question. The word 'compare' is quite obvious, but what does 'critically' add to the equation? It doesn't necessarily mean to give lots of criticisms. To take a critical approach means to seriously look at the strengths and weaknesses. Hence to critically compare means to weigh up the strengths and weaknesses of both ideas and form a view about their similarities and differences, suggesting which, if either, is better.

Sample answers

Exam question

Critically compare the use of symbol with the use of analogy to express human understanding of God. (35 marks)

Simon's answer

The issue of religious language has dominated 20th-century philosophy. It is difficult to know whether statements made about God are meaningful. The philosophers of the Vienna Circle argued that statements about God are meaningless. Only statements that can be verified by some empirical observation have meaning. Anthony Flew disagreed with the approach of verification and put forward a falsification principle. He used the story of the explorers in the garden to suggest that the difficulty of religious statements lay in the fact that they cannot be falsified. It is also difficult to know what statements about God would actually mean. Do words used of God have the same meaning as when they are used of human beings? If I say that 'Harry is good', does that mean the same as when I say that 'God is good'? Surely the words cannot have the same meaning?

Examiner says

I have a few concerns about this opening. It seems that Simon is giving a very general religious language answer. He is looking at whether religious language is meaningful whereas the question is focusing on two ways of examining what words about God mean. Can you spot his mistake on falsification? At the end of the paragraph he begins to address the question.

Examiner says

Simon understands analogy but has not explained it in detail. Technical terms like 'attribution' and 'proportionality' are missing. 'Univocal' and 'equivocal' could also be used. Can you see where?

One solution to the difficulties of religious language is to suggest that words used of God are analogical. This was the view of Aquinas. A word cannot have the same meaning when applied to human beings and God as God is so much greater than human beings. However words cannot have a completely different meaning as this would suggest that we cannot have any knowledge of God. Aquinas suggests that statements about God are analogical. This means that words have a similar meaning. Analogy is a part of everyday speech. We frequently use it when we have to explain something that is unfamiliar. For instance, we might explain what a wind turbine was by referring to a windmill or a helicopter. Likewise when we use words about God, a strength of analogy is that it enables us to have some awareness of what is being said.

However analogies have a number of weaknesses. One difficulty is knowing how far to stretch the meaning of words. How good is God's goodness when compared to human goodness? Perhaps the goodness of God is almost completely different to human goodness and there is little in common between the two uses of the word. Alternatively perhaps the meaning is stretched a little bit so that God's goodness is like human goodness just greater. Hence analogy gives some understanding of God but it seems difficult to know how much. Furthermore some thinkers might argue that analogy has the potential to reduce God to human level. This would be avoided if we adopted the via negativa.

Examiner says

Two weaknesses of analogy. Is Simon aware of the strengths? Could he have suggested some counterarguments to the points he has raised? This may have given a little more depth to his answers.

Examiner says

Simon gives us a very brief treatment of symbol which suggests he lacks a deep understanding of this topic. The conclusion does give a comparison between the two ideas but fails to give a judgement or really argue for anything. This is a reasonable answer on the topic but it lacks the detail and focus necessary for the highest marks.

One way of expressing ideas about God that avoids the difficulties of analogy is to suggest that religious language is symbolic. The philosopher Tillich argues that all religious language is symbolic, it participates in that to which it points. This gives us understanding of God but in a symbolic way. However it is difficult to see how symbols can participate in that to which they point so it may be that analogy is easier to understand.

In conclusion it can be seen that both analogy and symbol have difficulties in terms of conveying a clear understanding of God. God is logically above the abilities of our language. Both analogy and symbol recognise that statements about God do not have the same literal meaning as everyday statements but it is difficult to know how much knowledge is being conveyed by each use.

2

Religious experience

Millions of **people** worldwide have religious experiences. How are these **experiences** to be understood?

In this chapter you will learn about:

- different types of religious experience and consider what may be revealed about God through these experiences
- arguments from religious experience from William James and the aims and main conclusions drawn by James in *The Varieties of Religious Experience*
- the following different forms of religious experience: visions, voices, 'numinous' experience, conversion experience, corporate religious experience
- the concept of revelation through sacred writings
- how to discuss these areas critically and evaluate the strengths and weaknesses.

Religious experience

2.1 The importance of religious experience

In this topic you will consider the relevance and importance of religious experience today.

Experience and religion

The traditional arguments for the existence of God are at best inconclusive. Most philosophers would agree that the existence of a God cannot be proved or demonstrated to others. The phenomena of religious experience are different because, for those who have such experiences, these phenomena have authority and convince them that their religious beliefs are true or, in some cases, persuade them to change their religious beliefs.

Is religious experience widespread?

The Religious Experience Research Unit was founded in 1969 in order to discover more about religious experience. Some of its findings were presented in David Hay's book *Religious Experience Today*.

These findings, based on a random sampling of the public, include:

- 31% of British people and 35% of Americans have 'felt close to a powerful spiritual force' or have had an experience that they might consider religious.
- The experiences may last for just a few seconds in many cases but can last a lot longer.
- Those having experiences speak of the experience as being very different to all other experiences.
- They generally give awareness that there is more to reality than this physical world.
- They can produce a change in both behaviour and attitudes. These include a sense of altruism, increased self-esteem and a feeling of purpose.

What is also clear is that there is a huge variety of different religious experiences. These include **mystical experiences**, **numinous experiences**, visions, voices, conversion experiences, miracles (the subject of the next chapter) and **corporate experiences**. Each of these raises its own issues although to some extent the argument from religious experience and its challenges (pages 42–45) are relevant to all types of religious experience. These pages pose the central question of the topic: What, if anything, is shown by the phenomena of religious experience?

KEY WORDS

Mystical experiences: used to describe experience of direct contact or oneness with God or ultimate reality.

Numinous experiences: used to describe experiences of awe and wonder in the presence of God.

Corporate experiences: used to describe religious experiences that happen to a number of people at once in the same location.

FURTHER RESEARCH

You can read some modern accounts of religious experience by accessing the Religious Experience Research Unit website via www.heinemann.co.uk/hotlinks and entering the express code 3587P.

Religious experience

2.2 William James and *The Varieties of Religious Experience*

In this topic you will learn about the main aims and conclusions drawn by William James in his classic book *The Varieties of Religious Experience.*

The philosopher and psychologist William James' (1842–1910) book *The Varieties of Religious Experience: a study in human nature* summarises the author's Gifford Lectures given in 1902. It is arguably the most important book ever written on the topic of religious experience. In it James aims to survey the various types of religious experience as a psychologist and to present the findings of this survey and its implications for philosophy.

Religion and religious experience?

James defines religion as:

> *the feelings, acts, and experiences of individual men in their solitude, so far as they apprehend themselves to stand in relation to whatever they may consider the divine…*
>
> *Varieties*: Lecture 2

ACTIVITY

Explain how James defines religion using your own words.

For James, religious experience stands at the very heart of religion. Religious teachings, practices and attitudes are 'second hand' religion. These develop later as individuals reflect on their common experience. It is the actual experiences themselves that can be regarded as true religion.

FOR DEBATE

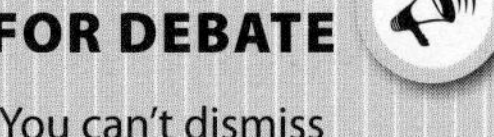

'You can't dismiss traditional religions as second hand.'

Varieties of religious experience

James analyses various forms of religious experience including conversion, prayer and the phenomenon of saintliness (the idea of the holy man or woman). James viewed conversion as a transformation from a divided or imperfect self to a more unified consciousness.

Much of *The Varieties of Religious Experience* concentrates on descriptions and first-hand accounts of experiences. Although sceptics viewed some of these as examples of psychological disorder, James disagreed and placed such accounts as central to any understanding of religion.

ACTIVITY

Display James' arguments about religious experience in a diagramatic form.

James' criteria for mystical experience

The term 'mystical experience' has many uses, including the everyday use which is little more than suggesting that the experience is strange or unexplained. In philosophical thought, mystical experiences refer to experience where God is revealed directly and there is a sense of oneness with the divine, or ultimate reality.

James recognised the difficulty of providing a definition of mystical

experiences and proposed that the following four criteria were the characteristics of all mystical experiences:

- **Ineffable**: The experience is beyond proper description. No adequate description can be given in words.
- **Noetic**: Despite the ineffability mystical states are not just feelings, the experience gives the mystic a deep and direct knowledge of God.
- **Transient:** The experience is a temporary one that cannot be sustained, although its effects may last a long time. It can develop and deepen with each subsequent experience.
- **Passive:** The experience is not initiated by the mystic but rather they have a sense that something is acting upon them.

James' conclusions

James draws on his knowledge of psychology and neurology in accepting that religious experiences are psychological phenomena that occur in our brains. However, this does not mean that they are just psychological phenomena. James argues that these experiences may well have a supernatural element as well as a physical element. James' conclusions rest on three key principles: **empiricism**, **pluralism** and **pragmatism**.

Empiricism

James is committed to an empirical approach. The many case studies he produces are empirical evidence of the effects of religious experience. This evidence provides us with clues as to the reality beyond what we see and hear. In response to those who might object that he is interpreting the data, James argues that we interpret all our experiences.

> *I think it may be asserted that there are religious experiences of a specific nature…I think that they point with reasonable probability to the continuity of our consciousness with a wider, spiritual environment from which the ordinary man is shut off.*
>
> James, *The Varieties of Religious Experience*

Pluralism

James' research into experiences in different faiths led him to conclude that they were similar. Those having experiences may be experiencing the same ultimate reality, which is then interpreted into the 'second hand' religious belief structure that is most familiar to them. A Christian might interpret an experience as the presence of the Holy Spirit, whereas a Hindu might interpret it differently.

Pragmatism

This concept is vital to an understanding of James' work. As a pragmatist, James believed that truth was not fixed and that what is true is whatever has great value for us. Therefore, on observing the effects of religious experience, we have to conclude that there is truth to be found in religion.

> *be ready now to judge the religious life by its results exclusively.*
>
> James, *The Varieties of Religious Experience*

ACTIVITY

Find some examples from scripture or modern accounts to illustrate each of James' points on mystical experience.

KEY WORDS

Ineffable: the idea that an experience cannot be properly described.

Noetic: the idea that an experience imparts or reveals knowledge.

Empiricism: the idea that observations via our senses lead us to understanding the world.

Pluralism: the idea in religion that truth is to be found in many faiths.

Pragmatism: an account of truth that states that the truth is not a fixed thing but is whatever has value or works for us.

STRETCH & CHALLENGE

'James' conclusions are psychological and do not prove anything philosophically.'

Write a couple of paragraphs discussing this statement.

Religious experience

2.3 Numinous experience 

In this topic you will learn about different understandings of religious experience, particularly numinous types of experience.

What is 'numinous' religious experience?

Numinous religious experiences are experiences of awe and wonder in the presence of an almighty and transcendent God. It is an awareness of human nothingness when faced with a holy and powerful being. The name comes from the Latin 'numen' which means to bow the head.

Many cases of numinous religious experience appear in religious texts, for example, Isaiah's experience recorded in the Bible:

> *'Holy, holy, holy is the Lord Almighty; the whole earth is full of his glory.'*
>
> *At the sound of their voices the doorposts and thresholds shook and the temple was filled with smoke.*
>
> *'Woe to me' I cried. 'I am ruined! For I am a man of unclean lips, and I live among a people of unclean lips, and my eyes have seen the King, the Lord Almighty.'*
>
> Isaiah 6:3–5

Other numinous experiences have been documented right up to the present day. The philosopher and mathematician Blaise Pascal (1623–62) wrote of his numinous experience.

> *From about half past ten in the evening until half past midnight, Fire!...'God of Abraham, God of Isaac, God of Jacob,' not of philosophers and scholars.*
> *Certainty, certainty, heartfelt, joy, peace.*
> *God of Jesus Christ....*
> *Joy, joy, joy, tears of joy...*
> *I have cut myself off from him, shunned him, denied him, crucified him.*
> *Let me never be cut off from him!*
> *Sweet and total renunciation.*
> *Total submission to Jesus Christ and my director.*
>
> Caillet and Blankenagel *Great Shorter Works of Pascal*

FOR DEBATE 

'The unsettling nature of numinous experiences means that they are less likely to be something that our minds have made up.'

Look at the experiences of Isaiah, Blaise Pascal and others in considering your response.

Otto and the numinous experience 

In *The idea of the Holy* Rudolf Otto (1869–1937) argued that all religious experience was numinous in nature:

> *It is an experience of being acted upon by something outside of ourselves, a 'Wholly other'. It makes us aware that we are creatures of an almighty God. This contrasts with a 'mystical experience' which tends to seek the unity of all things.*

It is described by Otto as being *'mysterium; tremendum.' Mysterium* because of the mystery of the experience, it is felt but cannot be described. *Tremendum* because of the awe-inspiring terror, almost a sense of dread in the presence of an overwhelming being. Yet, despite this, it is *fascinans*, we are drawn to the experience with a strange fascination.

These experiences provide a reference point. From then on, believers interpret the world through the experience and the beliefs attached to it. Ideas about God may be developed when believers reflect on their experiences but ultimately the encounter with God is inexpressible.

The numinous experience is key to understanding the spirituality of many religions. Otto claimed that 'there is no religion in which it does not live as the innermost core and without it no religion would be worthy of the name.'

Otto was greatly influenced by the philosophy of Immanuel Kant (1724–1804). Otto recognised that God could not be known via sensory experience or logical argument. For Otto, God is 'wholly Other'. He is a being that is completely different and distinct to human beings. We are not able to know God unless he chooses to reveal himself. However, the numinous experience is where God reveals himself and his revelation is felt on an emotional level.

Is all religious experience numinous?

Otto's account may be seen as confusing regarding the issue of whether knowledge of God is gained through the experience. He states that the experiences come from the 'deepest cognitive apprehension'. Yet he also states that the theological ideas come after the experience.

Otto seems to imply that the numinous experience is a 'once and for all' experience, which implies there can be no further religious experience.

To suggest that all religious experience is numinous is too simplistic. Other types of experience are well documented.

Other understandings of religious experience

Friedrich Schleiermacher (1768–1834) agreed with Otto that religious experiences are primarily emotional. These emotions are deeper than reason. For Schleiermacher, the experiences are not numinous but are at their core a feeling of absolute dependence upon the divine. It is this awareness of absolute dependence upon 'a source of power that is distinct from the world' that is at the heart of religion. Theology arises afterwards as people reflect on their experiences.

Martin Buber (1878–1965) viewed religious experiences as being analogous to intimate personal relationships that he called I–thou relationships. This differs from the I–it relationship that we have with objects or when we treat people as objects. The I–thou relationship is a mutual interaction. We may experience such I–thou relationships when we encounter nature, in deep friendships and most importantly, by experiencing God.

MAKING LINKS

Remind yourself of Kant's ideas by looking back at your AS notes.

ACTIVITY

'It is the emotion of a creature submerged and overwhelmed by its own nothingness in contrast to that which is supreme above all creatures.'

Explain in one or two sentences what Otto means by this quote.

STRETCH & CHALLENGE

Read about the ideas of religious experience of Schleiermacher, Buber or Stace. To what extent are their views compatible with those of Otto?

Religious experience

2.4 Visions and voices

In this topic you will learn about the religious experiences of seeing visions and hearing voices.

We live in a world of sights and sounds. We observe and hear the things around us. When we are unsure of whether to believe our eyes and ears, we can usually check our perceptions by asking a friend. ('Is the unicorn really there or am I imagining it?') What is unusual about the religious experience of visions and voices is that they are often described in terms of ordinary perceptions using the phrases 'I saw' or 'I heard'. However, usually the sights and sounds are not public or shared by others.

Both visions and voices share certain characteristics with other experiences and descriptions overlap. For instance Isaiah's experience (page 36) is a vision and is numinous. St Teresa's vision described below is also a mystical experience.

ACTIVITY

There are a number of good examples of visions in the Old Testament. What characteristics can be found in the visions of Exodus 3:1–17, Ezekiel 1:1–28 and Amos 7:1–9?

Visions

Visions occur in a variety of forms and in various faiths.

Muhammad's vision

The Muslim celebration of Lailat-ul-Qadr (Night of Power) remembers the experience of the Prophet Muhammad (pbuh) who had a vision of the Angel Jibril (Gabriel). The Angel gave the Prophet messages to recite and proclaim to the people of Makkah. This vision gives Muhammad a purpose and calling.

> *Proclaim! In the name of thy Lord and Cherisher, Who created – Created man, out of a clot of blood. Proclaim! And thy Lord is Most Bountiful – He Who taught the use of the pen – Taught man that which he knew not.*
>
> Surah 96:2–5

St Teresa's vision

Some types of visions are 'inner visions' as described by St Teresa of Avila (1515–82).

> *I saw Christ at my side – or, to put it better, I was conscious of Him, for neither with the eyes of the body or of the soul did I see anything.*
>
> *The life of Teresa of Jesus*, ed. E.A. Peers

Some thinkers refer to these as intellectual visions. The vision is not the same as seeing an external object with the eyes. It is instead a clear vision in the mind's eye. Religious believers who have these types of vision would argue that they are far too profound to be confused with the imagination.

Voices

One dramatic type of religious experience is the hearing of voices. These are usually the voice of God or, in the case of the revelation to Muhammad (pbuh), the voice of an angel mediating the words of God or Paul's conversion in Acts 9.

As with visions, the experiences of voices carry authority and have a profound effect. It is also worth noting that the voice heard need not be an audible voice as in Paul's case. Some Christians refer to the 'still small voice' of the Holy Spirit which speaks in the mind of the believer.

Augustine's experience

The conversion of Augustine is an unusual example of voices.

> *I was asking myself these questions, weeping all the while with the most bitter sorrow in my heart, when all at once I heard the sing-song voice of a child in a nearby house. ... it repeated the refrain 'Take it and read, take it and read.' At this I looked up, thinking hard whether there was any kind of game in which children used to chant words like these. I stemmed my flood of tears and stood up telling myself that this could only be a divine command to open my book of scripture.*
>
> Augustine, *Confessions*

In Augustine's case, the voice may have been the natural voice of a child playing. (This is uncertain even to Augustine.) However Augustine interprets this to be a means of God communicating with him. This shows that religious experiences may not always be supernatural. They may be natural events that we interpret as having religious significance.

Are visions and voices genuine religious experiences?

St Teresa of Avila offered two tests to determine whether an experience was genuine:

- does it fit in with Christian teaching, and
- does the experience leave the individual feeling at peace?

However, some thinkers have raised the issue of how we might prove that an experience is from God. For instance, some schizophrenics hear voices telling them to kill people, which they believe are genuine messages from God.

Also, some thinkers have observed that experiences such as visions and voices are often linked to physical factors such as fasting. Could putting the body into a weakened state lead a person to have an auditory or visual experience they believe to be a genuine religious experience?

FOR DEBATE 

If Augustine merely heard children playing, can this qualify as a religious experience?

ACTIVITY

Read and analyse the Bible's account of Paul's conversion in Acts 9:1–19.

ACTIVITY 

Look at some examples of visions and voices and write a newspaper article reporting the event. You may wish to put in quotes from expert witnesses such as Freud or James.

FURTHER RESEARCH 

Watch the film *A Beautiful Mind* about the mathematician John Forbes Nash. Are there any criteria for distinguishing between his experiences as a schizophrenic and those of religious believers?

Religious experience

2.5 Conversion and corporate experiences

In this topic you will learn about conversion experiences and corporate experiences and discuss some of the issues relating to them.

KEY WORD

Convert: to change in form, character or function. To cause a person to change beliefs. (*Oxford English Dictionary*)

Becky

I'd always gone to church but at sixth-form college I became aware of different types of church and was confused as to which was the 'right' way. I started searching for answers. At this time I began working at a charity shop run by the church. Then I started going to church. I felt welcomed and had the sense of peace I was missing.

12 months ago I knew something about God; but I was drinking three bottles of whisky a day, and smoking heavily. I was working and staying up late. It was destroying me. I got to know some Christians and began to discuss the Bible. I was born again. When I prayed the prayer of repentance, I couldn't stop smiling. Situations are much easier with Jesus.

Paolo

Layla

I've always believed in God and always prayed, but when I started to go to church I realised that there was something more to it. You can know God personally. It's been a gradual change but I feel fulfilled and a real joy inside.

ACTIVITY

These four young people have recently become practising Christians. Do their stories suggest the direct action of God or could there be another explanation?

I wasn't at rock bottom before, I was average Matt. I've been involved with drink and drugs. I suppose I was looking for fulfilment. I played rugby, tried boxing. Then I came to church. I know it's a cliché but it's as if a God shaped hole has been filled. I didn't realise how good life could be until I found Jesus. It's as if he gives a permanent fix.

Matt

Conversion as evidence for God

Examples of conversion experiences recorded in scriptures and in the modern day raise interesting issues. Although the inner experience is not empirically detectable, the resulting changes in behaviour are something that can be empirically observed. Had the profound changes described opposite occurred slowly over a period of 20 years, no one would think it unusual. For such change to occur so dramatically over days and weeks is for many believers a powerful piece of evidence for the existence of God.

William James argued that, as with all religious experience, its truth was to be found in the results. Hence dramatic changes in the character and lifestyle of an individual does count as empirical evidence in favour of spiritual claims.

Psychological views on conversion

However, some thinkers saw the process of conversion in different terms. Transformations in terms of our priorities and ideas do occur for all of us as we go through life. The changes are usually gradual. Sometimes 'crisis' type events can cause rapid transformation, so conversion could be seen in the same psychological light.

Edwin Starbuck's (1866–1947) study of conversion prompted him to draw parallels with the normal process of finding our identity in adolescence. Most religious conversions occur to people between the ages of 15 and 24. However what is worth noting in Starbuck's study is that non-religious adolescents appear to go through similar stages of anxiety and depression before finding 'happy relief' and a sense of identity.

Not everyone agrees with Starbuck's conclusions. Although in conversion, there is a sense of the individual choosing to believe and follow God, there is also an element of 'passivity'. Believers speak of a sense that someone or something is acting upon them. Also some theists recognise that there are psychological aspects of conversion experiences but argue that to reduce conversion to just a psychological phenomenon fails to address the question of the cause of the experience.

ACTIVITY

Look at the arguments for and against religious experience given in 2.6 and 2.7. Which of these can be applied to conversion experiences?

FOR DEBATE

'Conversion experiences are just another form of teenage rebellion.'

Corporate religious experiences

One of the most intriguing phenomena in religious experience is a corporate religious experience that happens simultaneously to a number of people. For example, the Toronto Blessing in 1994, when large numbers of believers reported being affected by the Holy Spirit. Some of the subsequent phenomena in these meetings including uncontrollable weeping, laughing, rolling on the floor and animal noises. Supporters of the blessing took these events as a sign of a 'new move' of God. However sceptics suggested that the explanation was more likely to be mass hysteria.

Corporate experiences may seem more impressive as there are a number of people having the experience. All other experiences are private and impossible to verify. Ultimately such experiences should be judged on what effects are produced. Are the experiences life changing in a positive way?

Critics of corporate experiences such as the Toronto Blessing examine sacred texts such as the Bible and question whether the experiences fits in with what is revealed of God's nature elsewhere.

FOR DEBATE

'Corporate religious experiences are just a form of mass hysteria.'

ACTIVITY

Investigate accounts of the Toronto Blessing and report your findings to the group.

Religious experience

2.6 The religious experience argument

In this topic you will learn about the argument for the existence of God based on religious experience as presented by William James and others.

'If there is a God there are likely to be experiences of him.

There are religious experiences, therefore there is a God.'

This argument seems plausible at a glance but unfortunately the two sentences are not logically connected. Let's assume the first sentence is correct and that if there were a God, he would interact with us in some way thus causing religious experiences. If we swap the sentences around, we are committing the error known as 'affirming the consequent'. Religious experiences may be caused by God but they may not. It's a little bit like saying: 'If I drink too much wine I will fall over: I have fallen over therefore I drank too much wine.'

Just as there may be other explanations for falling over, there may be other possible explanations for experiences that we call religious.

ACTIVITY 

Look at a modern mystery such as an alleged UFO sighting. Does this prove that there are aliens? Might there be another explanation?

William James' argument

William James took a psychological approach to religious experience (see earlier on pages 34–35). He believed that all religious experiences indicated the probability of God, although as a pluralist James does not directly speak of God but of 'the spiritual' and 'higher aspects' of the world and the self:

FOR DEBATE 

The phrase 'wider spiritual environment' is vague, James isn't really saying anything.

> *I think it may be asserted that there are religious experiences of a specific nature…I think that they point with reasonable probability to the continuity of our consciousness with a wider, spiritual environment from which the ordinary man is shut off.*
>
> James, *The Varieties of Religious Experience*

James was particularly interested in the effects of religious experience on people's lives. The validity of a religious experience rests upon the effects it produces, e.g. are lives changed? His concern was more 'Does it work?' as opposed to 'Is it True?'

So James offers an argument for God in very general terms, the phenomena of religious experiences point to a higher order of reality.

Swinburne's argument 

Modern philosopher Richard Swinburne (1934–) has come up with an interesting and some would say brave defence of religious experience. He suggests that there is no reason why claims to religious experience should be treated any differently to ordinary perceptual claims. Swinburne offers two principles to support this.

The *Principle of credulity* states that we must accept what appears to be the case unless we have clear evidence to the contrary. The clear evidence to the contrary might mean that you have good reason to doubt the person, you prove that God does not exist, or you show that the experience was not caused by God.

The *Principle of testimony* states that, unless we have positive evidence that they are misremembering or are untrustworthy, we should believe the testimony of the experience. Swinburne claims that 'other things being equal, we usually think that what others tell us that they perceived, probably happened'.

FOR DEBATE 

Is Swinburne right to say that religious experiences are no different to ordinary experiences and that we should just believe people?

Quantity: Religion, based on the experience of its founders, has been a powerful force in history. Recent research such as that of David Hay (page 33) suggests it is widespread.

Strengths of the experience argument

Effects: The effects of these experiences are powerful and positive. They change the lives of individuals and communities in a way that is very difficult to explain without reference to outside agency such as God.

Similarities: There are considerable similarities between descriptions of religious experiences that would not be present if these experiences were made up.

Weaknesses of the experience argument

There are various alternative explanations of religious experience found in psychology, physiology and sociology. If we can explain experiences naturally, then the force of the argument may be limited. (See pages 44–45.)

Religious experiences are usually private experiences. An experience may convince the experiencer of God's existence but do nothing for those nearby. This led Bertrand Russell (1872–1970) to reject the argument as it is impossible to confirm or deny what is happening inside someone else.

Believers tend to interpret experiences in the light of their religious beliefs and traditions.

Believers in different faiths claim their experiences prove the truth of their faith. They cannot all be right.

ACTIVITY

Look at some examples of religious experiences such as those of the young people on page 40. Use the information on this page to write a report on whether these experiences prove there is a God.

ACTIVITY

The people in the cartoon are certain that they are describing the elephant correctly. Do different religious groups interpret their experiences in this way?

Religious experience

2.7 Four challenges to religious experience

In this topic you will learn about the various ways in which thinkers have challenged religious experience and some responses to these challenges.

Challenge 1: psychological explanations

There are well-documented psychological explanations of various forms of religious experience.

Ludwig Feuerbach (1804–72) argued that the idea of God is a human projection. All the attributes of God are in our nature, they are human aspirations or desires. We create God in our image. 'God is man written in large letters.'

Sigmund Freud (1856–1939) believed that human religious behaviour was a neurosis caused by childhood insecurities and the desire for a father-figure to protect us. According to Freud, religious experiences are hallucinations that have a simple psychological explanation. Just as dreams are caused by deep desires we are unaware of, religious experiences are also the product of our subconscious and are caused by the desire for security and meaning.

ACTIVITY

Is God really man written in large letters? What reasons might people have for inventing the idea of God? How might a believer respond to this suggestion?

Countering the argument

Not all psychologists reject religious experience. Carl Gustav Jung (1875–1961) accepted the reality of numinous experiences and argued that development of the spiritual aspect of us was essential to psychological wholeness. He claimed that each of us has the archetype (idea) of God within a shared collective unconscious.

William James accepted that religious experience had a psychological dimension, but did not agree that this meant religious experiences were just psychological events.

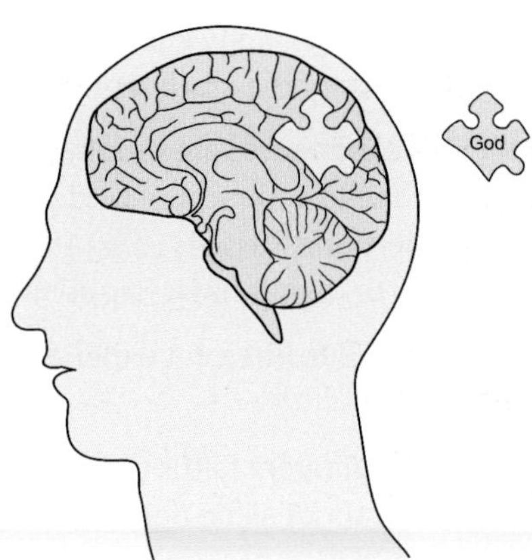

Do we really have a psychological need for God? Is it just psychological or did God cause this?

Challenge 2: physiological explanations

In recent years there has been considerable interest in physical explanations of religious experience.

Much work in the last 20 years has focused on the function of various areas of the brain. Some scientists suggest that there are neuropsychological mechanisms which underlie religious experiences. They refer to the 'causal operator' and the 'holistic operator' within the brain. These seem to show up on brain scans done on meditating Buddhist monks.

Countering the argument

As with the psychological explanation, the fact that there is a physical dimension to religious experience need not lead us to reject the experience completely. All experiences can be reduced to a series of neurological blips that show up on brain scans yet we don't doubt the reality of objects we see. Some thinkers have suggested our brains are constructed in such a way that we are almost wired up to experience God.

FOR DEBATE

'The existence of God is the best explanation of our psychological need for God.'

Challenge 3: difficulties of interpretation

Religious experiences tend to be described in terms of people's prior religious faith. For example a Catholic may interpret their experience as caused by the Virgin Mary, whereas a Hindu is unlikely to give this explanation.

Countering the argument

It can be argued that all our experiences are interpretations. Whatever happens to us, we describe it in our own way. You may have had the experience of discussing an event afterwards with a friend, and you both think something different happened. This does not logically mean that the event you are describing is false.

It could also be argued that a pluralistic interpretation is possible. Experiences in different faiths might be genuine experiences of an ultimate reality or God. These ideas are then expressed through the beliefs of a particular faith.

ACTIVITY

Create a diagram showing the four challenges to religious experience and their counter argument.

Challenge 4: it is logically impossible to experience God

A key objection to religious experience is derived from the philosophy of Immanuel Kant (1724–1804). Kant argues that our senses can only experience things in the empirical realm which Kant refers to as phenomena. There may be a reality beyond our experience (*noumena*) but it is impossible for us to experience it as a matter of logic.

Perhaps a clearer way to express this is to say that given our human senses are finite and limited, it is impossible for humans to experience an unlimited God.

Countering the argument

Whilst accepting that humans can't cause an experience of God, it may be possible for humans to experience God if he chooses to reveal himself to them.

William Alston (1921–) argues that religious experience is similar to our normal sensory perception. There may be an aspect of our human minds that is able to experience God.

C.D. Broad (1887–1971) gave an interesting analogy of a society of blind people where some evolve the capacity to see. Those who were still blind would be sceptical of the information given by those who could now see.

STRETCH & CHALLENGE

Use the information on these pages to write a dialogue on whether religious experience proves God's existence.

Religious experience

2.8 Revelation

In this topic you will learn about the concept of revelation.

Revelation

'The disclosure from the divine of something previously hidden.'

ACTIVITY

Explain the link between non-propositional revelation and religious experience.

Natural Theology/General Revelation

What information is available about God to all people at all times?

What is the role of reason and philosophy?

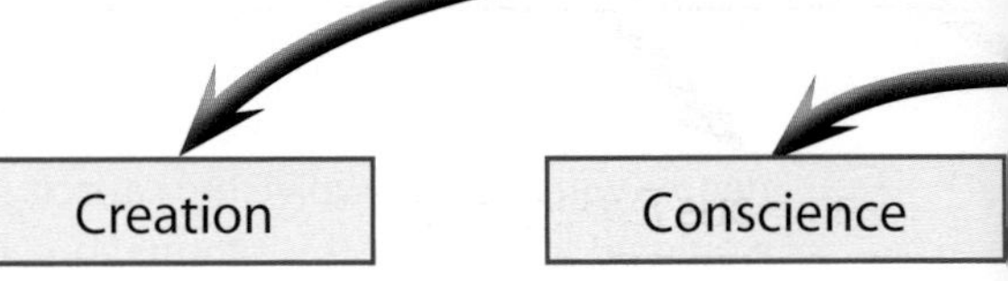

Revealed Theology/Special Revelation

What is revealed about God to certain people at certain times and places?

What is the nature of God's revelation?

Propositional

Non-Propositional

What is the method of God's revelation?

Religious Experience

Scripture

Miracle

STRETCH AND CHALLENGE

'Revelation through scripture has more authority than religious experience.'

Write a 400–500 word essay in response to the quote above.

Religious experience

2.9 Revelation through sacred writings

In this topic you will learn about the concept of revelation through sacred writings and how this might affect our ideas of God.

KEY WORDS

Revelation: the act of God revealing himself or knowledge about himself and his will to human beings.

General revelation: revelation of God available to all people at all times.

Special revelation: revelation of God to specific people at specific times.

Discussing revelation

Amir: I seem to remember that you weren't too impressed with the arguments for the existence of God; but aren't you a Christian?

Mike: I am a Christian but I don't think you can prove God's existence through logic and reason. For me, it's about accepting the revelation God gave in the Bible.

Amir: What do you mean by revelation?

Mike: Revelation is the communication of God to human beings. Human beings are not capable of working out and understanding God. God has to tell us the things he wants us to know.

Amir: I see. As a Muslim I believe that the Qur'an was supernaturally revealed to the prophet Muhammad, peace be upon him. I think I share your view that arguments cannot prove God's existence.

Revelation may be defined as communication of knowledge to man by a divine or supernatural agency. In monotheistic religions, revelation is the process in which God makes himself, his will, and/or other information known to humankind.

This topic will look specifically at some of the issues relating to revelation in the Bible, and will discuss what, if anything, is unusual or unique about revelation of God via scripture.

ACTIVITY

Look at the quotation opposite. What are the difficulties of saying that '*all Scripture*' is inspired by God?

> *all Scripture is divinely inspired and has its use for teaching the truth and refuting error, for reformation of manners and discipline in right living.*
>
> 2 Timothy 3:16

General and special revelation

There are two broad forms of revelation:

General revelation is available to all people at all times and in all places. Examples of these types of revelation would include the beauty of creation and the 'still small voice' of conscience, which is interpreted as the voice of God.

Special revelation is defined as God's revelation of himself to particular persons at definite times and places. It is in this category that the revelation of sacred writings, e.g. the revelation of the Torah to Moses, would logically fall.

FURTHER RESEARCH

Judaism, Christianity and Islam are religions of the book. Find out about the concept of revelation in one of these faiths and produce a PowerPoint® for the rest of the group.

If we assume that the revelation of the Bible is a special revelation, the question remains as to the way in which the scripture was revealed. Was God revealing facts or information (a **propositional revelation**), or was he merely making himself known during the process or revelation (a **non-propositional revelation**)?

Propositional revelation

Traditionally revelation of scripture has been understood in a propositional sense. When God revealed himself to the writers of scripture, he revealed truths or facts about himself. This means that for Aquinas, a supporter of this view, faith can be described as 'belief that'. In order to accept God's revelation, we are required to believe that certain propositions are true. For example, in Christianity, the belief that Jesus is God's Son.

Non-propositional revelation

A more modern approach to scripture has been to see the writings as the product of non-propositional revelation. When God is revealed to the writers via religious experiences, facts and truths are not communicated. The experience is ineffable, meaning the experience is beyond what can be described. However, the writers attempt to put their experience into words later by reflecting on it. Friedrich Schleiermacher (1768–1834) believed that the biblical texts came about as writers reflected on their religious experiences. For supporters of this view, faith is 'belief in'. It is not a matter of facts and information, it is more of an attitude of trust and relationship. For example, if you say that you have faith in a friend, you are likely to mean that you trust them, rather than you believe factual information about them.

STRETCH AND CHALLENGE

'Believing in revelation means that philosophical arguments are no longer relevant.'

Write a short essay either agreeing or disagreeing with this statement.

KEY WORDS

Propositional revelation: the idea that the process of revelation involves God revealing facts or information.

Non-propositional revelation: the idea that God does not reveal facts or information during the process of revelation. God makes himself known during the experience.

Can we trust the Bible?

Religious people persecuted scientists such as Galileo, and rejected Darwin, because they contradicted the Bible.
The writing of the Bible was a very human process. Stories may have been passed down by word of mouth before being written down.
The Bible is interpreted in so many different ways. Some of the moral commands of the Old Testament make no sense in the modern age.
Belief in the Bible causes all sorts of difficulties and conflict between those who believe it and those who follow other faiths.

The difficulties between religion and science are due to reading parts of the Bible too literally.
The fact that human beings were involved in the writing of the Bible doesn't mean there are mistakes. God guided the process of revelation throughout.
I agree that the Bible can be difficult to interpret. There are different types of writing and each type is interpreted differently.
The Old Testament standards of purity are no longer applicable now that Jesus has come.
You have to think about the influence of the Bible. Millions of people believe it and follow it. It changes lives.

ExamCafé

Relax, refresh, result!

Relax and prepare

Examiner says

Occasionally as an examiner, you get an odd script that stops trying to answer the question and launches into a complaint how their teacher never taught them a certain topic! It's not the candidate's fault is it? However it's strange that in the same packet of scripts there are several responses from students at the same college who clearly do understand the topic in question. I wonder what the explanation could be.

Exam question

Evaluate the claim that corporate religious experience is no more than an illusion. (35 marks)

Alan

When I saw the question I was a bit puzzled by the word corporate. Still we had done religious experience in class and I enjoyed the topic so I thought I'd do this question. When I came out of the exam, I found out that corporate religious experience is something that happens to a group of people. I was gutted! Our teacher had never mentioned it and then this question came up.

Sue

To be fair, we did do this but we spent only one lesson on it; I think Alan was away. It was the morning after Ricky's party. It was an interesting lesson but I didn't realise that it was something that was on the syllabus and you could get actual questions on it. I decided I would complain but when I read the syllabus, I realised it was there all along.

Hot tips

- Know your specification: The specification (spec) is a guide to what the examination is going to test. If you don't know what is in it, you won't know what to expect in the exam.
- Take responsibility: You are responsible for your learning on each topic. When you finish a topic, look at the spec and check your notes. Perhaps you were away for a lesson and need to copy up work missed. Perhaps your teacher only gave a brief treatment of some parts of the topic due to limited time. Did she say something about extra reading?
- When in doubt, ask: Sometimes even teachers are right! Your teacher is the expert about the spec and how the work done in class fits in. If you don't understand the relevance of something, ask.

Use the checklist on the next page to check your progress on this topic.

Refresh your memory

Revision checklist for religious experience

In order to do well in this area of the course you will need to:

- Explain the aims and conclusions of William James on religious experience.
- Explain the argument of James (and others*) that religious experience provides evidence for the existence of God.
- Be able to assess the above ideas.
- Explain and assess numinous type experiences.
- Explain and assess religious experiences of visions or voices.
- Explain and assess conversion experiences.
- Explain and assess corporate religious experiences.
- Explain the idea that God is revealed through sacred writings.
- Assess the view that God is revealed through sacred writings.

*Although other versions of the argument from religious experience are not strictly required, you will be credited if they are relevant.

Did God do this? What arguments are there for thinking that the phenomena opposite might be the result of divine intervention?

Corporate religious experience: Toronto

The arguments below relate to the phenomenon known as the Toronto Blessing. These are the bricks of the answer that Emma will give on the next page. When you read her answer, look at the 'mortar'. How has Emma put these bricks together to make one structure, her essay?

- The effects of the Toronto Blessing are a renewed sense of commitment to the faith. William James argued that all experiences should be judged by their effects.
- Trying to question the experiences naturally might be seen as a lack of faith. The Bible teaches that God's ways are higher than our ways. We ought not question how God acts.
- Strange phenomena often accompany religious experiences of God. The Old Testament prophets were moved to do strange acts. Ezekiel lay on his side for over a year and symbolically shaved his hair.
- The Toronto Blessing raises issues about the goodness of God. Surely God has bigger priorities than causing people to laugh or bark like dogs.
- The renewed enthusiasm is not for God but is a chasing of these types of experiences. The Toronto Blessing distracts believers from serving God.
- If God is omnipresent, why would people need to go to Toronto to experience this and bring it back to their churches?
- Events like the Toronto Blessing are classic examples of mass hysteria.

Look back at pages 40–41. Which of the arguments considered on these pages are also relevant?

Get the result!

Sample answers

Exam question

Evaluate the claim that corporate religious experience is no more than an illusion. (35 marks)

Emma's answer

One example of corporate religious experience is the Toronto Blessing of the 1990s. This first occurred in the Toronto Airport Church in 1994 when the visiting preacher Rodney Howard Browne was speaking. Members of the congregation began to laugh hysterically and other strange phenomena occurred such as believers being slain in the spirit and making animal noises. These events were believed by the church leaders to be manifestations of a new move of God's Holy Spirit. More sceptical people dismissed these as being illusions.

Examiner says

Emma's introduction is fine. A brief explanation of an example of a corporate experience. Not too much as the question requires evaluation rather than description. The last sentence might lead to an explanation of Freud's view.

Examiner says

At first glance, this seemed to be going off the question as there was no link sentence at the start of the paragraph stating why Emma was discussing James. This is addressed at the end of the paragraph.

The philosopher William James famously studied religious experience and he concluded that religious experience provides evidence that there is a higher realm that humans can be in contact with. His famous test for the validity of religious experiences was to test the 'fruits' of the experiences. In other words we should look at the effects and ask whether the person is changed for the better. James was a pragmatist and believed that this was the only test that could be given to experiences; the effects are in some way empirical. A psychologist can observe different behaviour after the experience. Supporters of the Toronto Blessing would argue that the experience passes this test as believers have a renewed sense of commitment to their faith. Others disagree and suggest that the effects produced are not renewed vigour for the faith but a craving after such experiences. As such they may distract believers from the mission of sharing the good news and serving God. Indeed one of the more unpleasant side-effects of the experiences are an intolerance by the supporters for Christians who question such experiences. Hence it is unclear whether it can be claimed that such experiences are more than illusions.

Examiner says

This is a key paragraph in terms of addressing the question. It's OK but there are some opportunities to go into more detail that are missed. How are Freud's conclusions disputed? What is mass hysteria and how does it apply?

One thinker who would argue that all religious experiences are illusions is Sigmund Freud. Freud studied mental patients and observed that religious belief had similar obsessional tendencies. He believed these to be caused by the Oedipus Complex and the subconscious desire for a father-figure. Freud observed that the subconscious is powerful in generating illusions, this is what happens in dreams. Religious experiences like dreams are hallucinations brought about by subconscious desires. Freud's conclusions are disputed; although religious experiences clearly have psychological effects, this is not the same as suggesting that the experiences are entirely psychological. In some ways, corporate experiences may escape Freud's challenge as these are not founded on the individual's psychology but are experienced by many different people. However this in turn brings in the possibility of the phenomena of mass hysteria which may be a possible explanation.

The question also raises theological considerations. If these experiences are to be more than illusions and attributed to the actions of God, then the question needs to be raised as to whether God really would act in this way. Supporters of corporate experiences such as the Toronto Blessing claim that 'God's ways are higher than our ways' and that human beings ought not question the action of God. They cite various examples from the Old Testament to prove their case. However one objection to this is the difficulties raised in claiming that these are actions of a benevolent God. Surely God would have better things to do than cause people to bark like dogs or laugh hysterically during sermons? Either these are not genuine actions of God or God is some sort of cosmic joker who finds these things amusing and cannot bring himself to deal with the big challenges in the world such as war and famine. The spreading of the blessing also raises difficulties with the omnipresence of God. If God is omnipresent it is unclear as to why church leaders need to go to Toronto to 'bring the blessing' back. These difficulties lead to the conclusion that this particular experience is not one of God but is more likely to be an illusion.

Examiner says

A good discussion and cleverly tied to the question. Without the opening and concluding sentences, this material might seem to be 'general topic'.

Examiner says

A slightly disappointing conclusion. There are a few things in this paragraph that may have benefited from further explanation. Nevertheless this is a solid answer to the question.

Philosophers studying religious experience have observed that interpretation and prior expectations play a big part in the type of experience that believers ultimately have. Psychologically there are good grounds for suggesting that if believers go to Toronto type meetings expecting strange things to happen then it is more likely that they will. However it must be noted that this does not necessarily prove that such events are illusions; it may be that the psychological phenomena do have some supernatural origin and each case of alleged corporate experience must be treated differently.

Now it's your turn

Look at the mark scheme and decide what marks Emma's answer might have got. What changes would make the answer even better?

3

Miracle

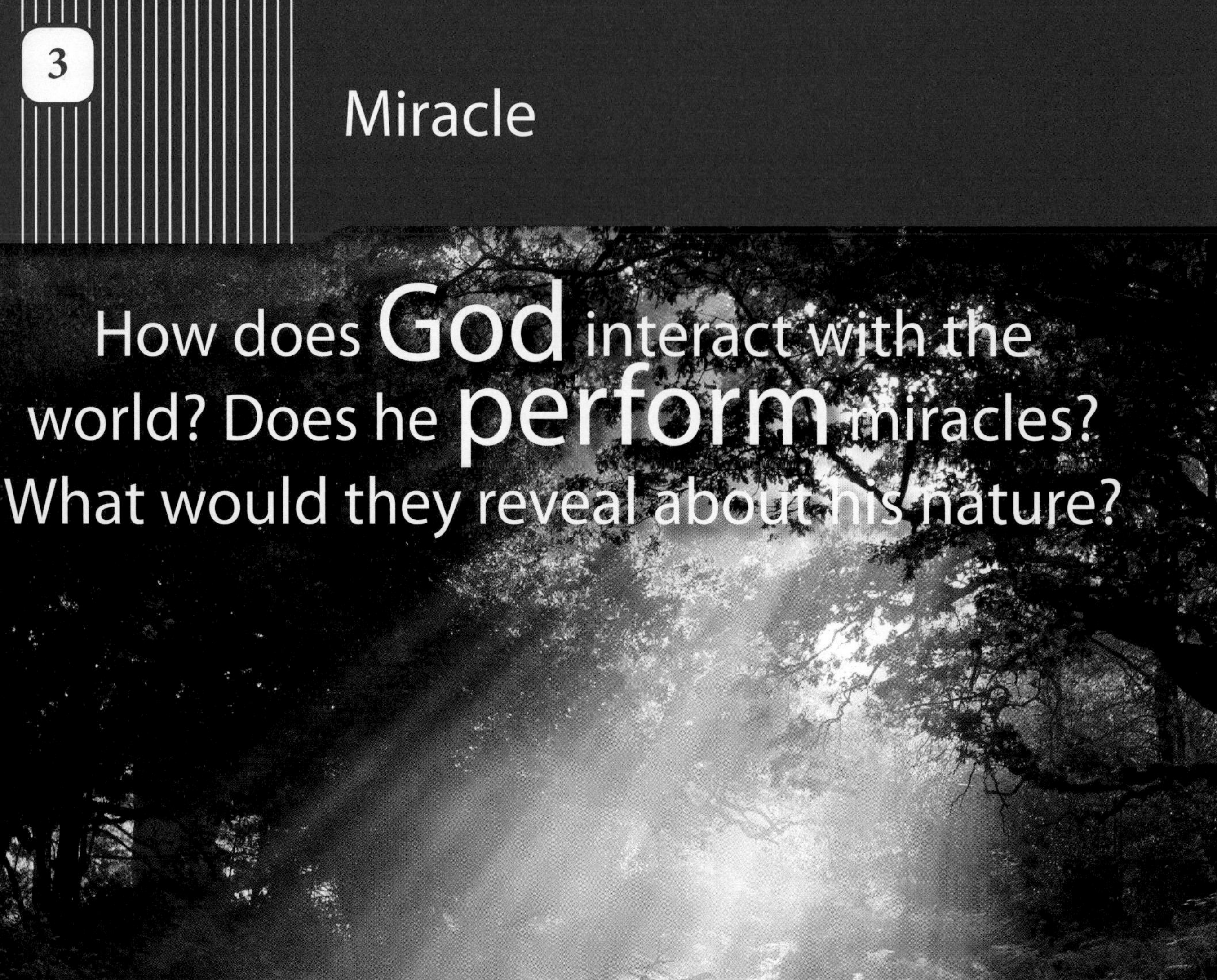

In this chapter you will learn about:

- the different definitions of miracle, including an understanding of Hume
- the biblical concept of miracle and the issues this raises about God's activity in the world
- the concept of miracle, and criticisms made by Hume and Wiles
- the implications of the concept of miracle for the problem of evil
- how to discuss these areas critically and evaluate the strengths and weaknesses.

Miracle

3.1 Introduction to miracles

In this topic you will consider the issue of miracles in modern times.

GOD GAVE ME A GOLD FILLING!

From the church that brought you the Toronto Blessing comes a new phenomenon, the gold filling. It was reported in several newspapers that God was miraculously transforming ordinary fillings into gold. The Toronto Airport Christian Fellowship reported over 300 instances of dental miracles one month, gold fillings appeared in people's mouths whilst they were being prayed for. This phenomena has since spread worldwide and similar miracles have been claimed in churches in Britain.

But Simon Jenkins, editor of the Christian website *Ship of Fools*, is not convinced:

> 'My criticism is for church leaders who do not think it through, who do not put a break on these claims before they have been whipped up. …Many will be thinking, why is God concerning himself with people's fillings, while there is such serious trauma in the world as Kosovo. They are bound to ask, hasn't God got anything better to do?'

FOR DEBATE 

Is the event described opposite possible if there is an omnipotent God? Does it seem like the sort of thing that God might do?

Strange, but is it true?

Every now and then, events such as the one above make the headlines; they are generally reported sceptically by the press. In the last couple of years there have been stories such as the name of Allah being written in perfect Arabic on a naan bread, the face of Jesus appearing in toast, together with the more 'usual' stories of healings at Lourdes. These leave us with several questions that philosophers consider:

- Can miracles really happen? Presumably, if God exists, he is able to do anything?
- How do alleged miracles demonstrate the goodness of God?
- What can we learn about the nature of God from miracle stories?

FURTHER RESEARCH

Whilst studying this topic, keep a look out for newspaper or TV coverage of unusual phenomena. Can any of them be described as miracles?

Miracle

3.2 Defining miracles 

In this topic you will learn about different ways in which philosophers have defined the concept of miracle.

It is not unusual to hear philosophers respond to questions by suggesting that it depends what is meant by a certain term. The question of whether miracles occur and what their significance might be is one of these classic cases. It really does depend upon what we mean by the term miracle. The two standard definitions are that:

- miracles are violations
- miracles are events having religious significance.

Are miracles violations?

Perhaps the classic definition of the term miracle was given by the philosopher David Hume (1711–76). Although, as we will see on pages 60–61, it's fair to say that he was sceptical about their occurence. Hume defined a miracle as: 'a transgression of a natural law by a particular volition of the Deity'.

This is known as the violation definition as its key claim is that a miracle is a violation or breaking of a natural law. For example, if you drop a pencil out of the classroom window and it hovers unsupported in mid air, then the law of gravity has been broken.

Examples of miracles as violations of the natural order can be found in many sacred texts, including the Bible:

> *Then Moses stretched out his hand over the sea, and all that night the Lord drove the sea back with a strong east wind and turned it into dry land. The waters were divided, and the Israelites went through the sea on dry ground, with a wall of water on their right and on their left.*
>
> Exodus 14:21–22

Objections to the violation definition

The violation definition assumes that we know what the laws of nature are. Scientific knowledge is constantly changing. Perhaps the law of gravity isn't as constant as we assume. Maybe at the exact moment you release the pencil, it will coincide with an odd lack of gravity that we did not expect but turns out to be a natural phenomenon. The point is, unless we know exactly all of the laws of nature, we are unable to comment on whether something is a miracle, however unusual.

A more complex objection comes from Alastair McKinnon. If the laws of nature merely describe the actual course of events, then to define a miracle in this way is to call it an event that disrupts the actual course of events. This is of course self-contradictory.

What might have needed to happen in order to satisfy each definition of the idea of miracle?

ACTIVITY

In the example of the West Side Baptist Church, each member of the choir was usually late on no more than one in four practices. What is the probability of all 15 members being late? Is this significant? You can check out the full story on the internet. Go to www.heinemann.co.uk/hotlinks and enter the express code 3587P.

Are miracles events with religious significance?

One problem with the definition above is that events that may appear to be coincidences are excluded.

A famous example of this is given by R.F. Holland (1932–). He gives the story of a boy playing on a railway line. The express train is about to come around the bend and will not be able to stop in time. Remarkably the train does stop a few metres short of the boy. It later emerges that the driver had fainted and the automatic cut off switch had stopped the train. These events are perfectly natural, but the boy's mother sees them as being significant, she sees the whole chain of events as an act of God. Hence Holland argues that miracles are not necessarily violations of natural laws but are any event that a person experiences as having religious significance.

A further example of this type of miracle was reported in *Life* magazine in 1950.

On Wednesday March 1st 1950, West Side Baptist Church exploded due to a gas leak. It was 5 minutes after choir practice was due to begin and normally most of the 15 members of the choir would have already been inside. Remarkably, no choir members were there; had they been they would have probably been killed or seriously injured. There were a variety of reasons why the members were late: car trouble, finishing homework, ironing a dress, finishing a letter, listening to a radio show, and just plain fallen asleep. Yet as the members arrived to see the ruins of the church, they were in no doubt that their lateness had been the direct result of divine intervention.

Whilst this definition allows us to include more natural events as miracles, it comes down to a subjective interpretation. If your teacher, who always gives you homework, decides not to on the evening you are going out, there is nothing to stop you from seeing this as a direct act of God.

ACTIVITY

Look for stories in newspapers or on the internet that contain the word 'miracle' or 'miraculous'. Which of these do you think are miracles? How might each of the definitions apply?

STRETCH & CHALLENGE

An unusual attempt to define miracles has been put forward by Gareth Moore. Find out what his definition is and consider whether it improves upon the two standard definitions.

Miracle

3.3 Biblical miracles

In this topic you will learn about the concept of miracles as presented in the Bible.

FOR DEBATE

According to the biblical account, the Egyptians were killed because God caused the sea to go back. Does this still count as a miracle even if the effects are not good?

ACTIVITY

Read and analyse a different miracle in the Old Testament.

KEY WORD

Covenant: a binding agreement. In theology it describes the agreements made between God and humans. Jesus is seen as bringing in a new covenant.

FURTHER RESEARCH

Some thinkers suggest that Old Testament miracles show a vengeful punishing God, whereas the New Testament miracles generally show compassion. Is this an oversimplification of the issue?

The Bible contains a number of miracles in both the Old and New Testaments.

Miracles in the Old Testament

Miracles in the Old Testament are generally acts of God that support and help the faithful. They demonstrate the glory of God and bring punishment on the wicked or those who oppose God's people.

The central miracle in the Old Testament is the events surrounding the exodus from Egypt. The scriptures tell of Moses standing before Pharaoh and asking that the Israelites be freed. With each refusal, plagues follow which only affect the Egyptians. These culminate in the death of the first born and the crossing of the Red Sea. The Egyptians who attempt to follow the Israelites are killed as the waters of the sea return to their normal place.

Miracles in the New Testament

The miracles in the New Testament centre on the person of Jesus. There are over 30 recorded miracle accounts in the four gospels. Scholars tend to divide the miracles into categories:

- Healings.
- Exorcisms.
- Nature miracles (such as walking on water).

These miracles are recorded by the writers of the gospels as demonstrations of the Kingdom of God. They bear witness to the fact that Jesus is the promised Messiah and that a new era is being unveiled in the person of Jesus. They show that God will have the final victory in the age to come. John's gospel refers to the miracles as signs; they point to the fact that Jesus is the Son of God and that the new **covenant** is a far better replacement for the old way of doing things.

The purpose of miracles

For a Christian, the miracles in the Bible have several purposes:

- They demonstrate the love and goodness of God. God is compassionate and responds to prayers and demonstrations of faith.
- They demonstrate God's power over nature, illnesses and even death.
- They show that God is continually involved and active in the world that he has created.
- They are signs pointing to the person and message of Jesus, they demonstrate that he is from God.

How miracles are understood

▌The nature miracle of Jesus walking on waves is well known. Should it be taken literally?

In the last 200 years, interpretation of the biblical miracles has been a contentious area. Advances in science led many educated Christians to abandon belief that the events described in the Bible actually happened. They argued that the important thing about the stories is the message contained in them.

Form critics such as Gunkel (1862–1932) argued that the key to understanding miracle accounts was understanding the period where the stories were passed on by word of mouth prior to being written down. What we see in the gospels are the miracles in the 'form' that they were told in the early Church.

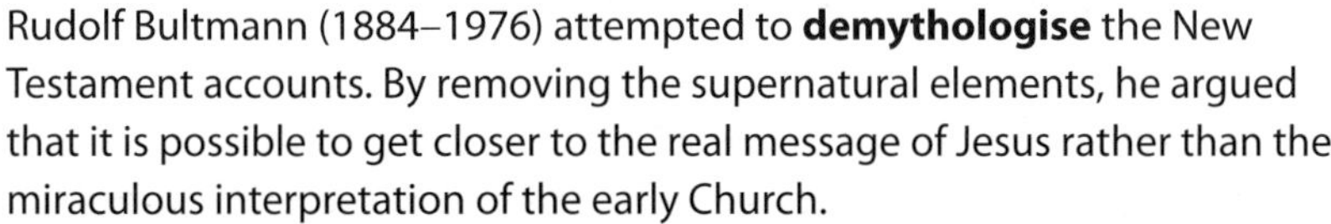
Rudolf Bultmann (1884–1976) attempted to **demythologise** the New Testament accounts. By removing the supernatural elements, he argued that it is possible to get closer to the real message of Jesus rather than the miraculous interpretation of the early Church.

These approaches are controversial amongst conservative scholars who argue that the miracles are part of the original accounts and not later additions.

Is the resurrection of Jesus a special case?

The resurrection of Jesus is the central miracle of the New Testament.

> *If Christ has not been raised, then our preaching has been in vain and your faith has been in vain.*
>
> 1 Corinthians 15:14

It can be seen as the key event in the history of Christianity. It confirms the claims that Jesus is the Son of God and is a demonstration that he is able to give his followers eternal life. For most Christians, it is essential to believe that the resurrection was a real physical event even if they have doubts over some of the other miracles.

For others, including the former Bishop of Durham, Rev. Dr David Jenkins, the resurrection of Jesus need not be believed literally:

> *I personally do not know whether the grave was empty or not. The evidence of the texts, the nature of the tradition and the general facts about the way people all over the world rapidly believe appropriate stories to support the religious beliefs leave me wholly uncertain about the Empty Tomb as literal historical fact.*
>
> Jesmond Parish Church website

KEY WORDS

Form criticism: a theological movement that analysed biblical texts in order to discover what form they were originally used in.

Demythologising: the process of removing the elements of the biblical accounts that are purely 1st-century myth in order to discover the essential message of Jesus.

FURTHER RESEARCH

Find out some of the arguments for and against the resurrection of Jesus. What reasons are there for thinking that this actually happened? You might want to look at what the former Bishop of Durham said about resurrection – there is some useful information on *The Daily Telegraph's* website. Visit www.heinemann.co.uk/hotlinks and enter the express code 3587P.

3.4 Hume's case against miracles 

In this topic you will learn about Hume's classic argument against miracles.

> *A Wise man proportions his belief according to the evidence.*
> Hume, *Enquiries Concerning Human Understanding*

ACTIVITY

Use the internet to research the most miraculous cure of Jean-Pierre Bely at Lourdes that was validated in 1999. How would David Hume respond to this claim?

In order to understand Hume's case against miracles, you need to be aware that he is both an empiricist and a sceptic. Hume is empirical in the sense that he believed that our knowledge of the world comes from the observations made by our senses. However he is also a sceptic as he argued that we cannot reason accurately beyond what we see and hear as this requires us to make assumptions.

The theoretical case against miracles

Hume appears to suggest that miracles are impossible. The laws of nature that we experience are uniform and constant; we assume that these laws will not be changed in the future and that they were constant in the past. However, in order to understand Hume's criticism of miracles it is necessary to consider his ideas on induction. Hume notes that we establish cause and effect relationships based on our experience of the world. This leads to us making predictions about what will happen in similar cases in the future. So for example, you will predict that the water you heat up tomorrow in a science lesson will come to the boil at 100 degrees, just as it always has done. The more experiences we have of an event, the less likely it is that the opposite will occur. Each experience we have of 'normal events' seems to make miracles less likely, yet there is no way of absolutely disproving them.

ACTIVITY

Produce a leaflet that would be useful for revision entitled 'Hume on Miracles'.

Faced with this difficulty, Hume suggests that the only evidence available to us is the testimonies and accounts written by others. Look back at the key quote from Hume at the top of this page, and ask yourself how useful these accounts are. What is more probable – that a miracle occurred or that the accounts are mistaken? Hume suggests that we ought only to believe a miracle story if it would be more incredible that all witnesses were mistaken than if the event were true. He says:

> *No testimony is sufficient to establish a miracle unless the testimony be of such a kind, that its falsehood would be more miraculous, than the fact which it endeavours to establish.*
> Hume, *Enquiries Concerning Human Understanding*

ACTIVITY 

Working in pairs, choose a biblical miracle account. Imagine you are David Hume and explain why the story is improbable. Present your conclusions to the class.

Hume does not believe in chance or in supernatural intervention. Hence, he appeals for us to go with the evidence and consider which state of affairs is more probable, a miracle or a more ordinary explanation.

Hume's practical arguments against miracles

Hume also gave four practical arguments against miracles – regardless of whether miracles are theoretically possible, Hume tries to persuade us that, practically speaking, they just don't (or can't) happen.

1. Hume observes that:

> *There is not to be found in all history any miracle attested by a sufficient number of men, of such unquestioned good sense, education and learning, as to secure us against all delusion in themselves…*

Hume's point speaks for itself here; miracles do not generally have many sane and educated witnesses.

2. Hume's second point is psychological. We have a natural interest in things that are unusual. This tendency towards things of surprise and wonder is exploited by religious people. Hume suggests that some religious people know that the stories they recount are false, but continue to spread them because it is in a good cause.

3. Prior to the age of political correctness, Hume suggests that it is mainly amongst the 'ignorant and barbarous nations' that miracles are reported and believed. According to Hume, these things don't seem to happen with such regularity in modern times.

4. Almost all religions carry miracle stories, yet they cannot all be right. The sets of testimonies would seem to cancel each other out because each faith alleges that the miracles they believe in provide evidence that their particular faith is true.

Responses to Hume

Hume's arguments against miracles have been criticised.

Hume's appeal to the laws of nature is inconsistent with his own writings. He suggests that our idea of scientific laws may just be a psychological habit based on what we repeatedly see. He famously observed that there was no good reason to expect the sun to rise in the morning, yet we do expect this.

Hume's practical points can be seen as sweeping generalisations. It is unclear how many witnesses Hume thinks would be sufficient. He also fails to define what 'ignorant and barbarous nations' are. Miracles are also claimed in modern western societies, as some of the accounts in this book demonstrate.

Swinburne has also noted that testimonies may not be the only evidence available. Physical traces of events, such as recent footprints on both sides of a lake and no boat or bridge, and dry clothes, would count as evidence of someone walking on water.

ACTIVITY

Look at Hume's four practical arguments. Rank them in order putting the strongest one first.

ACTIVITY

Millions of visitors flock to Lourdes every year – a site famous for its miracle cures. Are these people being exploited as Hume suggests, or is there a genuine reason for them to believe in the miracle cure? Using arguments from this page, write two or three paragraphs giving reasons for and against this argument.

STRETCH & CHALLENGE

Read chapter 10 of Hume's *Enquiries Concerning Human Understanding* to enhance your understanding of Hume's argument.

Miracle

3.5 Responding to Hume: modern thinkers on miracles

In this topic you will learn about how modern thinkers following on from Hume have criticised or defended belief in miracles.

ACTIVITY

Summarise the key points of each philosopher's argument. How does each link to Hume?

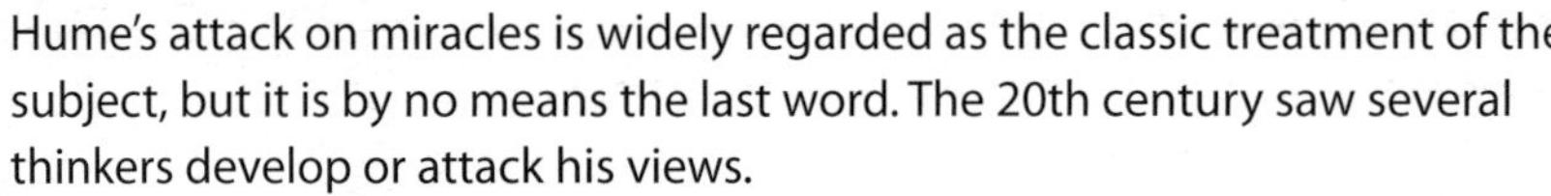

Hume's attack on miracles is widely regarded as the classic treatment of the subject, but it is by no means the last word. The 20th century saw several thinkers develop or attack his views.

Antony Flew (1923-)

I accept that Hume is technically correct to say that miracles cannot be proved and agree that the wise man should go with the evidence and reject miracles. I use a historical approach to attempt to strengthen Hume's argument. A historian could only have direct evidence of a miracle if they were actually present when it occurred. This does not tend to happen! So we have to resort to indirect evidence. In other words, we make an analogy or comparison to what we know about how the world works now. When we're presented with a story about a resurrection from the dead or water turning into wine, historically we have to reject this as our repeatedly tested experience tells us that dead people stay dead and water does not suddenly become wine. These are the only conclusions that we can make based on the evidence that is still available to us.

C.S. Lewis (1898-1963)

I am the author of the Narnia series – do you remember *The Lion, the Witch and the Wardrobe?* I wrote that. I converted to Christianity in 1929 after being an atheist. I wrote defences of a number of Christian ideas, including the belief in miracles. Basically, we are faced with a choice about how we view the world. We are either naturalists and believe that reality is totally physical and material and that nothing else exists. Or we are supernaturalists, which means that we believe that non-physical things such as God and souls may exist. For me naturalism is self-defeating. If you are just a physical being subject to laws of cause and effect as all physical objects are, then your decision to believe in naturalism is physically caused, you have no choice about what you believe. Your decision is caused by physical factors. However if you accept the possibility of a supreme God, then you can also accept the possibility of miracles. In rejecting this, the naturalist is making assumptions that the world is a purely physical thing.

Richard Swinburne (1934-)

I have defended belief in miracles in several recent works. I argue that it is important to be clear about what the laws of nature are. They are not necessarily fixed truths. Many of the scientific laws we adopt, such as Kepler's law on planetary motion and quantum theory, are merely statistical laws – they tell us what will almost certainly happen, but the individual particles in question are all behaving randomly. In my Concept of Miracle, I said that 'One must distinguish between a formula being a law and a formula being (universally) true, being a law which holds without exception.'

Perhaps God can suspend natural laws on occasions. Take the analogy of a loving parent who gives a child boundaries. This parent may sometimes relax a certain rule in response to a child's pleading. This may be like God – if he is all-loving, he would want to interact with his creation and may do so via occasional miracles.

I think that miracles by their very nature have to be occasional. If miracles were more regular, life would be confusing as we would not know whether laws such as gravity were going to operate. It also encourages humans to be active in trying to make progress. For example if we knew that God regularly healed cancer, humans would not actively seek a cure.

FOR DEBATE 

'Modern people can believe in miracles just as easily as people in olden times.'

John Polkinghorne (1929-)

I defend the possibility of miracles particularly the resurrection of Jesus. All that science can tell us is that a given event is against normal expectations. It cannot completely disprove its happening. I believe that the key theological question is whether it makes sense to say that God has acted in a new way. It may be perfectly possible for God to act in new and unexpected ways when circumstances change.

The laws of nature do not change yet the consequences of these laws can change when one moves into a 'new regime'.

Consequences of the laws of nature may change if God begins to deal with humans in a new way. The resurrection of Jesus is a crucial miracle as it brings a new age in God's dealing with people.

STRETCH & CHALLENGE

Choose one of the thinkers on these pages and find out more about their views. Prepare a presentation on this for the group.

3.6 Wiles on miracles 

In this topic you will learn about the criticism of miracles given by Maurice Wiles and consider the implications for our understanding of God.

Is God arbitrary and partisan?

The modern theologian Maurice Wiles (1923–2005) argued that any occasion where God intervened with the natural order to help individuals or groups would raise issues of consistency and fairness. He believed such a God would be **arbitrary** and **partisan**.

Wiles claimed that the goodness of God and the existence of miracles were two incompatible ideas. A God that chooses to help some and not others, often ignoring those in greatest need, would not be morally good. Wiles believed it is better theologically to believe in a God that does not do any miracles, than in one that was not morally good.

Wiles on God

In order to fully understand the objection that Wiles has to miracles, it is necessary to understand his ideas on the nature of God. For Wiles, God is the creator and sustainer of the world. To talk about God's actions is to consider his relationship to the world as a whole rather than looking at specific events. Wiles believed that there was in effect a single miracle of creation and that God's creation was good and did not require intervention in the form of specific miracles.

> *the world as a whole (is) a single act of God.*
>
> Wiles, *The Remaking of Christian Doctrine*

Some critics have argued that Wiles' view is a form of **deism** not theism. Although this may be seen as justified in that God does not intervene, Wiles rejects the claim as God is still actively sustaining his creation.

KEY WORDS

Arbitrary: an action based on random choice.

Partisan: a strong supporter of a certain party or group, often in times of war.

FOR DEBATE 

'If someone is religious, they have to believe in miracles.'

ACTIVITY

'the Lord hurled large hailstones down on them from the sky, and more of them died from the hailstones than were killed by the swords of the Israelites.' (Joshua 10:11)

How might someone use this text to argue that God is partisan?

ACTIVITY

Look at the picture. Does it seem unfair when another student is helped instead of you? Might the teacher have reasons for helping that student that you may not be aware of? Explain how this may fit in with the topic of this chapter.

Wiles on miracles

In creating the world, God puts in place certain natural laws. Given that there are natural laws, miraculous events would be very rare by definition. If this were not so, we could have no confidence in the laws of nature and our life would be difficult never knowing whether God might intervene or not.

Given that miracles have to be infrequent, the question remains, would God do such things? Wiles observes that:

> *...even so it would seem strange that no miraculous intervention prevented Auschwitz or Hiroshima while the purposes apparently forwarded by some of the miracles acclaimed in traditional Christian faith seem trivial by comparison.*
>
> Wiles, *God's Action in the World*

One target that Wiles has in mind is the New Testament miracle where Jesus turns water into wine. The biblical accounts suggest that this is done to prevent the embarrassment or shame of the hosts. In a world where suffering occurs on such a large scale, this would seem to be a bizarre arbitrary whim of God. For Wiles, the biblical miracles, including the resurrection, have a symbolic value and teach believers about the nature of God and the importance of obedience.

KEY WORD

Deism: the belief that God creates the world but is then separate and uninvolved in its continuing affairs.

STRETCH AND CHALLENGE

What are the advantages and disadvantages of deism? Is Wiles justified in claiming that he is not a deist?

Strengths of Wiles' argument

Supporters of Wiles' approach suggest that there are several attractions.

- Wiles' view may appeal to educated believers as it allows them to believe in God and uphold scientific laws.
- It may be seen as solving the problem of evil. God does not intervene either because he cannot or because he is willingly bound by the laws of nature.
- It allows believers to reinterpret the idea of prayer. It is not about presenting wish lists to God that make God act; it is rather about allowing an individual to connect to God's will.

Weaknesses of Wiles' argument

Consider the following weaknesses of Wiles' approach:

- What Wiles is suggesting does not accord with traditional religious teaching about God. It requires the claim that believers have completely misunderstood the notion of miracles for almost 2000 years.
- To suggest that miracle stories show God's love and power loses impact if God is not able to intervene in the world.
- It is not appropriate to make God conform to human rationality. God may act in ways that are beyond our human reasoning.

ACTIVITY

Wiles concluded that ***either*** God does random and arbitrary miracles in which case he would not be worthy of worship, ***or*** he does not intervene at all.

The latter option is Wiles' own view as this preserves the goodness of God. Using the arguments on this page, write one or two paragraphs stating your own view and your reasons why.

Miracle

3.7 Miracles and the problem of evil 

In this topic you will learn about the link between the topic of miracles and the problem of evil.

ACTIVITY

Recap on what you have learned about the problem of evil so far. Display your notes in a diagramatic form.

What is the link between miracles and the problem of evil?

The definition of all-powerful would seem to include the ability to do miracles.

The idea of goodness includes fairness; If God is 'all-good', he ought to treat everyone equally. But if God performs miracles, he is helping the selected few, and is being unfair.

The seeming incompatibility has led to many different conclusions:

- Rejecting miracles on theological grounds.
- Rejecting miracles scientifically.
- Defending miracles as symbolic stories.
- Defending literal belief in miracles.

Rejecting miracles on theological grounds

Maurice Wiles would agree that a miracle-working God does not help us to solve the problem of evil. This is because miracles would compromise the goodness of God. It is unfair if God helps some people in their suffering but not others (see page 64).

It could also be argued, using an Irenaean-type theodicy, that the world presents us with opportunities to grow and develop our character. Therefore repeated intervention by God prevents us from growing and developing ourselves. We might become lazy and expect God to constantly perform miracles rather than work to make things better and alleviate suffering.

Counterargument

However, it is not inconceivable to suggest that God may act seemingly randomly in performing miracles in order to have an impact on humans. God gives humans freedom to choose to believe in him and to choose to love him and others. It may be that miracles act as signs and encourage some people to respond to God. Indeed the Bible refers to miracles in some instances as signs (see John 2:11).

MAKING LINKS

Look at chapter 4 on the attributes of God. How does this link in with the problem of evil?

Rejecting miracles scientifically

Many scientists argue that nature is a closed system with fixed causal laws.

This raises another difficulty. Presumably nature was created by God, and natural evil such as earthquakes is the direct responsibility of God. If he were to intervene to prevent it, that would indicate the world was not made perfect. If he did not intervene, questions would be raised regarding his goodness.

Counterargument

These objections may ignore the effects of human free will and sin. In Augustine's theodicy, the blame for both natural and moral evil is laid at the door of human beings who misuse their free will. This would indicate that God may choose to intervene occasionally but is not morally obligated to clear up the mess!

MAKING LINKS

Review your work on the Irenaean and Augustinian theodicies from the AS course. Consider how each may be strengthened or weakened by a belief in miracles.

Defending miracles as symbolic stories

Rudolf Bultmann regarded the stories of miracles in the New Testament as later additions to inspire us to follow God and be morally good.

Miracle accounts should be read symbolically. They teach us about God's power or Jesus' compassion and should inspire us to help people in a similar way.

This eases some of the difficulties regarding the problem of evil as God does not literally intervene in people's lives in an arbitrary manner, which would raise issues of fairness. However one question that remains is whether the lack of divine intervention is because God cannot or because God chooses not to.

ACTIVITY

Read the story of Jesus turning the water into wine. In what way is this a sign of who Jesus is and what his ministry would involve?

Counterargument

Bultmann may be right that the miracle stories contain theological truths and may inspire us to do good things. But wouldn't the stories have more effect if they were true? Admittedly they do seem mystical and sometimes impossible but surely God's power allows him to do such things?

Defending literal belief in miracles

Christians see miracles as a way that God reveals his power, and miracles usually go against the natural law of the universe. In some biblical miracles, God punishes the wicked as well as helping the righteous. But does this solve the problem of evil or add to it?

Believers point to God's overall plan for the Kingdom of God and the return of Christ. Here, evil will finally be defeated by God and goodness will triumph. God is omniscient and knows the future in a way that humans cannot. What makes no sense to us now may form part of God's plan. It is argued that we ought not to question the workings of God (see pages 66–67 on faith and reason).

Counterargument

This position may well be correct but it becomes impossible to engage in dialogue about it. It is neither verifiable nor falsifiable.

3.8 Faith and reason

In this topic you will consider the place of faith and reason in relation to miracles.

Faith

'Belief is not subject to rational analysis'

FOR DEBATE

'People should not hold beliefs that are not reasonable.'

Faith over Reason

Key Idea

Fideism: the belief that faith takes priority over reason.

Key Thinkers

Soren Kierkegaard (1813–1855): One must take a leap of faith contrary to reason.

Martin Luther (1483–1546): Philosophy is the devil's whore! It will never lead to faith in God.

A bit of both...

Key Thinkers

Augustine (356–430): Reason is fallen and must be used carefully.

Anselm (1033–1099): Faith must come first so that reason can be used properly.

ACTIVITY

Produce a PowerPoint® giving a more detailed explanation of the ideas of one of the thinkers named on pages 68–69. Swap your PowerPoint® with other members of the class.

Reason

'Philosophical logic and science determine what is to be believed'

Reason defends Faith

Key Idea

Far from defeating faith, reason supports faith and may enable us to prove some religious claims.

Key Thinkers

Thomas Aquinas (1224–1274): God's existence can be proved.

Richard Swinburne (1934–) and C S Lewis (1898–1963) defend ideas such as God and miracles.

Reason defeats Faith

Key Thinkers

David Hume (1711–1776) and Bertrand Russell (1872–1970) seek to demolish traditional arguments for God.

Sigmund Freud (1856–1939), Karl Marx (1818–1883) and Charles Darwin (1809–1882) seek to show the absurdity of faith from psychological, sociological and scientific perspectives respectively.

Exam Café

Relax, refresh, result!

Refresh your memory

Revision checklist for miracle

In order to do well in this topic you will need to:

- Know and understand the main definitions given to the concept of miracle.
- Explain Hume's views on miracles including his criticisms of the concept.
- Assess whether Hume's criticisms of miracles are successful.
- Understand the concept of miracle as presented in the Bible and have an awareness of some of the issues that it raises.
- Explain and assess the view of Wiles that miracles would lead to an arbitrary and partisan God.
- Explain modern views on the concept of miracle.
- Assess whether modern people can be expected to believe in miracles.
- Explain the connection between miracles and the problem of evil.
- Assess whether a belief in miracles solves or adds to the problem of evil.

Relax and prepare

Hot tips

Nicola

I wonder if anyone can help me. It may seem like a trivial problem but I can't stop getting Bs on my essays. I learn my notes really well and try to make sure I'm answering the question but I'm always a couple of marks short of getting the A grade I need for my university. Just how do you get A or A*? I daren't ask the teacher in case she thinks I'm blaming her for not teaching me well.

Ashifa

You idiot! Ask your teacher, they're the expert.

Dan

Do you do any reading other than the notes you did in class? When we did the topic of miracles I really got into it and read a couple of short books by modern thinkers. I saw the topic in a new way. Things kinda clicked and I got A* on an essay for the first time. I don't normally do top grades, me.

Get the result!

A* anyone?

Some people will get top grades, others will just do ok. So the question is, what exactly is the difference? If you look at the mark scheme for band 5 you will see some statements regarding what the best candidates are likely to do. Although the exact location of grade boundaries is discussed at the end of each session, it is a reasonable bet that candidates who are around the A/A* are likely to give answers with some of the following characteristics.

- Understanding: This means that rather than an essay that seems to just state ideas and arguments, there is real evidence that you have grasped them for yourself. If you're just repeating things that you've memorised without understanding them, it shows.
- Engagement with the material: Have you spent time wrestling with some of the issues and reading up on things rather than sticking to your teacher's notes or the same textbook?
- Technical terms: You understand RS words and use them confidently in the right context.
- Critical analysis of different viewpoints: You don't just accept points or put forward philosophers' arguments. You analyse them also.
- Comprehends the demands of the question: You understand all the implications of the question and have substantial understanding of a range of material that is relevant. In other words, your response is detailed and no major area is overlooked.

Examiner says

Too many students are like babies! They expect to be spoonfed all the time. This may have happened for them at Key Stage 3 and even GCSE where their teachers' notes saved the day. They didn't ever need to think for themselves. Ironically the fact that they did reasonably well at GCSE was the worst thing that could happen; they become lazy and think that their teacher will continue the feeding. A Level RS is not like that, it can't be taught by formulas. You have to study issues, engage with them and ultimately think for yourself.

Nicola

I realised I had to broaden my study of each topic. On the miracles topic I just had ten pages of my teacher's handouts and made revision notes from them. I'd never looked at anything else. I found a book in the library with a good chapter on miracles and a good website. This helped me see the topic in a new way. I did the miracles question on the actual exam and was well chuffed with my grade!

4

Attributes of God

What is God like? What **difficulties** are there in the traditional definition of God? Is the idea of God a **coherent** concept?

In this chapter you will learn about:

- what it means to describe God as eternal, omniscient, omnipotent, and omni-benevolent
- the philosophical problems arising from these concepts
- the views of Boethius on eternity and foreknowledge
- the question of whether a good God should reward and punish.

Attributes of God

4.1 What are the attributes of God?

In this topic you will learn about the difficulty of combining some of the attributes of God.

God and the suitcase

Most of you will have packed a suitcase for a holiday. As you reach the end, you realise that it will be difficult to fit everything in. As you put in items that are large but essential, there is a knock-on effect on the other items in the case. They are either squashed or left out.

Traditional definitions of God include the idea that God is:

- eternal (everlasting or timeless)
- omnipotent (all-powerful)
- omniscient (all-knowing), and
- omni-benevolent (all-good).

Which items are essential to the definition of God? What would happen if some of the items on the floor were to be added?

Like the holiday suitcase, it is a matter of debate as to whether these items fit together and are coherent. It may depend on how we choose to define each one of them. Adjusting our definition of just one of these items has implications for the others, and may cause knock-on effects to theological problems.

Religious believers are aware that the idea of God may be slightly **paradoxical**. There is a tension in asserting that God is both **transcendent** and **immanent**. However, many would argue that this is due to our human limitations. We are not able to accurately reason regarding the nature of God.

Greek philosophy and the Bible

One issue in Christianity is whether the concept of God has been affected by Christianity's links with Greek philosophy. It is certainly true that great thinkers such as Augustine and Aquinas were influenced by Plato and Aristotle. The solutions that they bring to the issues of this chapter attempt to be both biblical and philosophical. Other thinkers feel that some aspects of the traditional idea of God have too much of the Greek influence.

Difficulties in reconciling all the different pieces of the jigsaw led some thinkers in the 17th and 18th centuries in particular to become deists. For deists it seemed more logical to believe in an all-powerful creator God who was no longer actively involved in the world.

ACTIVITY

Draw a spider diagram showing the key ideas involved in the concept of God, together with definitions of some of the key words.

KEY WORDS

Paradox: a situation where two contradictory statements both appear true.

Transcendent: the idea that God is separate from the physical world. He is far above all things.

Immanent: the idea that God is active and closely involved in the world.

Immutable: the idea that God cannot change.

4

Attributes of God

4.2 God as eternal

In this topic you will learn about different ideas on what it means to suggest that God is eternal.

KEY WORDS

Timeless: the belief that God stands outside of time and that all time is equally present to him.

Everlasting: the belief that God moves through time along with creation but has no beginning or end.

Process theology: a reformulation of the concept of God which rejects the immutability of God and teaches that God is also in the process of becoming and change.

ACTIVITY

Look up the word eternal in a dictionary. Apart from God, are there other things that could be eternal?

MAKING LINKS

Look at your AS work on Plato and the Forms. Why did Plato believe them to be unchanging? How similar is this to the idea of timelessness?

Whilst there is agreement between believers that God is eternal, it soon becomes clear that this idea is understood in very different ways. Different thinkers suggest that:

- God is **timeless**: past, present and future are all alike to him
- God is **everlasting** within time
- God moves through time with his creation, but changes with it (**process theology**).

Eternal means 'timeless'

Although everything that we experience as human beings occurs in time, this is not necessarily the case with God. God is outside of time and sees all events in an eternal present. In other words, your fifth birthday party, your GCSE results and the birth of your first grandchild are all immediately visible and are 'now' as far as God is concerned. As Augustine writes, 'thy years neither come nor go; whereas ours both come and go'.

So time is something that is bound up in creation and created things but does not affect God. The link with Greek thought is obvious. Ideas such as change and motion are part of the world of appearances. The forms are eternal and unchanging. Plato taught that time was the moving image of eternity. In the middle ages thinkers such as Boethius, Anselm and Aquinas worked with the contrast between the real world and this world. In this world things are changing in time. God is unchanging and is outside of time.

The idea that God is timeless has attracted a number of criticisms.

The idea of time not applying to God seems to contradict the plain reading of scripture. The Bible speaks of God promising and remembering. Supporters of the view that God is timeless argue that we ought to understand these texts metaphorically or analogically.

'He who goes along the road does not see those who come after him; whereas he who sees the whole road from a height sees at once all those travelling on it' (Aquinas). How does this analogy help us to understand the idea of God as timeless?

The idea of God being personal and active within the world is harder to fit with a timeless God. God would seem to be logically too far removed.

But if God is timeless, it is easier to affirm the traditional belief in the immutability of God. If God is in time, as those who believe God is everlasting would claim, then God may be subject to change. For example his knowledge that England will win the World Cup in 1966 changed to knowledge that they had won it after the event.

ACTIVITY

Read Genesis 17:4–8, 9:15, 8:1. Do these texts imply that God is within time? Write a short paragraph explaining your views.

Eternal means everlasting

The belief that eternal means everlasting is probably the most widespread view of eternity amongst those who have not studied philosophy. To describe God as eternal is to say that God moves through time with us. He has always existed and always will exist.

One prominent defender of this view is Richard Swinburne (1934–) who states that:

> *there was no time at which he did not exist…He is backwardly eternal. He also exists at any other nameable time…will go on existing forever…he is forwardly eternal.*
>
> Swinburne, *The coherence of Theism*

ACTIVITY

'I, the Lord, do not change.' (Malachi 3:6)

Explain why this text may imply that God is timeless.

ACTIVITY

Explain how a belief in God as everlasting may be more beneficial to believers than the idea that God is timeless.

Some scholars, such as Oscar Cullman (1902–99), argue on the basis of textual analysis of the Bible that eternal should be understood as everlasting and not timeless. The most logical translation of eternal is to mean 'endless duration' not outside of time.

One criticism of the belief that God is everlasting is that it is difficult to see how God could be in time and not be affected to some extent by creation and hence change. After all, we are changed by our interactions with others as time progresses.

Despite the difficulties, some thinkers argue that this is the only alternative that allows us to preserve God's omnipotence and his action within the world.

Other ideas on eternity

Process theology accepts that God moves through time with his creation – that eternal means everlasting and not timeless. However, for process thinkers such as A.N. Whitehead (1861–1947) and Charles Hartshorne (1897–2000), God is affected by this interaction. God is in the process of becoming and changes with us. So for process thinkers, God is involved in his creation. Although he is powerful, he is in no sense omnipotent.

FURTHER RESEARCH

Find out more about process theology. Explain why traditional Christianity finds this view to be a problem.

D. Z. Phillips (1934–2006) suggested a very different concept of eternity. For Phillips, the idea of eternity is not related to the notion of time but expresses something of a qualitative nature. God does not exist as just another object amongst objects even if he is the greatest being. He is a completely different being that cannot be comprehended; the notion of God as eternal attempts to convey this idea.

4

Attributes of God

4.3 God as omnipotent 

In this topic you will learn about the issues surrounding the definitions of the omnipotence of God.

KEY WORD

Omnipotent: the idea that God is all-powerful.

The problems of omnipotence

If you were asked to define the word '**omnipotent**', you would probably reply that it means that God can do anything. But ask yourself the following questions:

- Can God sin? Most of us find it really easy to make mistakes and hurt others. If God can't sin, does this mean we are something better than God?
- Can God run, jump or do other things that people with bodies can do?
- If God can do everything, could he create a five-sided triangle? Can he make 2+2 = 5?
- Can God change the past? One scenario raised by Michael Dummett (1925–) concerns hearing on the news that the ship your loved one was on sank two hours ago with few survivors. Does it make sense to pray in that situation? Could God change what happened or is your loved one already safe because God knew that you would pray?

God can do everything!

Given some of the difficulties above, it seems hard to suggest that this is the correct definition of omnipotence. Yet this is the definition favoured by René Descartes (1596–1650). There are at least two distinct types of problems that this definition encounters.

Logical and philosophical problems

Does being omnipotent mean that God ought to be able to do what is logically impossible? Aquinas argued that logically impossible actions, such as 2+2 = 5, are not actions at all. They are not 'proper things' that one can or cannot do. C.S. Lewis (1898–1963) agreed observing that:

> *meaningless combinations of words do not suddenly acquire a meaning because we prefix to them two other words: 'God can'*
> C.S. Lewis, *The Problem of Pain*

Can God create a stone too heavy for him to lift? If you answer yes to this problem, then you have found something God can't do, lift the stone. If you answer no, then you also find something that God can't do, create the stone. Is there always one thing that God can't do?

Theological problems

Many argue that it is incorrect to suggest that God can sin, lie or engage in immoral behaviour. Hebrews 6:18 states that it is impossible for God to lie.

God can do all things that are logically possible

In view of God's goodness, and the fact that he is not a being that possesses a body, it seems that this definition may be more appropriate. In the words of Anthony Kenny (1931–), God's omnipotence must be defined as:

> *a narrower omnipotence, consisting in the possession of all logically possible powers which it is logically possible for a being with the attributes of God to have.*
>
> Kenny, *The God of the Philosophers*

Alvin Plantinga (1932–) took this further. He argued that an omnipotent being may not have omnipotence as a necessary quality. He may choose to limit his powers in certain circumstances in order to preserve human free will.

For many, this view of omnipotence is coherent and seems to solve the paradoxes that arise in this topic. However, a weakness of this view might be the feeling that it doesn't really say anything. We are effectively saying that God can do all things that God can do!

God is 'Almighty'

An alternative suggestion comes from Peter Geach (1916–). He notes that the word omnipotence comes from the Latin 'Omnipotens'. However, the New Testament was written in Greek and the word 'Pantokrator', which translates as 'almighty', was used to describe God. Geach argues that this is best understood as a capacity for power, power over everything rather than a power to do everything.

Are there solutions to the paradoxes?

Look again at the paradox of the stone on the previous page. George Mavrodes suggested a solution. If the task is defined as 'to create a stone that God cannot lift' and God, by definition, is a being of unlimited power, this would make the idea of a stone he cannot lift self-contradictory. So to create such a stone is a logically impossible task for an all-powerful being.

Look again at the paradox of changing the past on the previous page. William of Ockham (1285–1349) came up with a solution that distinguishes between the two powers of God.

The 'absolute power of God' refers to the options available before God committed himself to a particular course of action. Prior to creation, God could have done anything – he could have created the world or not created it.

The 'ordained power of God' refers to the options currently available to God. Now that God has created the world he can exercise his power over it in many ways but he cannot 'uncreate it' once he has chosen to create it in the past.

ACTIVITY

Look again at the problems of omnipotence. Does the theory that God can do all things that it is logically possible for him to do solve these problems? Why or why not?

FOR DEBATE

'Changing the word to Almighty doesn't solve anything. We still have to work out what it means.'

Discuss Geach's solution in pairs and consider whether you agree with this quote.

FURTHER RESEARCH

Find out more about the famous paradoxes of omnipotence. Are there any that cannot be solved? Can you think of your own paradoxes?

ACTIVITY

Design a poster entitled 'Things God cannot do' and give reasons for each one.

Attributes of God

4.4 God as omniscient

In this topic you will learn about some of the difficulties in understanding God's omniscience.

FOR DEBATE

'O Lord you have searched me and you know me. You know when I sit and when I rise; you perceive my thoughts from afar.'
(Psalm 139:1–2)

Does the idea of God knowing all things about you provide comfort or is it unsettling?

FURTHER RESEARCH

Watch the film *Bruce Almighty*, particularly the clip where Morgan Freeman guesses the number of fingers that Jim Carrey will hold out. What problem might be raised by claiming that God is omniscient?

KEY WORD

Middle knowledge: the idea that God knows all the possibilities of what would happen in different scenarios.

The word omniscience means all-knowing. Judaism, Christianity and Islam all teach that God is omniscient. Does this mean that God knows everything that it is possible to know? What limits might there be on God's knowledge?

Knowledge and the senses

As human beings we gain knowledge through our senses. If God does not have a body with senses such as ours, can God have knowledge of tastes, smells and sounds? For instance does God know what chocolate tastes like?

Imagine a scientist who has studied chocolate for 20 years and knows all facts about it, but has never eaten it, does the scientist know more about the chocolate once he actually tastes it?

Intuitively we may say yes. This might suggest that God's knowledge is restricted in terms of a lack of sensory experiences. However, one response to this is to separate knowledge from sensation. To taste or smell something is not knowledge, it is merely a pleasant or unpleasant sensation. God knows all that we know, and more, about experiences but does not have the accompanying sensation of pleasure or pain.

Middle knowledge

One area of possible knowledge that is discussed among philosophers is whether omniscience includes **middle knowledge**. Middle knowledge consists of knowledge of what would happen if certain choices were made or if certain things happened differently.

For instance God knows that you will pass your A levels, marry a man called Sid and become an accountant. His middle knowledge is detailed knowledge of what would happen if your decisions had been slightly different. He would know exactly what would happen to you if you didn't pass your A levels, or if you won the lottery and gave up your job. Clearly this would involve a whole range of possible scenarios, involving not just you but everyone around you.

The issue at stake is whether there is such a thing as middle knowledge for God. Are the thousands of 'what ifs' in each of our lives genuine facts or not?

Does omniscience include knowledge of the future?

The Bible seems clear that God has knowledge of the future.

> *Your eyes saw my unformed body. All the days ordained for me were written in your book before one of them came to be.*
>
> Psalm 139:16

Philosophers debate whether knowledge of the future really can be called knowledge if the future has not happened yet. However, God's knowledge may be different to ours. He may know all the choices we will make and the outcomes of these choices.

One area where this causes problems is when we look at God's omniscience in the light of his omnipotence. Thinkers such as Anthony Flew (1923–) and John Mackie (1917–81) have argued that, given God could have foreseen the consequences of creation, it ought to have been possible to create free creatures who always chose to do the right thing.

Omniscience and free will

God's knowledge of the future may also have great implications for the idea of human free will.

The problem can be stated in the following way:

God is omniscient; this means that he knows the past, present and future.

If God knew that you were going to eat cornflakes, were you free to choose differently?

If he believes that you will have cornflakes for breakfast tomorrow morning, then his belief is true. He knows it is the case. It is not possible for you to do anything else.

If you make a last-minute decision to have toast (possibly to outwit God!), he knew that was going to happen.

So it would seem that these two properties, omniscience and free will, are incompatible.

Ways around the dilemma

There are various attempts to answer this question. Some concede that these concepts are incompatible, others offer solutions.

Some thinkers concede that free will is not possible. They argue that God is omniscient and that our free will is only apparent. **Calvinistic** views on **predestination** fall into this category.

Some thinkers concede the idea of omniscience. Process theologians reject omniscience in the traditional sense.

The timelessness of God is offered as a solution. Because God is outside of time, he knows but does not cause our actions.

The everlasting nature of God is given as a solution. God moves through time with us and knows all that it is logically possible to know. He knows our future actions but does not cause them.

MAKING LINKS

'God is omniscient and knows what we will do, and omnipotent and could prevent us doing evil. No theodicy can cope with this problem.'

Look again at the theodicies of Augustine and Irenaeus and consider whether the statement is correct.

STRETCH AND CHALLENGE

'Middle knowledge is not really knowledge'.

Write one or two paragraphs assessing this claim.

KEY WORDS

Calvinism: theological system named after John Calvin (1509–64) which emphasised grace, faith and predestination.

Predestination: the belief that God chooses some to be saved.

4.5 Boethius, eternity and foreknowledge

In this topic you will learn about different views on God's foreknowledge and how it has implications for humans' free will, including the views of Boethius.

MAKING LINKS

This topic relates to the free will and determinism topic in ethics which you may have already studied. Apart from omniscience, what else is believed to affect human free will?

It depends what you mean by freedom!

It is perhaps worth noting that there are two standard definitions of free will:

- Liberty of spontaneity – freedom is doing what we want. These 'wants' may have causes we are not aware of.
- Liberty of indifference – freedom is the ability to do otherwise. This type of freedom may be incompatible with God's omniscience.

Boethius and Lady Philosophy  

In *The Consolation of Philosophy*, Boethius (480–525 CE) presents the difficulty of eternity and **foreknowledge** as a dialogue between himself and the Lady Philosophy (or wisdom):

> *'Now I am confused by an even greater difficulty', I said.*
>
> *'What is it?' Philosophy answered, 'though I think I know what is troubling you.'*
>
> *'There seems to be a hopeless conflict between divine foreknowledge of all things and freedom of the human will.'*
>
> *The Consolation of Philosophy*, chapter 5

Boethius observes that what the omniscient God foresees in the future must happen. Whether it happens because he sees it or he sees it because it will happen is irrelevant. God may not directly cause our actions but, in seeing them, they become necessary and we cannot do otherwise. Boethius sees that this produces several problems:

- It is pointless or unjust to reward the good and punish the wicked, as all actions are predestined to happen.
- If these actions are foreseen but not prevented, does this not make God responsible?
- There seems little point in prayer as the outcome will not change.

KEY WORD

Foreknowledge: the knowledge of what will happen in the future.

Boethius' solution

In *The Consolation of Philosophy,* Lady Philosophy states that God's foreknowledge is not the cause of future events happening. The free will of human beings causes these things; God surveys the whole of time in an eternal present. In other words, all of what we call time is 'now' to God.

Boethius understood the word eternal to mean timeless, rather than everlasting (see page 74). He argued that if God is eternal, he cannot be subject to time; to be in the eternal is to be outside of past, present and future.

Boethius is influenced in saying this by Plato's views:

> *'we should follow Plato in saying that God indeed is eternal but the world is perpetual. The world is subject to change, motion and time but God is completely different in all respects.'*
>
> *'Then,' Philosophy went on, 'if we may aptly compare God's present vision with man's, He sees all things in his eternal present as you see some things in your temporal present. Therefore, this divine foreknowledge does not change the nature and properties of things; it simply sees things present before it as they will later turn out to be in what we regard as the future.'*
>
> *The Consolation of Philosophy*, chapter 5

Assessment

Whilst this approach is coherent and avoids the idea of God seeing the future, there are several criticisms:

- Anthony Kenny notes that the idea of all of time being equally present to God is incoherent, although it may just be that we as human beings cannot comprehend it.
- It is difficult to understand how a God that is outside of time can have knowledge of what is occurring in time. Might this knowledge compromise the immutability of God?
- In order for God's relationship with the world to have genuine **providence**, God would require middle knowledge to know what the outcomes would be if human choices had been different.

In order to reconcile the idea of omniscience with an everlasting God, Peter Geach offers the analogy of playing chess with a grandmaster. Although you are free to move wherever you like, the grandmaster will undoubtedly win the game.

Omniscience and the everlasting God

Some thinkers have defended the compatibility of omniscience and human free will without the idea of timelessness.

Richard Swinburne believes that God is everlasting and progresses through time. Swinburne defines omniscience in a similar way to omnipotence. Basically, omniscience is not to know everything, but knowledge of everything that it is logically possible to know. As the future has not yet happened, it cannot logically be known. God's knowledge may include all future events that are predictable by physical laws but leaves aside free will choices. Swinburne suggests that omniscience may even leave room for God's free choices; e.g. to respond to people's prayers.

This view of omniscience weakens the definition of omniscience and it may appear similar to process theology, which is rejected by traditional Christianity.

ACTIVITY

Look at the quote opposite from Boethius. Re-write it in your own words.

STRETCH & CHALLENGE

Read chapter 5 of *The Consolation of Philosophy*, available on the internet.

FOR DEBATE

'Given that we feel we are free regardless of whether we actually are, it seems impossible to resolve the issue one way or the other.'

KEY WORD

Providence: God's goodness and continuing activity on behalf of his creation.

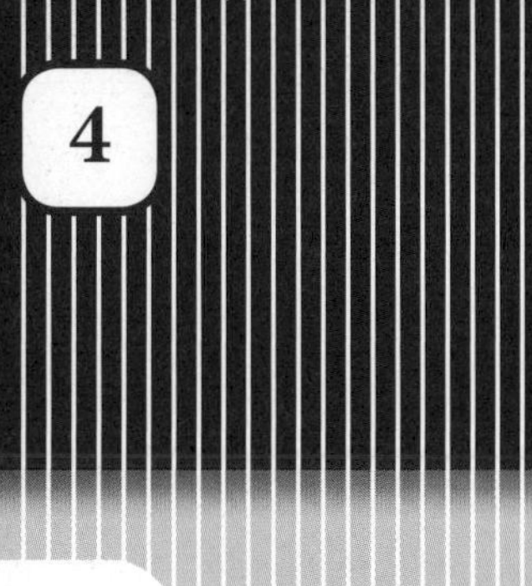

Attributes of God

4.6 God as omni-benevolent

In this topic you will learn about what it means to refer to God as good, and consider whether a good God ought to reward and punish.

MAKING LINKS

Review your AS notes on the goodness of God. How does the God of the Bible differ from the idea of goodness that the Greek philosophers had?

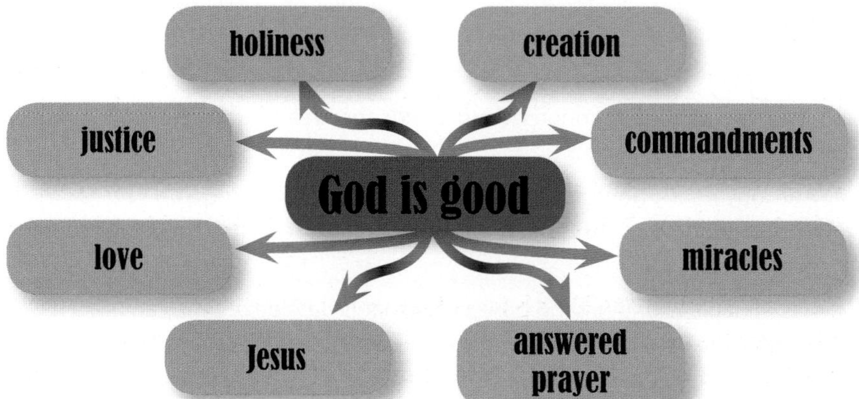

▌ How does each of these things illustrate the goodness of God?

The Bible proclaims the goodness of God:

> *He is good; his love endures for ever.*
>
> 2 Chronicles 7:3

God is not just good in the way that we might be good, he is perfectly good or to use the technical word, omni-benevolent. This prompts various questions amongst philosophers.

What exactly does it mean to say that God is good?

The medieval philosophers, influenced by the Greeks, held that God was simple rather than complex. To describe God was to describe a perfect being. Aquinas stated that: 'the perfections of everything exist in God, he lacks no excellence of any sort' (*Summa Theologica*).

Only a perfect being could be worthy of worship. God's goodness, along with omnipotence and omniscience, were held to be part of this perfection.

To say that God is good is more than saying he is nice! God's goodness may include concepts such as love, holiness and justice. Some modern thinkers such as Swinburne have drawn analogies between God's goodness and the role of a parent. Therefore, God's goodness may at times involve both rewarding and punishing his creation, as a parent would.

Issues regarding God's benevolence

What is the relationship between God and goodness?

The Euthyphro dilemma poses the question of the link between God and goodness. Does God set the standards in determining what is good and bad or do these standards exist regardless of the views of God? For example, would murder have been good if God had said so, or was it already wrong before God gave the commandments?

Can God do evil?

One tricky issue is whether God could in theory do evil actions. Some thinkers have argued that God's goodness is of lesser value if he *has* to do good and is not freely choosing to do good actions.

For example, if you saw an old woman crossing the road and *chose* to help her across, would this make you a better person than if you *had* to help her across? If you had no choice but to be good, is your goodness of lesser value?

For other thinkers, goodness is part of the essential nature of God and it is logically impossible for God to do evil. This links in with the topic of omnipotence previously studied. It all depends on whether you think that the inability to do evil is a genuine limitation.

Should a good God reward and punish?

The idea that God rewards or punishes people at the end of their lives is well established in theistic faiths. In the Christian faith, you are ultimately rewarded in heaven or punished in hell.

Some thinkers are concerned that the idea of rewards and punishments may lead to religious morality being selfish, people may just 'be good' purely to get to heaven. However, it must be noted that if God were omniscient, he would see through such motives.

The concept of omniscience brings further difficulties to the issue. If God knows what our actions will be and that they cannot be otherwise, it does not seem just for God to judge those actions.

If God is omni-benevolent, can hell exist?

The concept of hell is thought to be incompatible with the notion of the goodness of God. Universalists such as Hick argue that ultimately all human beings will be saved. However, Richard Swinburne rejects this and has argued that human freedom must include the freedom to damn ourselves if necessary (see also pages 108–109).

Some philosophers give a symbolic interpretation to the rewards and punishments of heaven and hell. Heaven and hell are not real places that your souls go to after death but are intended to inspire commitment to the teachings of Jesus and to persuade others that it is worthwhile following his teachings.

FURTHER RESEARCH

Find out more about the Euthyphro dilemma. What solutions have thinkers come up with?

ACTIVITY

Look at the destruction of Sodom in Genesis 19. How could a believer justify these actions as being the acts of a good God?

ACTIVITY

Write a letter to a newspaper responding to an atheist who has previously written to reject the notion of a good God.

MAKING LINKS

God's goodness is likely to be very different from ours. Look again at Aquinas' idea of analogy from the religious language topic. How helpful is this theory?

FURTHER RESEARCH

Find out more about the idea of **universalism**. What are the arguments for and against this view?

KEY WORD

Universalism: the belief that all people will ultimately achieve salvation.

4.7 A theological minefield

In this topic you will consider the implications of different philosophers' beliefs about the attributes of God.

This world is constantly changing as time progresses. The realm of the Forms is eternal and unchanging. What is perfect does not change.

God is sovereign and human beings have free will. Free will has been weakened through sin. God foresees what human beings will do.

God is not in time as human beings are. So although human actions are all known to God, our being in time means that we freely act.

God is simple and is ultimate perfection. It is not possible to conceive of anything greater than good.

God is timeless and self existent. We may use reason to prove his existence but his nature is known through revelation.

Plato (428–348BCE)

Augustine (256–430)

Boethius (480–525)

Anselm (1033–1109)

Aquinas (1224–1274)

hell

predestination

heaven

problem of evil

process theology

ACTIVITY

Choose two of the key terms in the theological minefield and write a paragraph explaining why they may cause theological problems.

STRETCH & CHALLENGE

Choose one of the key thinkers covered in the chapter. Imagine they were being interviewed on the attributes of God. Write a script for the interview.

Exam Café

Relax, refresh, result!

Refresh your memory

Revision checklist for attributes of God

In order to do well in this topic you will need to:

- ▷ Know about different views on what it means to say that God is eternal.
- ▷ Understand the difficulties in defining God as omnipotent and some possible solutions to these difficulties.
- ▷ Understand the difficulties involved in discussing God's omniscience.
- ▷ Understand what it means to describe God as omni-benevolent.
- ▷ Assess the coherence of these concepts and explore the philosophical problems of asserting all of these attributes.
- ▷ Assess the view that a good God ought not to reward or punish people.
- ▷ Consider the views of Boethius and others on the issue of eternity and omniscience.

Common mistakes

Aynsley

I was just wondering, what are the main reasons that candidates don't do well in the exams? Is it just that they don't know enough?

Examiner says

It is true that some answers show a lack of preparation and revision but there are other issues as well. The following is a list of some of the common 'sins' if you like at A2.

- Writing all you know about the topic and not really answering the question specifically. Often the answer starts on the question and then rambles in the second half.
- Failing to explain your points in detail. I know that your examiner is a specialist who knows what you mean anyway, but the exam is a test of the depth of your knowledge and understanding.
- A failure to argue. The essays at A2 require argumentative writing. You are attempting to defend a view. You will have to consider both sides and reach a conclusion.

Get the result!

Reaching conclusions

One problem that candidates often have in examinations is reaching conclusions and then writing them. Compare Shoaib and Sally's conclusions. Which is better?

Sample answers

Exam question

'If God knows what we are going to do, he has no right to reward the good and punish the wicked.' Discuss. (35 marks)

Shoaib's conclusion

If God knows the future, then it does seem that we do not have free will. So our actions cannot be helped. On the other hand God is good and would not punish people undeservedly. Having looked at the various different viewpoints it seems that God has got the right to reward and punish people.

Examiner says

Shoaib's approach to writing conclusions is not unusual. However, it is not the conclusion or summary of an argument. It is merely a statement of two different points of view. Shoaib's idea of writing a conclusion seems to be a statement of what he thinks without backing it up.

Sally's conclusion

Although the argument regarding God's omniscience is a strong one and seems to rule out human freedom; this would only be the case if God's foreknowledge were in time. Hence Boethius' solution that suggests God is timeless is the only hope of preserving the goodness of God. Despite its reliance on Platonic philosophy, it is coherent and means that God does not affect or determine our actions. They are our own and we can be justly rewarded or punished for them.

Examiner says

Sally's approach is to use her conclusion to sum up the argument. It reads as a concise summary of the argument she has advanced during the essay. I know what her views are and why. They sum up an excellent essay.

Life and death; the soul

Do you have a soul? Is life after death possible?

In this chapter you will learn about:

- different views on the body and soul in the thinking of Plato and Aristotle
- materialistic views of Dawkins and Hick that reject the idea of the soul
- the different views of life after death: resurrection of the body and reincarnation
- the issues surrounding the nature of disembodied existence
- the relationship between ideas of the Afterlife and the problem of evil.

Life and death; the soul

5.1 Life, death and me!

In this topic you will be introduced to two views concerning the nature of human beings and learn how these relate to the issue of life after death.

What makes a person?

Animals, plants and humans are all living beings. Yet, you probably think of yourself as quite different from a chimpanzee, and very far removed from a simple carrot! You are able to think, you are conscious and you have a mind. This means that you are capable of intelligent thought and decisions. You are also capable of having experiences such as falling in love.

You may also believe that humans have souls. But exactly what is a soul and how do you know if you have one? Is it the same as your mind or your brain?

Souls and life after death

Death is the end of the functions of your body, it no longer has life. Does this mean that you no longer have life? Thinkers divide themselves into two broad camps on this subject:

Dualists, who argue that there are two aspects to human beings, a physical body and a non-physical soul. Dualists tend to believe in life after death.

Materialists or **monists**, who argue that human beings are made of only one substance, the physical body. Materialists reject the idea of life after death.

Although it is generally true that thinkers who reject the idea of a soul also reject life after death, you will soon see that this is an oversimplification.

What makes you 'you'? 

Philosophers raise the issue of personal identity over time. What is it that makes you one and the same person despite the changes you experience?

The Queen's physical appearance and character have changed over the years. Is she still essentially the same person?

KEY WORDS

Dualism: the idea that there are two aspects to human beings, the physical and the mental. The mental may be identified with the soul.

Materialism: the idea that human beings consist of physical matter alone.

Monism: the idea that human beings are made up of one substance, the word is often used synonymously with materialism.

FOR DEBATE 

Is there such a thing as a 'soul' that does not change and is the real you journeying through life?

ACTIVITY

Write a description of yourself aged one, aged 17 and (predicting the future) aged 30. What physical and mental changes occur between stages? What stays the same?

Life and death; the soul

5.2 Plato's dualism

In this topic you will explore the ideas of Plato and begin to assess his views on the soul.

MAKING LINKS

Look back at your work on Plato from AS. Produce a mind map to show the various things the cave analogy was attempting to teach. Add links to show its connection to the Forms.

Plato at the double

The Greek philosopher Plato (428–347 BCE) is probably the most famous dualist. Plato's whole philosophy relies on drawing contrasts between opposite ideas. You may recall his division between the Forms and the particulars. He also draws a contrast between knowledge and opinion as well as the philosopher and the non-philosopher. There are also two aspects of human beings.

Body and soul

Plato argued that the soul is more important than the body. The body is part of the empirical world and like all objects is subject to change. This is one of the reasons why Plato thought that the body and its senses cannot be a reliable guide to the truth. The body allows us to gain opinions via our senses. The soul, however, enables us to have knowledge.

In Plato's own words:

> *The body is the source of endless trouble to us by reason of the mere requirement of food; and is liable also to diseases which overtake and impede us in the search for true being: it fills us full of loves, and lusts and fears, and fancies of all kinds, and endless foolery, and in fact as men say, takes away from us all power of thinking at all.*
>
> Plato, *Phaedo*

So our bodies are, according to Plato, constantly distracting us from our real purpose, philosophical thought. This could be conclusive proof that philosophy really is better than sex!

FOR DEBATE 

Think about a time when your spirit has overridden your appetite – for example, when you were revising for your AS exams, you were tired and hungry, but persisted and went back to your revision notes. Does this mean that you have a soul? How else could this inner conflict be explained?

Key to Plato's understanding of the distinction between body and soul is the idea of the soul as 'simple'. Unlike the physical matter of the body, the soul cannot be split into parts nor can it change. It is also capable of knowledge of other simple and pure ideas, i.e. the Forms.

What does the soul consist of?

Plato draws an analogy to describe the inner workings of the soul. He asks us to imagine a charioteer in charge of two horses. One of the horses behaves but the other is a little wayward. Plato explains that there are three aspects present within the soul: the reason, spirit, and appetite or desire. The soul works best when the charioteer or reason is in charge. Unfortunately the horses often pull in different directions. Our appetites can lead us to things that are not helpful. We also need spirit or will to make us determined to do the right thing. Plato's idea of a good person is one whose soul is properly balanced with reason at the helm.

Plato thinks that reason needs to rule within the soul. What would happen if reason were not in charge?

Soul: past, present and future

Plato believed that the soul was eternal. It existed prior to its incarnation in a human body; it will also exist after death. Given that the soul cannot change, Plato argues that it cannot come into or pass out of existence as beginning to exist or ceasing to exist are pretty significant changes!

In the past, the soul was in the realm of the Forms. The soul has knowledge of the Forms before being pulled to earth by the appetites.

In the present, it is incarnated in a body and experiences all the tension of the conflict between body and soul. Plato views the body as a prison and talks of the soul being liberated from it at death.

In the future, it will be freed from the body and will be reincarnated into another body or eventually return to the realm of the Forms. Unlike the body, the soul is 'simple' and cannot be broken into parts.

> *...for if while in company with the body the soul cannot have pure knowledge, one of two things seems to follow – either knowledge is not to be attained at all, or, if at all, after death. For then, and not till then, the soul will be in herself alone and without the body.*
>
> Plato, *Phaedo*

Plato's arguments for dualism

Plato argues for the soul on two main grounds:

1. The soul has knowledge of eternal ideas and is able to recognise forms such as beauty. Plato uses the example of Socrates questioning a slave boy about geometrical problems he had never faced before. The slave's answers demonstrate an awareness of Pythagoras' theorem, which demonstrates that the soul has knowledge from its prior existence. Learning is therefore merely remembering.
2. The body and soul are opposites. One makes the other necessary just as the concept of light logically makes us aware of the idea of darkness. Life and death are two opposite things. Plato argues that death is a thing (rather than nothingness) and this leads him to suggest that death is an event, the soul leaving the body.

ACTIVITY

Make a table summarising the differences between the body and soul.

FURTHER RESEARCH

Read sections 69e–88b of the *Phaedo* to get Plato's description of dualism in his own words.

ACTIVITY

Investigate further the story of the slave boy that Plato told. What other explanations do you think are possible?

STRETCH & CHALLENGE

Look at Plato's arguments for dualism. Write a paragraph backing up his arguments using examples of your own. Then write a paragraph countering his arguments. Which paragraph do you agree with most? Write a conclusion to support this paragraph.

5.3 Dawkins and the rejection of the soul 

In this topic you will learn why Richard Dawkins rejects the traditional idea of the soul.

FURTHER RESEARCH

Richard Dawkins' website has a number of excellent articles and links to other sites sympathetic to his views. To go to his website visit www.heinemann.co.uk/hotlinks and enter the express code 3587P.

Who is Richard Dawkins?

Richard Dawkins (1941–) is one of the most influential scientists of the last 30 years. His view is that we are purely a product of our genes. Our bodies enable our genes to survive and ultimately our genes are passed on via reproduction. All that our genes are concerned with is survival and replication. In this sense we are no different from any other plant or animal on earth. He argues that nature, although having an appearance of design, is the product of random favourable variations that were necessary in order to get to where we are now. (Dawkins is currently the Charles Simonyi Professor for the Public Understanding of Science at Oxford University, however, this doesn't mean that you can sue him over your GCSE science grade!)

Soul as a mythological concept

Dawkins' views on the concept of the soul are probably as far removed from those of Plato as it is possible to be. Dawkins argues that the idea of a 'soul' is a mythological concept invented by the ancients to explain the mysteries of consciousness. In the same way that the concept of God provided an easy explanation for the gaps in science, so the notion of the soul provides a convenient 'explanation' of the mysteries of human personality and consciousness. However in doing this we are not actually explaining anything. It is, according to Dawkins, 'Not an explanation but an evasion'.

MAKING LINKS

Look back at your work on religious language. What does it mean to consider the soul as mythical?

Although Dawkins admits that consciousness is still mysterious, he points to the advances in genetics where scientists are able to make statements about personality based on genetic codes. This was thought to be impossible at one stage. Dawkins predicts that scientists will eventually be able to unlock the mystery of consciousness. This will mean that there will be no need for anyone to believe in old-fashioned religious ideas, such as the soul.

Soul One and Soul Two

Although Dawkins strongly rejects the notion of a soul in the religious or Platonic sense, he suggests there may be a place for talking about 'soul' in a metaphorical or symbolic way. It depends what you mean by soul!

Soul One: the traditional view of a principle of life, a real separate thing that is spiritual and contains personality. This is a concept which Dawkins rejects.

Soul Two: as defined by the Oxford English Dictionary refers to 'intellectual or spiritual power. High development of the mental faculties. Deep feeling and sensitivity'. Dawkins argues that this is a meaningful way of describing ourselves provided we are clear that this does not refer to a separate thing.

In the sense of Soul One, science has either killed the soul or is in the process of doing so. Probably within the next century, Soul One will finally be killed, and good riddance. But in the process, Soul Two, far from being destroyed, will still be finding new worlds to conquer.

Richard Dawkins in a debate with Stephen Pinker, 2001

Dawkins believes that our 'soul' refers to the development of our intellectual faculties and nothing else. Do you support this view?

Dawkins and life after death

Richard Dawkins was asked how he as an atheist prepared for death:

You prepare for it by facing up to the truth, which is that life is what we have and so we had better live our life to the full while we have it, because there is nothing after it. We are very lucky accidents or at least each one of us is. If we hadn't been here, someone else would have been. I take all this to reinforce my view that I am fantastically lucky to be here and so are you, and we ought to use our brief time in the sunlight to maximum effect by trying to understand things and get as full a vision of the world and life as our brains allow us to, which is pretty full!

Interview with Sheena McDonald, Channel 4 News, 1994

Dawkins argues that the consolation religion provides can only truly be consolation if religion is true and we are able to survive death. Dawkins says death should not be feared. It is the 'extinguishing' of our consciousness and it will be no different to the time before we were born. We will not know about it or experience it.

ACTIVITY

Read Dawkins' thoughts on life after death in the Channel 4 interview quote. Religious believers might say that this is a very negative view. Dawkins would argue that he has a positive view of life and death. In pairs, decide which argument you are most in favour of and why. Present your conclusions to the class.

FOR DEBATE

'I am against religion because it teaches us to be satisfied with not understanding the world.' (Richard Dawkins)

FURTHER RESEARCH

Dawkins has suggested that religious instincts are also the product of evolution. Find out more about his view that religion is like a virus of the mind. What would the implications be for the reason why some of us believe in life after death?

Life and death; the soul

5.4 Aristotle and the soul

In this topic you will find out about Aristotle as well as other thinkers who have developed a concept of the soul.

Like Plato or Dawkins?

Given that Aristotle was Plato's pupil and lived over 2000 years before Dawkins, it is perhaps logical to expect that his views will be closer to those of Plato. However this is not necessarily the case. Aristotle's views on human beings are complex and it is not unusual to find that both dualists and materialists enthusiastically claim him to be one of their own. Hence, it is important to unpick his view with a little care.

The soul is not something extra!

Many thinkers have criticised Plato's belief that the soul and body are two separate substances. His argument for innate knowledge in the *Meno* seems to rely on the character Socrates asking some quite leading questions. The main problem, however, seems to revolve around the idea of 'form' which for Plato is something separate from the object. Aristotle criticises this as unnecessary and argues that properties are not additional to the object.

One helpful way of understanding this debate is provided by Bertrand Russell (1872–1970) via the example of a game of football. Football could not exist if there were no footballers, likewise redness could not exist as a property if there were no red objects. If we consider the idea of beauty, Plato would argue that beauty exists as a form even if there were no beautiful things. For Aristotle, beauty is a property of beautiful objects. Without beautiful things there would be no beauty.

For Aristotle, the soul is the formal cause of the body. It is the characteristics and attributes that we each have. It is not an extra that exists in addition to the body. The body is the raw material, like the marble of a sculpture; the soul is the form, like the characteristics of the sculpture when finished. So:

- the soul is merely a description of the essence or properties of the body. It is our personality and abilities. The soul is the form of the body.

> *It indubitably follows that the soul is inseparable from the body.*
>
> Aristotle, *De Anima*

- the soul cannot be divided from the body. The body is not just a prison for the soul as Plato thinks, but is essential to us. We are body and soul.

Aristotle provides several illustrations of the relationship between the body and the soul. He suggests that if the body were an axe, the soul would be its ability to chop. If the body were an eye, the soul would be the ability to see. These illustrations help reinforce his view that there can be no soul present without the body.

ACTIVITY

Draw a cartoon to show Aristotle's idea of the relationship between body and soul. Annotate it so it will be helpful as a revision aid.

Types of soul

Aristotle believed that every type of living creature had a soul.

Our particular soul is a human soul with human properties. Aristotle suggests that human souls are made up of an irrational part and a rational part. The irrational part consists of abilities that plants and animals have. It is made up of a vegetative element and an appetitive element. Plants have only the vegetative element which is essentially the ability to gain nutrition. Animals have this vegetative element and an appetitive element which involves movement and desires. For Aristotle the human soul is different as it has the ability to reason. This is what separates human beings from animals.

Life after death

At first glance, it seems obvious that Aristotle does not believe in life after death. However, there is some evidence that he feels the ability to reason in some way survives death. If this is the case, it does not mean that our identity or personality survives death but that a kind of abstract property of intellect or reasoning carries on without us.

Is Aristotle right to view humans as different to other species? What do you think?

Descartes and his critics

Rene Descartes (1596–1650) can be considered the heir of Platonic thought on the soul. Descartes realised that it was logically possible to doubt all things including the existence of the body. (Think of the film *The Matrix*.) However, it is not possible to doubt that 'I' exist as a 'thinking thing.' Whenever I think, there must be something doing the thinking. This Descartes calls the mind or soul. Hence, if the body can be doubted and the soul proved, this suggests that they are different things. I am more than just a body.

Twentieth-century philosopher Gilbert Ryle (1900–76) rejected Descartes' argument, claiming that belief in a soul was a category mistake. Ryle gave the example of a foreign visitor being given a tour of Oxford University. After seeing the colleges, meeting lecturers and visiting the libraries, the visitor asks: 'Where is the university?' Just as the visitor makes a category mistake in thinking that the university is something over and above what he has seen, so dualists such as Descartes make a category mistake in assuming something that is additional to the body and its behaviour.

ACTIVITY

Draw a diagram to display Aristotle's ideas about the soul.

MAKING LINKS

Refer back to your work on the Four Causes. Explain why the soul is the efficient, formal and final cause of the body.

FOR DEBATE

Russell said Aristotle is 'Plato diluted by common sense. He is difficult because Plato and common sense do not mix easily.'
(*History of Western Philosophy*, 1946)

STRETCH & CHALLENGE

Find out what is involved in the following theories of mind: Property dualism and functionalism. Both claim to be following the tradition of Aristotle. Can you see why?

FOR DEBATE

'Descartes has proved that dualism is true.' Discuss whether this statement is correct.

Life and death; the soul

5.5 The views of John Hick 

In this topic you will learn about John Hick's views on the body–soul debate and how this might be applied to life after death.

Hick's rejection of substance dualism

The Christian theologian John Hick (1922–) is one of the leading theistic thinkers in recent times. Hick rejects the traditional belief in body-soul dualism by essentially adopting a materialist position and arguing that this does not weaken the possibility of life after death.

He argues that the dualist view of the body and soul owes more to Plato than to Judeo-Christian tradition. When we talk about the soul, we are really describing mental characteristics or aspects of our personality. They describe what a person is or does, or in Hick's words 'behavioural dispositions', (what we are likely to do). Hence to talk of the soul is a way of expressing the value of human beings. For example the SOS distress call literally means 'save our souls'. When someone makes such a call, they are not asking that some invisible ghost-like substance be saved (and their body left to die). Hence to talk of the soul is a way of talking about the value of our whole selves.

FACT BOX

'Ghost in the Machine': this phrase was first coined by Gilbert Ryle (1900–76). It is a criticism of dualism, particularly that of Descartes. Ryle suggests that dualism teaches that there is a mysterious ghost-like substance (soul) that 'rattles around' inside the machine (our body).

ACTIVITY

Sketch a quick cartoon with labels to show the ideas inherent in the 'Ghost in the Machine' concept.

There is no mysterious 'ghost in the machine'. All that needs to be said about us can be explained by reference to our physical selves both in terms of our genes and our upbringing. In Hick's own words:

'a package of genetic information has programmed the growth of a living organism in continuous interaction with its environment.'

Hick, *Death and Eternal Life*, 1976

Hick and traducianism

The Roman Catholic Church teaches that individual souls are created and implanted by God. However, Hick questions whether an idea that was denounced as a heresy might not provide a better understanding. The 3rd-century bishop Tertullian had argued that souls were passed down from parents. This idea was known as **traducianism**. This idea seems to be more in keeping with modern science and fits in with Hick's idea that soul does not refer to an extra something implanted by God.

Hick argues that we are unique due to the random arrangement of our genetic material. In this sense our being is still dependent upon God.

KEY WORD

Traducianism: an early Christian teaching that souls were passed down from parents rather than uniquely implanted by God.

Is there more than just the physical?

Hick does not completely rule out the possibility that the mind and body are different entities. Hick suggests there may be some aspect of us that is non-physical. He examines alleged cases of telepathy and ESP and concludes that these offer interesting and strange evidence. Hick calls this mind-brain dualism. This would mean that the physical and mental aspects of us could interact and affect each other. However these aspects would be dependent on each other and this would not be anything like dualism in the traditional Platonic sense.

The replica theory and life after death

In *Death and Eternal Life*, Hick introduces the **replica theory**. He argues that God can recreate the whole person in another realm after death.

> *I wish to suggest that we can think of it as the divine creation in another space of an exact psycho-physical 'replica' of the deceased person.*
>
> Hick, *Death and Eternal Life*, 1976

Hick aims to show that the concept of life after death does not depend on human beings having souls in the Platonic sense. Humans are a psycho-physical unity, the death of the body is the death of the person, there is no separate soul to live on. Hick argues that this does not rule out our existence after death. It is logically possible for an all-powerful God to recreate us in another world, i.e. heaven. Hick defends this view with three thought experiments:

1. Suppose John Smith were to suddenly disappear in London and reappear in New York. Presumably we would believe that he was the same person who disappeared in London. There would be tests that could be done to establish that the 'replica' was identical.
2. Suppose that John Smith were to die in London and be recreated in New York. Presumably we would identify John Smith as being the person in New York rather than the body in London.
3. Finally, suppose that John Smith dies in London and is buried. Is it not logically possible that God could recreate him in another world? Hick argues that this is close to what St Paul teaches about the resurrection body in 1 Corinthians 15.

In each of the examples, Hick argues that the key to identity is true memories. If the recreated replica remembers their former existence, there are grounds for claiming that it is the same person. Although Hick's contribution to the debate is original and well argued, some philosophers have objected to his view by arguing:

- there is a break in continuity between the original body and the new body. This means that it is difficult to say that it is the same person.
- it is logically possible that many replicas could be created. Which of them would be 'me'?
- identity is not just about memories, a person with Alzheimer's disease is still the same person.

FOR DEBATE

Hick cites an example of a woman during the war who claimed to have seen an apparition of her brother. She discovered two weeks later that he had been killed in action around that time.

Does this show that minds can communicate with each other regardless of physical location?

KEY WORD

Replica theory: the name given to John Hick's theory that God can recreate an exact copy of us in the Afterlife.

ACTIVITY

Produce a PowerPoint® presentation comparing Dawkins' and Hick's views on body and soul. Make sure the contrasts between their views are drawn out.

STRETCH AND CHALLENGE

'Hick gives the best solution to the mind-body problem. He is both scientific and theological in his approach.'

Explain what you think about this view. You will need to review other thinkers as the quote invites a comparison.

Life and death; the soul

5.6 The case for and against dualism 

In this topic you will look at the arguments for and against dualism and assess them.

The case for dualism

ACTIVITY

Divide yourselves into two groups. Using the material on these pages, prepare for a debate about whether humans have souls. You ought to be able to argue for either viewpoint regardless of what you believe.

■ The felt experience of falling in love cannot be reduced to purely physical phenomena

■ There is an 'explanatory gap' between what we know about consciousness as we experience it and the brain as described by science

■ Paranormal experiences may indicate there is something more than the body

The case against dualism

STRETCH & CHALLENGE

Take four or five of the arguments on these pages and prepare a counter-argument to each of them.

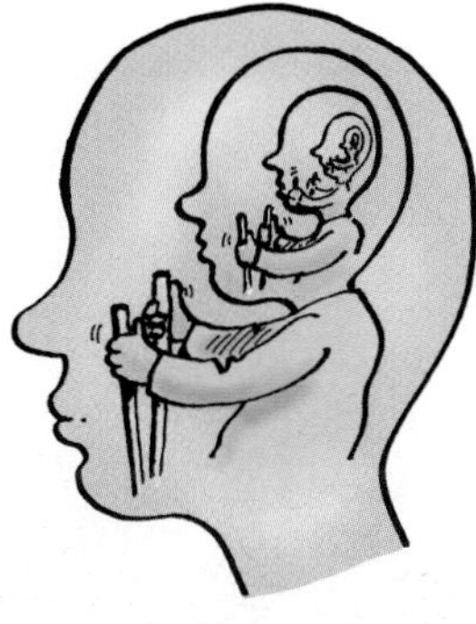

- Dualism seems to treat the soul as a little man in our head controlling us. Would this man need another littler man to control him and so on?

- If my mind is non-physical, how do I know that other people have minds like I do? It seems easier to believe in other minds if the mind is purely the physical brain

- It is difficult to see how two completely different substances (body and soul) can affect each other. It is like asking 'How does a ghost ride a bike?'

Life and death; the soul

5.7 Resurrection

In this topic you will learn about the idea of resurrection of the body as expressed in Judaism, Christianity and Islam.

KEY WORD

Resurrection: the belief in an Afterlife that involves the embodied existence of individuals.

ACTIVITY

Analyse the biblical passages listed below and list the information given about the nature of Jesus' resurrected body.

Luke 24:15–16, 31, 36–43. John 20:11–16, 19–20, 26–27.

ACTIVITY

What problems do you foresee if everybody was bodily resurrected, regardless of their beliefs and how they lived their life?

ACTIVITY

Draw a spider diagram entitled 'Afterlife' briefly showing different views held by religions.

Christianity and Resurrection

A belief in a continuation of human existence after death has always been central to Christians. The Christian belief in the **resurrection** of the body is based upon the belief that Jesus rose from the dead. This is why it is important to most Christians to believe that the resurrection was a physical event and that Jesus had more than a spiritual ghost-like body. As early as the 1st century, the apostle Paul can be seen defending a bodily resurrection by using the example of the resurrection of Jesus in 1 Corinthians 15: 12–14.

Christians base their belief in resurrection on the resurrection of Jesus. Can this be considered good evidence?

The resurrection body of Jesus is described by Paul as being the 'first fruits' of the resurrection of the dead. Yet the resurrection body of Jesus had different powers: according to scripture, he walked through walls, was not easily recognised, yet was still sufficiently physical to need food and drink. This is taken by many to indicate a belief that the resurrected bodies of the dead will be different in character to our present bodies. This seems to be what Paul has in mind later on in 1 Corinthians 15: 42–44.

So it will be with the resurrection of the dead. The body that is sown is perishable, it is raised imperishable; it is sown in dishonour, it is raised in glory; it is sown is weakness, it is raised in power; it is sown a natural body, it is raised a spiritual body.

What do Christians believe about life after death?

According to traditional Christian belief, the resurrection of the body occurs at the end of time when Jesus returns. The Bible indicates that the dead in Christ will rise first followed by those who are still alive at the time of his coming

(1 Thessalonians 4:16). This may prompt the question of what happens prior to the resurrection of the body. Are the dead simply asleep or is there an intermediate stage?

Many Christians would argue that although the body dies, the soul is immediately united with God. They point to biblical material such as the story of the thief on the cross (Luke 23:39–43). Jesus promised that the thief would be with him in paradise that day.

Catholic beliefs

Catholic Christians believe that most souls go to **purgatory** where they experience punishment or purification in order to prepare them for the **Beatific vision**. These souls are then ready to be united with a **resurrection** body. As Aquinas believed that a person is a composite of both body and soul, it would seem logical to say that only after the state of purgatory can we be said to be a person again. The timeless Beatific vision is the final end of humans. It is the state where, according to the apostle Paul, we 'see him face to face.'

Protestant beliefs

Protestant ideas about life after death are more varied. Some thinkers interpret the resurrection as a spiritual event that involves the soul going to God but does not require a physical body. Other thinkers argue that a resurrection body is distinct from present bodies in the same way that Paul argues in 1 Corinthians 15. Protestant ideas of the resurrection also tend to envisage a heaven that is more like a community where people meet and recognise one another.

The Afterlife in Judaism

The early Jewish scriptures do not contain much evidence for belief in the Afterlife. The 'life after death' that God promises the patriarch Abraham is via the deeds of his offspring. A belief in some form of immortality seems to be present in some of the Psalms (16:11, 23:6) but it is only in later Jewish writings such as the book of Daniel and the Maccabees that a fully developed belief in the resurrection of the dead is present.

The Afterlife in Islam

Like Christianity, Islam has always had a belief in the idea of life after death. The Afterlife, or **Akhira**, involves the separation of the righteous from the wicked. Muslims believe that life is a test and that the deeds done in the body will be either rewarded for the good that they have done and punished or forgiven for the wrongs they have done. The Qur'an describes paradise as a luxurious garden full of pleasures where the believer will see God. Hell is described as a place of fire and some Muslims believe that those who enter hell remain there eternally. However, others argue that this is inconsistent with the Muslim belief that Allah is all merciful.

MAKING LINKS

Look back at pages 90–91 on the distinction between body and soul. Can you see why these ideas of life after death might require belief in a soul?

ACTIVITY

Imagine that you are Plato or Dawkins. Write a couple of paragraphs in character giving your assessment of the belief in the resurrection.

KEY WORDS

Purgatory: a state or place where souls are purged or purified before entering heaven.

Beatific vision: the immediate sight and vision of God in heaven.

Akhira: literally, the hereafter, everlasting life after death.

STRETCH AND CHALLENGE

'Christian, Jewish and Muslim beliefs about the Afterlife are virtually identical.'

Research this claim and write a response.

Life and death; the soul

5.8 Reincarnation

In this topic you will learn about the idea of the soul's reincarnation as expressed in Eastern Religions.

MAKING LINKS

Look again at 5.2 Plato's dualism. What similarities can you see between his ideas and those of reincarnation?

KEY WORDS

Reincarnation: the belief that after death, our soul lives again in another embodied form.

Transmigration: a word used of the soul's passage or journey to another body after death.

Karma: the principle of actions, deeds and effects, that our actions in this life affect the next. Regarded as a law of the universe.

Brahman: God or the absolute in Hinduism.

Maya: the illusion or the unreal world of separate consciousnesses.

Atman: a word used to describe the soul or 'principle of life'. All forms of life have atman.

Monotheistic: the belief in the existence of one God, for instance in Judaism, Christianity and Islam.

Reincarnation in Hinduism

Reincarnation is the **transmigration** of the soul from body to body. It involves the idea that we have lived before, possibly many times, and we may live again. The soul is eternal and lives in many different bodies.

> *As a person cast off worn out garments and puts on others that are new, even so the embodied soul cast off worn out bodies and puts on others that are new.*
>
> Bhagavad Gita 2,13

How a person lives when they are embodied affects the next incarnation. A good person may be reborn as someone wealthy or successful whereas a bad person could be reborn to poverty and suffering. They may even be reborn as an animal. This process is operated by what is known as the law of **karma**. This is essentially a law of cause and effect which determines that any action carried out in this life has an impact on the next life.

Reincarnation and the soul

The more philosophical schools of Hinduism believe that **Brahman** (God) is pure consciousness or thought. The created universe is temporal and is in a sense unreal. The Hindu word for this is **Maya**. However all living things have soul or '**atman**' which is in some way united to the physical matter surrounding them. The aim of consciousnesses is for the atman to be liberated from the repeated cycle of death and rebirth and to be united with Brahman. Ultimately the atman is part of Brahman. For many Hindus, the separateness of individual consciousnesses or souls is an illusion. One helpful way of thinking about this is the idea of space within jars. The jars represent our bodies, and consciousness is the space in individual jars. So once the bodies are destroyed then the space can unite into one. Hence for many Hindus, individuality is an illusion and ultimately life after death is not the personal survival taught by the western **monotheistic** faiths.

Is it still me?

One of the key difficulties with the idea of reincarnation is the question of whether I will still be me when I am reborn. In order to be able to claim to be the same person, at least one of these three aspects: body, memory or personality should be present. With reincarnation, obviously I will not have the same body and there are many people who have a similar personality to me, so the key to identity might seem to be memory.

Advocates of reincarnation argue that the trauma of birth and death cause memories to be buried deep within our consciousness. We do not remember most of the events of our first two years of life, yet we don't dispute that it was us. However past life memories seem to be more problematic. Some people do claim to have experience of past lives but these are sometimes vague and are vigorously disputed by most scientists. If all of these links fail, we are left to argue that it is the soul that provides the continuity, but obviously this cannot be verified.

FOR DEBATE

More people are alive now than ever. Where have the new souls come from? Are they the souls of former animals or plants? What do you think?

Buddhist teaching on rebirth

Although the two concepts seem very similar, Buddhists use the term rebirth and do not believe in reincarnation. Buddhists believe that everything in the universe is transient or impermanent (Anicca), and so do not believe in a permanent soul that is reincarnated into other bodies . Buddhists also teach the doctrine of Anatta, which literally means 'no self'. Because of the changing nature of everything around us, there is no unchanging self that journeys through time. For Buddhists the rebirth is not a continuation of the person's identity. Rather the consciousness of the person becomes one of the contributory causes in a new group of materials from which new persons are formed. The new person is not identical to the old nor completely different. They are simply aspects of the continuing stream of consciousnesses. It is the awareness of these truths followed by right living and meditation that may enable one to escape the cycle of rebirth and reach **Nibbana** (Nirvana).

KEY WORDS

Nibbana: the state of being free from suffering and the cycle of rebirth.

Moksha: literally meaning 'release' or 'liberation'. In Hinduism this refers to the final escape from the continuous cycle of death and rebirth, which is known as Samsara.

Evaluation of reincarnation

There are several points of view on reincarnation and the problem of evil. Reincarnation could provide an interesting solution to the problem of evil. We are suffering as a direct result of our past actions. Others feel that reincarnation does not solve the problem of evil, it merely postpones it as there is no adequate explanation for the suffering experienced in the first life.

It is claimed that some people can remember past lives. On attaining **Moksha**, it is argued that the meditator will be able to see the connection between all lives. Others argue that reincarnation does not solve the personal identity issue adequately, as it is difficult to see how memories are transferred or stored between lives.

The game of snakes and ladders is derived from the Indian game Moksha Chitram. How might this game be connected to the concept of karma?

ACTIVITY

Role play a chat show programme interview between a sceptical interviewer and a guest claiming memories of their former life.

Life and death; the soul

5.9 Arguments about life after death 

In this topic you will compare different views about life after death.

Arguments for Life after Death

Near-death experiences are common amongst resuscitated patients. They may suggest that we are more than just physical beings.

Paranormal phenomena such as telepathy, ESP, mediums and psychic activity provide some impressive and puzzling cases. Not all can be dismissed scientifically.

There is an almost universal belief in life after death. Why do so many different cultures share these similar ideas?

The summum bonum cannot be achieved in this life. Moral perfection requires there to be an afterlife.

Hick's replica theory seeks to establish that life after death is still a logical possibility regardless of whether humans have souls.

Some people are able to recall details of past lives.

ACTIVITY

Produce a PowerPoint® giving a detailed explanation of one of these arguments. Swap your PowerPoint® with other members of your class.

Arguments against Life after Death

Much of what we used to attribute to the soul can now be explained by neuroscience and located within the physical brain.

Hume argues that given the fragility of the mind, it is more likely to be destroyed by death rather than to survive it.

It is difficult to establish how we can be sure that a person in the next life is the same person as the embodied person who died.

The phrase 'I will survive my own death' is meaningless.

Belief in life after death says more about human psychology, i.e. our own wishful thinking, than it does about reality.

FOR DEBATE

'Life after death is just wishful thinking.'

Life and death; the soul

5.10 Issues surrounding disembodied existence

In this topic you will examine the coherence of the idea of disembodied existence and consider some of the problems associated with it.

KEY WORD

Disembodied existence: literally the idea that we are able to exist in some form without our bodies.

ACTIVITY

Produce an ideas map showing the key features of each of the various ideas of the Afterlife. Suggest two or three strengths and weaknesses of each view.

Life without a body?

Regardless of which theory of life after death we subscribe to, it seems that some form of **disembodied existence** is required even if this is just an intermediate stage. Platonic views lead to some form of permanent disembodied state for the soul, whereas in reincarnation and resurrection theories there is generally an intermediate state where the soul is away from the body before acquiring a new body or a resurrection body respectively. Hence this leaves us with two related questions: is the idea of disembodied existence a logically coherent concept, and can the existence of a person without a body be proved?

Coherence of the concept

To accept the possibility of a disembodied existence after death, we must believe that the core of our identity is a non-physical soul or mind. However this belief is felt to contradict much of the findings of modern science. In our present form we recognise each other by our physical bodies and scientists indicate that much of what makes us the people we are is rooted in our physical DNA. If we are to claim that disembodied existence is a coherent concept, we are required to assert that our mental characteristics, perhaps our memory, is the key to our identity.

One thought experiment that might conform this view and suggest that disembodied existence is at least coherent was given by John Locke (1632–1704). Locke gave the story of a prince and a pauper who woke up in each other's bodies. He argued that the reason why each of them knew who they really were was based upon their true memories of their previous existence. This might be taken to suggest that if, hypothetically, I was to leave my body I could claim that I still existed, despite the death of my body, if I could remember 'being me' prior to death.

A second difficulty with disembodied existence is the question of exactly what our existence after death would be like. One philosopher who attempted to answer this question was H.H. Price (1899–1985) who argued for the possibility that our mind may survive the death of our body and exist in a mental world. He likens the perceptions of the mind after death to the perceptions that we have in dreams, that is, formed by our mental images and ideas. However unlike our dreams, these perceptions may be shared by other minds in this post-death world.

Price's view has been criticised by a number of thinkers including Hick. Hick argues that there is an inconsistency between stating that our mental world after death is created by our desires and that this world is shared. Presumably our desires would be quite different to those of others and would lead to a different world for each of us.

Evidence for the possibility of disembodied existence

Suppose we assume that the idea of disembodied existence is coherent, how might we set about proving such a phenomena? By its very nature, arguing for the existence of phenomena that cannot be seen or heard is problematic. To a sceptical scientist, the claims made below seem on a par with suggesting the earth to be flat. Nevertheless some thinkers have found some of the phenomena suggested below intriguing.

Near death experiences

The near death experience (or out of body experience) was first documented by Dr Ray Moody. Moody studied various patients who claimed to have had out of body experiences during traumatic operations. He found a number of similarities between cases including some where detailed descriptions of things within the room were given that could not have been known by the unconscious patient. However, many scientists, such as Susan Blackmore, believe these experiences to be chemical reactions generated by the dying brain.

ESP and mediums

A range of interesting and related phenomena are discussed by H.H. Price. Price examines the claims of mediums and concludes that these are either evidence that disembodied persons continue to survive in another world and can communicate with this world, or that there is an unconscious part of our mind that can transmit and receive information telepathically in a way that is beyond normal perception. Perhaps the two interpretations are related to each other. However, Price is cautious about concluding too much from these phenomena, and suggests that we should merely 'not be too sure that you will not continue to exist as a person after your physical organism has died' (Price, *The problem of life after death*, 1968).

Case study

In the Chaffin will case, a North Carolina farmer who died in 1921 appeared in a dream to one of his sons four years later to reveal the location of a missing will. This will was validated by a court and led to his farm being shared equally rather than just left to one of his other sons!

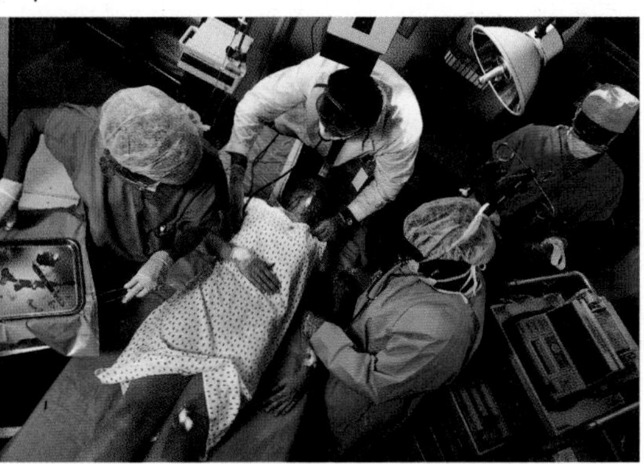

Does it seem sensible to say that we could look down on our own body from a position outside it?

ACTIVITY

Have you or any of your friends had a paranormal-type experience? If you feel comfortable, share it with the class and find out what they think about it.

FURTHER RESEARCH

Find out more about near death experiences using the International Association for Near-Death Experiences website. To go to this website visit www.heinemann.co.uk/hotlinks and enter the express code 3587P. Choose two examples of near death experiences and write a short report on them to present to the group.

5.5

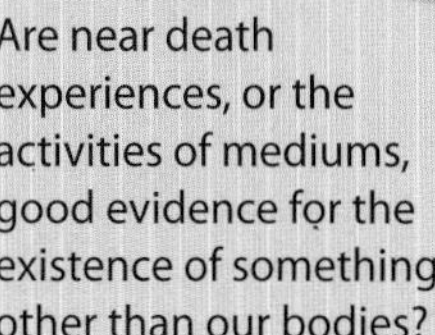

FOR DEBATE

Are near death experiences, or the activities of mediums, good evidence for the existence of something other than our bodies?

Life and death; the soul

5.11 The Afterlife and the problem of evil 

In this topic you will consider how different theories of life after death may affect the attempts at constructing theodicies to justify God.

MAKING LINKS

Review your work on the classic theodicies of Augustine and Irenaeus from the AS course. How do they use life after death to compensate for the evils of this world?

Resurrection and the problem of evil

The idea that our actions are rewarded or punished and that those who suffer unjustly are compensated in the next life is integral to religious ideas of the resurrection. Philosophically Kant's notion of the *summum bonum* expresses in logical terms the common sense notion that if goodness is commanded, it ought to be achievable, and good actions should be rewarded. Clearly this does not always happen in this life.

Does a belief in life after death help to justify such seemingly tragic and pointless events?

Both the Augustinian and Irenaean theodicies seem to require a belief in the Afterlife. Both thinkers rely heavily on the notion of free will. This in turn seems to require the idea of rewards and punishments if there is to be justice in the world and our free actions are to receive what they deserve.

Augustinian theodicy

For Augustine, death is a consequence of sin. Had the first human beings not sinned, there would be no death. Augustine believed that all human beings in a sense deserve suffering due to original sin, but God redeems the believer through the work of Christ. Not all are saved however; in his book *The City of God* Augustine's theology of the resurrection includes the idea of the damned being embodied and burning forever in literal flames. Augustine's idea has at least two weaknesses:

- Many modern thinkers find the idea of hell immoral. It is questionable whether God is morally justified in allowing an infinite punishment for a finite amount of sin.
- Augustine's views on heaven and hell are further damaged by his belief that God predestines some to be saved. This seems to be unjust and contradicts his view that humans have genuine free will.

ACTIVITY

Create a diagram of Augustine's theodicy and its connection with the Afterlife. Underneath, add modern responses to this theodicy.

Irenaean theodicy

The Irenaean theodicy regards the initial creation of God as being in a state of immaturity like that of an innocent child. Our life on earth enables growth through our experience of suffering. This leads humans to reach ultimate happiness, where they are able to see and know God. Irenaean-type theodicies have been used by modern thinkers to justify God's actions and to make links to the idea of life after death.

John Hick (1922–) has developed the idea of 'soul making' and argued for the idea of universalism. He argues that the idea of hell is not to be understood literally and that a benevolent God could not eternally punish people.

Richard Swinburne (1934–) argues that death is an essential part of a reasonable theodicy. It is only if our choices are limited by time that they acquire significance. If there will always be another chance, what we do does not matter. This unlimited freedom, Swinburne argues, has to include the possibility of damning ourselves to hell by our own actions.

Not all thinkers have approved of these ideas. D. Z. Phillips (1934–2006) has rejected soul making theodicies as they involve an instrumental use of evil by God. It cannot be morally right for a good God to permit evil, often on a massive scale, in order to bring about future good. An eternal life in heaven may be compensation but it does not correct the immorality. D. Z. Phillips lacked even that compensation as he did not believe in personal life after death.

Reincarnation and the problem of evil

Much of what makes for our quality of life lies outside of our control. We inherit genetic traits and we have no choice as to the social setting and status that we are born into. This leads to inequalities and, depending on where we live in the world, potentially great poverty and injustice. This may in turn affect our ability to live a 'good' life. Reincarnation solves this difficulty by suggesting that our situation is not random but is the direct result of the law of karma. Our actions in previous lives have led directly to the situation we now find ourselves in. At first glance there is no longer any problem of evil to be solved.

There are some potential difficulties with this solution:

- Reincarnation could be seen not as a solution to the problem of evil but a postponement of it. If we follow the causal chain and explain our present life in terms of the previous one and so on, the question arises as to how we explain our situation in our first life.
- The suggestion that we suffer directly for our individual past actions is plausible according to a basic theory of reincarnation. However, in Vedantic Hinduism and in Buddhism, it is taught that the idea of 'self' is an illusion. If there is no 'self', then it seems odd that individuals should be rewarded or punished.

MAKING LINKS

Look again at your work on God's omniscience and whether God should reward and punish (chapter 4). How is this relevant to the Augustinian theodicy?

ACTIVITY

Create a diagram of Irenaean's theodicy and its connection with the Afterlife. Underneath, add modern responses to the theodicy.

STRETCH & CHALLENGE

Find out more about Hick's soul-making theodicy as outlined in his book *Evil and the God of Love*. Swinburne's theodicy is outlined in several works including the accessible *Is there a God?* Produce a handout for the rest of the group on one of these theodicies.

FOR DEBATE

Discuss whether resurrection or reincarnation gives the best solution to the problem of evil.

Exam Café

Relax, refresh, result!

Refresh your memory

Revision checklist for life and death; the soul

In order to do well in this area of the course you will need to:

- Explain the body–soul dualism of Plato.
- Assess the coherence of his view.
- Explain Dawkins' rejection of the traditional idea of the soul.
- Assess whether Dawkins is correct in his view.
- Explain Aristotle's dualism and consider how it differs from that of Plato.
- Explain Hick's materialism and how his replica theory suggests the possibility of life after death.
- Assess the coherence of such views and consider the arguments for and against their positions.
- Explain what is meant by the idea of resurrection.
- Assess the arguments for and against the idea of resurrection.
- Explain the idea of reincarnation.
- Assess the arguments for and against the idea.
- Consider whether the idea of a disembodied existence makes sense.
- Compare the theories of resurrection and reincarnation and how they deal with the problem of evil.

Remember!

You need to take charge of your revision and use techniques that work for you. You could make spider diagrams of some of the bullet points listed above, or jot down 5–6 key words on a cue card. Alternatively you could approach each of the bullets as a possible exam area and make rough model answers to each.

Relax and prepare

Common mistakes

Examiner says

One of the problems with a topic like this is that there are a number of names and theories. Obviously if it is clearly just a slip of the pen where you have described Plato's views perfectly but called him Aristotle, we try to be positive in our marking. Unfortunately it is sometimes not possible as a candidate has partly remembered one thinker's ideas, for example Plato, called him Aristotle and then added a few of Aristotle's ideas for good measure. It is vital that when you revise, you try to draw clear distinctions between thinkers and theories. You could do a table to summarise the views as David suggests below.

Michael

I found this topic a little confusing as we seemed to be looking at two separate issues: whether we have souls, and whether there is life after death. I thought the teacher wasn't being very clear but eventually I saw that the two topics were connected. Whether we have souls or not affects whether we can believe in life after death.

Kelisha

Sort of right, most dualists like Plato believe that we survive death because we aren't really our bodies, the soul is the real me. People like Dawkins think we are just lumps of physical stuff and when we die there's nothing there to survive. But don't forget John Hick – he's a materialist but thinks that God can recreate us in another realm.

David

One way I sorted different ideas out on this was to do a table. I put Plato, Dawkins, Aristotle and Hick as column headings and then wrote questions like do they believe in the soul? Is the soul something separate? Am I my mind or just a body? Do they believe in life after death? I then ended up with a really clear account of their similarities and differences and I'd hardly written anything. Struck me as a good use of time!

Get the result!

Exam question

Critically assess Dawkins' claim that since life is no more than DNA reproducing itself, there can be no life after death. (35 marks)

Language of the exam

This may seem like a long and complex question but, once it is broken down and you understand the trigger word, it is actually fairly straightforward. (If you've studied the area and revised well!)

Critically assess: The question is asking you to 'critically assess'. You may be familiar with the word 'assess' as in weighing up the strengths and weaknesses of an idea. As stated previously, care is needed when we come across the word 'critically'. It does not mean that we should just state a lot of criticisms. To take a critical approach means to seriously and academically look at the strengths and weaknesses. It may help to think of it as 'giving a critique' of the view.

In order to do justice to the question above you will need to consider the statement in two parts. Firstly, is Dawkins correct about the nature of life? Could it be that more dualistic views such as those of Plato are more correct? You will need to assess (critically) the arguments. One of the key words in the question is the word 'since' so, secondly, suppose that Dawkins is correct that we are just DNA, does this lead logically to his conclusion that there can be no life after death? If he is right about the first claim, must we logically accept the second? You may wish to bring in the ideas of John Hick here.

Planning an answer

Before you turn over the page to look at the sample student answers, why not try writing a short plan of how you might go about answering the question.

Exam question

Critically assess Dawkins' claim that since life is no more than DNA reproducing itself, there can be no life after death. (35 marks)

Planning your answer

There isn't necessarily one correct way of structuring a response to this question and there is no requirement that you have to cover any specific thinkers other than Dawkins who is named in the question. However, in order to answer the question fully, you will need to explain and assess Dawkins' claim in detail and you may wish to bring in the ideas of other thinkers provided that the material stays relevant to the question that is being asked. A suggested plan follows.

Paragraph 1: Introduction and explanation of Dawkins' claim.

↓

Paragraph 2: Support for Dawkins' claim that life is just DNA: evidence of neuroscience & claim that it provides simplest and most scientific explanation.

↓

Paragraphs 3-4: Arguments against Dawkins' view considered: Consciousness/qualia, free will, Descartes divisibility argument.

→

Paragraph 5: Consideration of the dualism of Plato or Descartes; is this more coherent than the view of Dawkins?

↓

Paragraph 6: Assuming Dawkins is correct, does this rule out life after death? Explain views of Hick.

↓

Paragraph 7: Discussion of Dawkins *v.* Hick: Hick's view merely a hypothesis that requires existence of God. Is Dawkins more realistic?

↓

Paragraph 8: Conclusion summing up your argument.

Use the structure above, or a structure of your own if you prefer, and try writing an answer to the question above. You should aim to explain and discuss arguments fully when you present them. Paragraph length may vary but try to get around 200 words into most of your paragraphs.

Sample answers

Examiner says

Natalie has got the basic idea of what Dawkins has to say. If her aim in this paragraph is to unpack Dawkins' ideas in detail then this is not sufficient. More depth would be needed for a reasonable mark. There are a couple of issues with style here also. There are no marks available for biographical information so the opening, although not wrong, could be more concise. Natalie is not losing marks by putting in the biographical information but she is losing time. She is also distracted from the focus on Dawkins by putting in a brief introduction to dualism. This would be better done elsewhere and in a little more detail. The last sentence states the obvious and is unnecessary; it would be worrying if an essay written in response to this question didn't do this.

Natalie's original answer

The philosopher Richard Dawkins was born in 1941. He is a professor of science at Oxford University. He is famous for writing various books including the recent bestseller *The God Delusion*. Dawkins has famously attacked various religious ideas including the idea that human beings survive death. Dawkins believes that human beings are just 'bytes and bytes' of digital information. We are the sum total of our DNA. For Dawkins we are no more than our physical bodies, this means that he rejects the idea of the soul. Plato and others are dualists which means they believe that we are made up of two aspects: a physical body and a non-physical soul which can survive death. Dawkins rejects this idea and suggests that we are just physical and, as a result, when our body dies that is the end of us. This essay will discuss this claim and reach a conclusion as to whether this is true.

Natalie's improved answer

Oxford Biologist Richard Dawkins is a leading critic of various religious ideas including the idea that human beings survive death. Dawkins believes that human beings are just 'bytes and bytes' of digital information. We are the sum total of our DNA. For Dawkins the idea of the soul is not an explanation but is an evasion dreamed up by ancient people in order to explain the mystery of consciousness. Dawkins' view is that science is increasingly able to explain human personality in terms of DNA and the workings of the brain. All functions that were previously suggested to be the soul will be explained as science progresses. For Dawkins this logically leads to a rejection of the belief in life after death. Given that our identity is entirely physical, it is not possible for anything of us to survive the death of our bodies. Dawkins is famously quoted as saying that he believes that when he dies 'he will rot'. The only possibility of any life after death as far as he is concerned is via the reproduction of our DNA through our children, but this is not life after death in the traditional sense of our personal survival. This may seem like a straightforward argument, however, it is not clear that the link need be so obvious.

Discuss: In what way is Natalie's second introduction an improvement on the first?

6 Meta-ethics

In this chapter you will learn about:

- the use of ethical language – the ways in which different scholars understand how words such as 'good', 'bad', 'right', 'wrong' are used when ethical statements are made
- how meta-ethics differs from normative ethics
- the different approaches: cognitive and non-cognitive; ethical naturalism and intuitionism; emotivism and prescriptivism and how these apply to ethical statements
- how to discuss these areas critically and evaluate the strengths and weaknesses.

Meta-ethics

6.1 What does it all mean?

In this topic you will learn about the use of ethical language and how different philosophers argue that it can be meaningful or meaningless.

The human race has spent long periods of time trying to discover what 'things' mean. Things such as crop circles, star constellations to UFOs. In many ways the search for meaning provides some answers, for example after a long period of study archaeologists were able to translate and understand Egyptian hieroglyphics with the discovery of the Rosetta Stone. However in some areas answers are not easy to find. Some reasons for this are due to differences in culture, religion or upbringing.

In the same way the meaning of our language and words has fascinated and divided philosophical thinkers for centuries.

How can we decide what this means if we don't understand the language? Does it mean anything at all? Why is it important to know what language means?

Can we understand what 'good' really means?

Two friends might believe that they are drinking a good cup of coffee, however one might claim that a good cup of coffee is one that has milk and two sugars added, whilst the other believes that it is one that is black and unsweetened! Which one of these friends is correct? The drinks are clearly different, so why do they use the same word?

This example may seem unimportant in the grand scheme of things, however, the principle remains if we substitute an ethical word for coffee and therefore make it a statement that deals with morality. For example, substituting the word euthanasia then would suggest that the speaker has a specific meaning in mind. How do we understand what this person means? Can we make sense of these words in a way that we all understand?

This area of ethical theory is called **meta-ethics**. Meta-ethics is the discussion about the nature of ethical statements and whether these are useful and valid. Meta-ethics analyses ethical language and seeks to understand the meaning of moral judgements.

KEY WORD

Meta-ethics: the area of ethics that seeks to explore and discover the meaning of words used in ethical statements.

ACTIVITY

What does 'good' mean?

Is it something I approve of? (E.g. the Iraq War.)

Is it something that fulfils its purpose? (E.g. a knife that cuts.)

Is it someone or something that has moral worth? (E.g. Jesus or pacifism.)

Is it my own opinion? (The music of REM or U2.)

Is it what God/the Bible says that we should do? (E.g. do not steal.)

Write down whether you agree or disagree with each of these definitions of what 'good' means and give reasons to support your answer.

6 Meta-ethics

6.2 Meta-ethics and normative ethics – the differences

In this topic you will learn about the differences between meta-ethics and normative ethics and how they work together, and about the theories that claim that the ethical language we use has no useful meaning apart from as part of our own opinions.

FOR DEBATE

'Good means the same thing to everyone. We all understand it.'

Is this an accurate statement? Why might it be inaccurate? Try to apply both meta-ethics and normative ethics to the statement.

KEY WORDS

Normative ethics: the area of ethics that attempts to discuss whether something is right or wrong, good or bad.

Empirical evidence: information that is gained using sensory data (i.e. what we see, smell, hear, taste and touch).

Cognitive: a statement that is subject to being true or false. For example, 'the cat is asleep on the chair'.

Non-cognitive: a statement that is not subject to truth or falsity. For example, 'hurray' or 'ouch'.

Normative ethics deals with what things are right and wrong. They help people to understand what is right and moral and what is wrong and immoral. In some ways normative ethics are like a traveller's guide book – they tell people what to do and what not to do.

Meta-ethical statements deal with what it means to claim that something is right or wrong. In fact meta-ethics is closely linked to normative ethics and trying to understand the meanings of the terms in the theories. In some ways meta-ethics is like a foreign language, you have to know what the words mean to understand what is being said. In the statement 'This is a good gun', normative ethics would explore whether the gun is morally good, whilst meta-ethics would try to understand what we mean by using the word good, i.e. is it good because it fulfils its purpose or because I approve of it.

Fact or fiction?

For many people ethical statements are either true or false. They believe that they can be verified or falsified using evidence from observable facts (**empirical evidence**). This idea seems quite sensible, however it is flawed. It is possible for people to disagree with a moral statement without referring to empirical evidence, but by applying cultural or religious ideas that give an action its rightness or wrongness. An example of this is the Islamic and Evangelical Christian teaching that homosexuality is wrong.

Can we be sure we all mean the same thing when we use words?

Some philosophers believe that ethical language can have a true meaning – they are called **cognitivists**. They believe that the words we use can be meaningful because they have a factual basis. Other philosophers disagree and say that ethical language cannot have a true meaning – they are called **non-cognitivists**. They believe that the words cannot be meaningful because they are not subject to being true or false.

Is it all meaningless?

Non-cognitivists would say that it is difficult for ethical language to be meaningful, as it does not give us any objective information that is subject to being true or false. Therefore some ethical philosophers claim that to speak of ethical language as meaningful is nonsense.

The background

During the 1920s, a group of philosophers called the Vienna Circle developed a theory called logical positivism that wanted to look at ethical language and religious language from a more scientific perspective, rather than naturalistic or intuitive. They said that ethical statements cannot be verified or falsified as they are neither **analytic statements** or **synthetic statements**. The statements have no empirical facts that can be checked to be true or false, so they must be meaningless. For further discussion of these ideas, see page 12 in chapter 1.

FOR DEBATE 

Look at the following ethical statements and explore different ways that they can be understood using the ideas on these pages:

'The terrorists of 9/11 were wrong to fly into the Twin Towers.'

'Mother Teresa was a good woman.'

'Stealing is always a bad action.'

'If someone is in extreme pain, then euthanasia is the right solution.'

FOR DEBATE 

When Tony Blair outlined his government's decision to invade Iraq and said that it was the 'good and right thing to do', was he merely saying that he approves of military action or that it is intrinsically good to go to Iraq?

KEY WORDS

Analytic statements: statements that are true by definition, e.g. 1+1=2.

Synthetic statements: statements in which the predicate is not a necessary part of the description, e.g. 'The mermaid has a large comb.'

One of the most influential philosophic contributors to the language debate is Ludwig Wittgenstein. His most famous claims was 'Whereof we cannot speak, thereof we must remain silent.' Wittgenstein's ideas have provided many subsequent debates concerning language. So much so that it is suggested that the focus on *meaning* of the ethical language that we use is detrimental to any discussion of true practical ethical questions. Followers of Wittgenstein suggest that it is impossible to even discuss ethical theories at all before we understand the terminology used.

Meta-ethics

6.3 It is all meaningful!

In this topic you will learn about the theories that claim that the ethical language we use has meaning and is empirically provable.

KEY WORDS

Naturalism: the belief that suggests that all things are knowable (provable) using empirical evidence.

Non-naturalism: the belief that all things to do with meaning are knowable using intuition rather than empirical evidence.

ACTIVITY

Write out a response from an ethical naturalist giving a definition of what is a 'good knife', 'a bad student', 'a wrong decision' and 'a right action'. Your AS work on Aristotle's Final Cause may be useful here, see page 21 of your AS textbook.

MAKING LINKS

Use what you have learned about medical ethics at AS to give a naturalistic approach to these statements:

'Abortion is wrong.'

'The sanctity of life is a good argument.'

'Euthanasia is right.'

Within cognitivism there are two approaches as to how the ethical language used is meaningful. These two approaches agree in principle that the language is meaningful, but differ in the working out of the specifics. These approaches are called **naturalism** and **non-naturalism**.

Naturalism

According to this approach 'good' is something that can be defined and has a real existence. As a student you know what a good pen is and what makes it good! To a certain extent, a good pen is one that fulfils its purpose by writing properly. We can therefore say that good is something that is provable, using what is referred to as empirical evidence. Anything that is proved using one or more of the five senses is referred to as empirical data.

Ethical naturalists say that, in the same way that we can say that things are factually accurate by using empirical data (e.g. Tony Blair was once Prime Minister of the United Kingdom), we can also use ethical statements and say that they are accurate using empirical evidence (e.g. 'Genetic research is right').

Is a 'good' pen one that writes properly?

We prove that Tony Blair was once Prime Minister of the United Kingdom using newspaper records and other sources of evidence.

Ethical naturalists believe that the statement about genetic research is just as valid because you can use evidence to support or criticise it. Therefore, I could say that genetic research saves lives by curing diseases, and conclude that it is right to use it.

Non-naturalism 

In the non-naturalistic approach 'good' is something that cannot be defined using any type of natural experience. Good is not something that is found in things, but instead is used to describe an action or an object. G.E. Moore

(1873–1958) said that good is not a word that can be defined or explained using a more simple word. He compared it to giving a definition of a colour. If we are asked to give a definition of the colour green then we are stumped, as we can only define green by giving examples of things that are green. Moore says that we run into problems, however, as everyone has a sense of the meaning of green! Therefore for Moore the only way to understand goodness is to provide an example to illustrate it.

Moore believed that ethical language is made up of propositions that may be made true by objective features of the world, independent of human opinion. He did not consider that goodness and rightness could be natural properties, e.g. the roughness of a brick is a natural property that is empirically apparent, but the goodness of a right moral action is not measurable in the same empirical manner. Therefore Moore rejects ethical naturalism because it teaches that moral terms and properties can be reduced to the terms of non-moral properties.

Intuitionism

Moore's approach led to the emergence of the theory of **intuitionism**. Intuitionists claim that we understand basic moral principles using a special faculty called moral intuition. Using this special faculty we can still determine whether something is right or wrong, true or false. Moore's idea was that we recognise good when we see it – we just know it is good.

> *If I am asked 'What is good?' my answer is that good is good, and that is the end of the matter. Or if I am asked 'How is good to be defined?' my answer is that it cannot be defined, and that is all I have to say about that.*
>
> G.E. Moore, *Principia Ethica*, 1903, chapter 1

H.A. Pritchard (1871–1947) developed Moore's ideas a little further and said that it wasn't only goodness that was indefinable, but also the idea of obligation. In the same way that goodness is recognised by example, so are our obligations. We will always know when we ought to do a certain act. For Pritchard, intuitionism was the joining of reason and human intuition to help people to decide what to do based on facts. Therefore we know what is right/good and also what we ought to do.

He believed that everyone has a different moral intuition – some more developed and clearer than others. In a situation where moral obligations clashed he simply said examine the situation and choose the greater obligation.

W.D. Ross built a lot on the work of Moore and Pritchard and agreed that 'good' and 'obligatory' are intrinsically indefinable. He believed that a set of basic moral principles are apparent prima facie (at first appearance). Our moral obligations are apparent and must be followed unless there is another greater obligation that exists. He saw this as intuitionism at work, as our intuition identifies our **prima facie duties** and we then make our moral decisions based on this intuition that we have. Ross' approach tells us to obey the greater prima facie duty; however he doesn't expand this to tell us which duties are the greater ones.

STRETCH & CHALLENGE

In what ways does this naturalistic approach link closely with Natural Law? Can you connect the teachings on naturalism with those of Aristotle and Aquinas?

KEY WORDS

Intuitionism: a theory that ethical and moral truths are known and understood by our intuition.

Prima facie duties: this translates as 'at first appearance'. It means these duties are the primary ones.

FOR DEBATE

Is Moore correct in his idea that we just *know* what is good by employing our intuition? What would other cognitivist approaches say about his approach?

ACTIVITY

Using your understanding of non-naturalism, try to give an intuitionist understanding and approach to the following statements: an evil man, a good bomb, a wrong choice, a bad holiday.

Contrast your applications with the naturalistic approach to them.

Meta-ethics

6.4 It's just a matter of opinion 

In this topic you will learn about the two theories that believe that ethical language is just a response to emotions or a way of prescribing a course of action.

KEY WORDS

Emotivism: the idea that the meaning of ethical language is not knowable as its use is only an expression of emotion.

Boo-Hurrah Theory: another name for emotivism.

Prescriptivism: the idea that the meaning of ethical language is not knowable as it is a manner of prescribing a subjective belief or course of action.

Emotivism – Boo-Hurrah

According to A.J. Ayer all meaningful statements had to be verified either analytically or synthetically. He said that ethical and religious statements could not be verified using either so they aren't meaningful.

Ayer said that ethical statements can be problematic and therefore simply may be an expression (rather than an assertion) of an emotion. His approach to ethical language is called **emotivism**, as everything that is said could just be an expression of emotions. For emotivists, statements are presenting preferences and evincing emotions. In effect the statement 'theft is wrong' is a non-cognitive expression but it doesn't mean the same as 'I disapprove of theft', which is a cognitive expression. This approach is sometimes called the '**Boo-Hurrah Theory**', as what we are saying if we make statements about the morality and ethics of war is 'Boo to War' or 'Hurrah to War', and these are not significant because they are simply evincing expressions of approval or disapproval. We do not need to feel the emotion expressed.

The people who are protesting in this picture disapprove of war. Would it be true to say that they disagree with all wars?

FOR DEBATE 

'There is no point in making a statement of what is good or bad! It's just an opinion.' Discuss this with reference to emotivism.

Moral statements can sometimes simply express our liking or disliking for something – there are no claims to any truth in them. It could be as factually meaningful for me to say that 'The Arctic Monkeys are the best band in the world'.

C.L. Stevenson looked at the emotive meaning of words and how they affect other people by their use. It is easy to use words like honesty in a descriptive sense, however it also has an emotive meaning that aims to influence other people. Stevenson believed that ethical statements are subjective opinions that are there to influence the views of others and to explicitly give approval or disapproval rather than just give an emotive perspective.

Stevenson's approach gave more meaning to moral disagreements, as they were more than descriptive statements of emotions, they were aiming to express commands and to persuade and influence others. This dealt with fundamental beliefs and principles and this is what ethical disagreements are about.

Prescriptivism

R.M. Hare said that moral statements were more than an expression of personal values or emotions, they were in fact suggesting that other people should apply that same value and follow the same course of action in similar circumstances. He said that ethical language is intrinsically prescriptive and implies what ought to be done and that this is universal. In other words, everyone in the same position would be advised to take the same approach or course of action – if it is correct for one person, then it is correct for another person.

Ayer had suggested that moral statements don't describe anything factual, and Stevenson believed that moral statements were attitudes based on personal beliefs that attempted to persuade other people. Hare disagreed with this subjective approach in emotivism, as there was more to moral statements than expressing ideas or outlining behaviours. He saw statements as commanding behaviour and guiding actions because they prescribe attitudes, which can permit logical tests for consistency. He saw the statements as imperatives that must be consistent with logic.

Hare didn't see his approach as stating facts or something that is true or false, he saw prescriptivism as a way of expressing wishes and beliefs. In many ways these prescriptive statements are just like imperatives that are orders or requests to be followed.

When a prescriptivist says 'Murder is wrong' they mean that you shouldn't murder and neither will I. Prescriptivists believe in this idea of universalisability that not only prescribes actions for other people but also that these actions are to be followed by us too.

MAKING LINKS

Look back at the work that you have done on Kant's categorical imperative at AS. What are the important links between Kant's first maxim and the teachings of Hare? In what ways does Kant's categorical imperative help to validate the teachings of prescriptivism?

ACTIVITY

In pairs, prepare a presentation on the different non-cognitivist theories and approaches. You will need to show:

- an introduction into the background of non-cognitivism, e.g. logical positivism
- emotivism and its three main proponents
- prescriptivism
- the differences between emotivism and prescriptivism

Apply these non-cognitivist approaches to some ethical statements.

ACTIVITY

Choose a newspaper headline that includes a moral statement. Attempt to explore and analyse it with reference to both cognitivist and non-cognitivist approaches. Remember to evaluate not just to outline.

6 Meta-ethics

6.5 Evaluating meta-ethics

In this topic you will look at criticisms of the different approaches to meta-ethics.

KEY WORD

Naturalistic fallacy: It claims that good cannot be defined and that attempting to provide ethical conclusions from natural facts is wrong.

STRETCH & CHALLENGE

Does intuitionism make any sense? It is based on the idea of a 'sixth sense' that enables us to understand and know what moral statements mean. In what ways is it an easy explanation? What would other philosophers like Aquinas, Fletcher, Bentham and Kant conclude about it?

FOR DEBATE

By saying that 'Abortion is morally wrong', would people be justified in saying that 'We ought to stop all abortions'? Discuss this in pairs considering both naturalist and non-naturalist perspectives.

Evaluating naturalism

If the meaning of ethical statements is solely based on empirical evidence, we have some problems. If all ethical statements are the same as non-ethical statements, then they must stand up to scrutiny. However, they don't stand up to criticisms as they suggest that we know what is right based on what our sensory experience tells us, because they can be verified or falsified.

Moore claimed that by classing ethical statements and non-ethical statements together, naturalism was guilty of committing what he called the **naturalistic fallacy**. He said that people cannot be talking about facts and then switch into talking about moral values. What we 'ought' to do cannot be based on the facts of what 'is'.

Moore based his teaching on the naturalistic fallacy on the work of David Hume who thought that to derive an 'ought' from an 'is' would be logically wrong. All too often according to Moore we are talking about facts and then slip into speaking about ethical or moral values without making clear the basis of how we did so, because we ascribe natural properties to morality, which is fallacious.

Good cannot be defined in any simpler way, yet moral values about what is good are applied to the facts but are not discoverable among the facts like naturalism would suggest. Moore said attempting to define good using natural terms committed the naturalistic fallacy, he believed that it could be approached using the Open Question Argument. Suppose I believe that the natural quality of pleasure is the good. Now suppose I said 'I find hurting people pleasant'. It makes, most of us would say, perfect sense to ask, 'But is it good?' But, if pleasure = good, then it makes no sense to ask the question, because it would mean, 'Hurting people is good (= pleasant), but is it good?' As long as you can still ask, of any natural quality, 'But is it good?' (the Open Question), then that quality can never be the good.

Evaluating non-naturalism

It is important to note that non-naturalism doesn't seek to take away any meaningfulness from ethical statements, it takes the approach that facts are not adequate in proving them true or false.

Can intuitionism really provide a cognitivist answer that the meaning of language is knowable? This inbuilt moral sense the intuitionists refer to isn't ever fully explained or verified by Moore, he actually was quite dogmatic about his approach and said either you agreed with him or you need to think about it again properly.

Non-naturalism makes ethical discussion very difficult. If our understanding of moral statements is based on a person's intuition, then it is difficult to argue with it even when our own intuition disagrees with it. We can't know which intuition is correct and which isn't, we all perceive things around us in different ways and the same must be true of our intuitive understanding of good and bad.

Evaluating emotivism

One of the principle criticisms of emotivism concerns whether it is really an ethical theory at all. If everything is all about how we feel or what our emotions dictate, then how can we know anything at all?

James Rachels claims that Ayer and Stevenson are incorrect in removing the concept of reasoning from ethical judgements as there is so much more to statements than just expressions of feelings or desires. Moral judgements must appeal to reason otherwise they become arbitrary and therefore pointless.

It seems that emotivism would claim that moral perspectives and statements concerning the Rwandan Genocide or 9/11 atrocities would be reduced to being classed as subjective personal feelings rather than important meta-ethical statements.

Ayer does suggest that ethical statements are more than just expressions of feeling – he said they were 'expressing certain moral sentiments' (Ayer, *Language, Truth and Logic* page 107). Therefore they can be made without the assertions that suggest approval of a specific action. Stevenson's contribution to addressing the criticisms was to question why one person's understanding and perspective about a matter might be better than those of another person.

Evaluating prescriptivism

Hare proposed that moral statements were both prescriptive and universalisable and it therefore followed that he believed there were absolute ideas and principles to follow. However the relativist philosopher J.L. Mackie (1917–81) disagreed and said that morals are not universal. His reasoning was based on the concept that his preferences may be different from someone else's and that Hare's approach doesn't work in practice. It wouldn't help to suggest 'do unto others as you would have them do unto you', as what we would want done to us may not be the same as others would want done to them. We only have to look at cultural differences in other societies to see how this could be true, for example the fanaticism of al-Qaeda and the cult of the suicide bomber.

MAKING LINKS

Could the approaches that you have looked at concerning ethical language be used to examine religious language? Are the approaches in religious language applicable to the study of ethical language?

FOR DEBATE

Some people suggest that the emotivist approach to language could influence people's perceptions of moral issues if the language used is not subject to truth or falsity. In essence it reduces all our language to a relativist understanding (i.e. that every time we use a word it can mean a different thing depending on the circumstances). In light of this, can we ever truly state that child torture is objectively wrong?

STRETCH & CHALLENGE

If according to prescriptivism, moral statements contain prescriptions and are universally applicable, then does this not suggest that this approach is more of a normative ethical theory than a meta-ethical theory? Or is it just a radically different approach to normative ethics and the relativism of Mackie?

Meta-ethics

6.6 Meta-ethics: an overview of meanings

In this topic you will revisit the meanings and the different approaches to meta-ethics.

ACTIVITY

Look at the summaries of the theories on these pages.

- Do a mind map summarising them (use other sources too).
- Add criticisms of each in a different coloured pen.
- Discuss with someone which approach you find most acceptable.
- Do a presentation to the class on one of the sub-topics.

Emotivism: emotivists, like Ayer, believe that ethical statements and language are only statements that express emotions. If we say that 'war is good' or that 'abortion is wrong' then what we are saying isn't significant at all – we are merely evincing expressions of approval or disapproval. Therefore the use of these words could be suggested to be meaningless, they just express emotions which we might not even feel of what is right or wrong and have no factual significance or meaning.

Prescriptivism: this theory says that the ethical statements are prescriptive, they are universal and that they are logically consistent. They don't just express a personal opinion or emotion, they suggest that other people in similar circumstances should do the same and therefore the prescribed principle is universalised.

Non-cognitivism: this approach says that there can be no ethical knowledge because ethical language and statements give no factual information and therefore must not be meaningful as they are not subject to truth or falsity. It is suggested by this approach that they are expressions of emotion and prescriptive recommendations.

Naturalistic fallacy: Moore claimed that for naturalists to say that a moral statement can be proved like a non-moral statement was to commit the naturalistic fallacy. The philosopher David Hume taught that to take a fact and then to infer a moral action was logically flawed and he famously proposed that you cannot derive an 'ought' from an 'is'. A statement of fact cannot be transformed into a moral imperative. According to Hume what 'is' and what 'ought to be' are unrelated to each other. Naturalism makes the same mistake by suggesting moral statements and non-moral statements can both be verified and are reducible in the same way. Moore disagreed and it led to the emergence of intuitionist approaches to language.

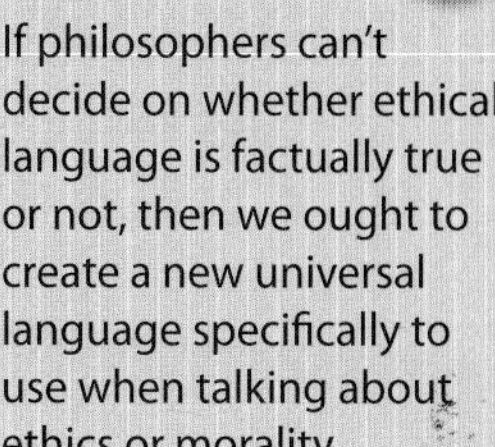

FOR DEBATE

If philosophers can't decide on whether ethical language is factually true or not, then we ought to create a new universal language specifically to use when talking about ethics or morality.

STRETCH & CHALLENGE

If ethical language is something that we use on a daily basis, how can it help us in our understanding and use of normative ethics and practical ethics? Apply this to the work you did at AS on Natural Law, Utilitarianism, Kant and medical ethics.

Meta-ethics: the area of ethics that deals with what ethical language/statements mean, e.g. what does the word 'good' really mean?

Cognitivism: a view that says that moral knowledge is possible. Therefore ethical statements can be meaningful because they can be proved true or false as they have a factual basis.

Ethical naturalism: the belief that goodness exists and can be described and validated as true with reference to some objective part of the world independent of human opinions. It relies on the use of empirical evidence (experience of the senses) to prove a statement as true or false. This theory teaches that all statements, ethical or non-ethical, are factual and can be verified or falsified through external verification. It believes that moral features can be reduced to non-moral features.

Ethical non-naturalism: the belief that ethical sentences express propositions and that some such propositions can be described and validated as true with reference to some objective part of the world independent of human opinions. It relies on the use of empirical evidence (experience of the senses) to prove a statement as true or false. This theory teaches that all statements, ethical or non-ethical, are factual and can be verified or falsified through external verification. But, in contrast to ethical naturalism, it believes that issues of morality are *not* reducible to non-moral features.

Intuitionism: This teaches that good cannot be defined with reference to the world or sensory (empirical) experience. Goodness is a tool to describe an object or action, but cannot be discovered in it. This is an approach that believes any attempt to define ethical statements solely in terms of statements about the natural world commits the naturalistic fallacy. This theory teaches that ethical statements cannot be factually proved like non-ethical ones, but that we can recognise good through intuition, which is a moral sense that is based on experience rather than inference.

Exam**Café**

Relax, refresh, result!

Relax and prepare

Hot tips

Rachel

Once I understood that this is not about deciding what is right and wrong but about the meaning of the words right and wrong, I understood what the different theories were trying to say.

Aisha

Murder is really horrible but this does not mean that murder ought to be wrong. This is the best way to think of the 'is/ought' idea.

Hamish

Knowing the difference between cognitive and non-cognitive is the key to understanding meta-ethics. Cognitive theories say that right and wrong are objective facts independent of humans, whereas non-cognitive theories say that right and wrong are subjective, they express feelings or tell people what to do.

Phil

To help me remember the different theories I reduce them to the key ideas such as 'you can't define yellow' or 'Boo-Hurrah Theory'.

Getting started...

Try setting out key concepts in a visual way, such as in the flowchart below.

Right and wrong are...

Observable facts
Objectively true or false.
Independent of humans.

Cognitive

Ethical naturalism
Ethical statements can be proved true or false.

Intuitionism
G. E. Moore: Cannot derive how the world ought to be from how it is.
We intuitively know what good is but we cannot define it.

Based on feelings and emotions
Telling people what to do.
Subjective.

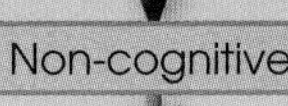

Emotivism
A. J. Ayer: Expression of feelings to stimulate action.

Prescriptivism
R. M. Hare: Not just our feelings to stimulate action but should be universal, we should all act the same.

Revision checklist for meta-ethics

You need to be able to demonstrate knowledge and understanding of:

- The use of ethical language – the ways in which different scholars understand how words such as 'good', 'bad', 'right', 'wrong' are used when ethical statements are made.
- How meta-ethics differs from normative ethics.
- The different approaches: cognitive and non-cognitive, ethical naturalism, intuitionism, emotivism and prescriptivism, and how these apply to ethical statements.
- You will need to be able to discuss these areas critically and their strengths and weaknesses.

Get the result!

How to answer an A2 exam question

You must include both the AO1 explanation and the AO2 critical discussion in your answer for each question. It is a bit like rolling both parts of an AS question together.

Questions are likely to have a statement which will ask you to discuss, but you will need to ensure that you include both an explanation of the key ideas and a critical discussion of them in order to get the higher marks.

You will have to answer two questions from a choice of four and you will get 1 hour and 30 minutes in which to answer the questions. That is 45 minutes per question. Each question is worth 35 marks and the total for the paper is 70 marks.

In the AO1 explanation you will need to:

- Select and demonstrate clearly relevant knowledge and understanding of the topic, the issues within the topic and the scholars relevant to the topic. The key word here is 'relevant', do not just write down everything you know about a topic, make sure it is relevant to the question.
- Use evidence, examples and the correct language and terminology in your answer to help demonstrate your knowledge and understanding to the examiner.
- Address the question specifically (which means answer the question set and not focusing on one word and writing everything you know about that) and select relevant material.
- Show comprehensive and accurate knowledge, which is expressed clearly. You will not receive marks for your written communication but if your ideas are not clearly stated you may not get the marks you deserve.
- Use a range of terminology accurately and consistently throughout the whole of your answer.
- Explain examples, relevant sources and scholars' views. Do not just stick Hume's name in or a quote from him without explaining why this is relevant to your answer and the question.

In the AO2 critical discussion section you will need to:

- Critically evaluate the ideas, not just saying if something is good or bad/strong or weak, but saying why and why not.
- Justify each view you give through evidence and reasoned arguments.
- Construct a well-organised evaluative argument. Remember the conclusion you reach is less important than the quality of your argument.
- Demonstrate an informed viewpoint and show evidence of your own thinking. Don't just write 'I like the Boo-Hurrah Theory'. Explain why you think that emotivism is a valid explanation of ethical language, or why it proves that ethical language is meaningless.
- You will need to show understanding of different views and arguments. You will need to show off about how much you know about each topic, this must include showing your knowledge and understanding of the different views put forward by scholars within each topic area.
- Use proficient, fluent and accurate language so ensure that you practise your essay writing style so that it becomes as proficient, fluent and accurate as possible. But whatever you do don't waffle, be precise. Give detailed explanations but not long-winded examples which involve your Nan's cat or Spiderman or anything that is not relevant to the question.

Sample essay plans

When it comes to the exam some candidates write essay plans. This is not required by the exam board and they are not marked. Many examiners don't even read them. However, the following sample essay plans highlight what you need to include in your answers in order to ensure that you achieve the highest grades possible.

Look at the three examples below. Which of these three do you think might produce the best answer?

Examiner's tips

Ensure that you know and understand the synoptic themes that run through the topic that you are studying. For example, in meta-ethics the synoptic theme is authority and truth in religion. This is a way of ensuring that you understand the wider themes involved in your study. It is quite clear how meta-ethics contributes to a discussion on authority and truth in religion if that authority and truth is based on language which can be argued to be meaningless.

Sample answers

Ethical language is subjective. Discuss. (35 marks)

Dean's essay plan

Ethical language is subjective	Ethical language is objective
Hume Hare Ayer Wittgenstein	Ethical naturalism Normative ethics – Kantian, utilitarian, virtue

Examiner says

Dean's plan shows that he is thinking about the discussion element to the question which is good but has he considered the explanation side of the answer? Also, he might be better off including intuitionism in the 'objective' column and leaving out the normative ethics.

Magda's essay plan

Meta-ethics

Hume – what does 'murder is wrong' mean?

Ethical naturalism – true or false

Naturalistic fallacy – Moore- intuitionism – what is yellow?

Emotivism – Ayer Boo-Hurrah

Prescriptivism – Hare – prescribing our views to others

Examiner says

Magda's essay plan shows knowledge of meta-ethics and could lead to a good explanation of this area of moral philosophy. However, it does not suggest any discussion will take place. Also, it might be a good idea to include a section on the difference between cognitive and non-cognitive meta-ethical theories.

Examiner's tips

If we merge the best bits of both plans together we would end up with:

Ethical language is subjective	Ethical language is objective
Hume Hare Ayer and Stevenson Wittgenstein	Ethical naturalism Intuitionism: Moore, Prichard and Ross

- The difference between cognitive theories and non-cognitive theories.
- Hume – what does 'murder is wrong' mean?
- Ethical naturalism – true or false
- Naturalistic fallacy – Moore – intuitionism – what is yellow?
- Emotivism – Ayer Boo-Hurrah
- Prescriptivism – Hare – prescribing our views to others.

This could produce a good answer to the question set.

Sample answers

Essay questions about meta-ethics are likely to ask candidates to discuss the strengths and weaknesses of the different meta-ethical views. Some questions may ask for a comparison between meta-ethics and normative ethics.

Discuss the strengths and weaknesses of emotivism. (35 marks)

Will's answer

Emotivism seems to be the most sound meta-ethical theory as it does not try to suggest we can derive how the world ought to be from how it is, such as ethical naturalism. This of course is a naturalistic fallacy. Neither does it suggest that we intuitively know right from wrong, but this not does take into account the differences in culture, time and society as Moore would want us to believe. Emotivism also refrains from giving a universal prescriptive statement as Hare would suggest, which encounters the same issues as any absolutist ethical theory. Therefore emotivism suggests that right and wrong are just our emotional responses: 'They are calculated also to arouse feeling and so to stimulate action' (A.J. Ayer).

Examiner says

This is a very different way to start a discussion essay on meta-ethics. It gives a brief introduction to each theory and a similarly brief criticism. What is good about it is that it is focused on emotivism, and criticises each theory in relation to the ideas presented by emotivism. Will could have given a description of emotivism or outlined the strengths of emotivism as part of his introduction.

In the rest of his essay Will goes back to look at each theory, describes the key features of each theory and the main criticisms, before focusing for the majority of his essay on showing the strengths of emotivism as well as highlighting and answering some of emotivism's criticisms.

Do ethical statements have any meaning?

Laila's answer

There are two views to answer this question. One from a cognitive point of view and one from a non-cognitive point of view.

A cognitivist believes that ethical statements contain facts which are objective and can be observed in the world. They are seen to be good or bad independent of humans. This is also known as moral realism. So for example a cognitivist would believe that if someone said 'euthanasia is right' we could go out and observe this. We could find objective evidence to support or reject the rightness of euthanasia.

A non-cognitivist would believe the opposite. They believe that we cannot find rightness or wrongness objectively. They are not independent of humans. Non-cognitivists believe that facts about ethics are actually facts about us as humans – they do not describe the world. They also suggest that ethical statements are an expression of our emotions or feelings towards an issue. They cannot be described as true or false and so are described as subjective.

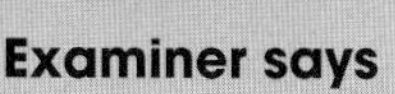

Examiner says

Laila gives a clear description of the difference between cognitive and non-cognitive approaches to ethical language. However, Laila could improve this by explaining each idea with examples rather than just giving a description.

7

Free will and determinism

If I make a choice, it means I am responsible for my actions, doesn't it?

In this chapter you will learn about:

- the theories of hard determinism, libertarianism and soft determinism
- the views of Clarence Darrow, Ted Honderich, David Hume and John Locke
- the religious approaches to free will and predestination (theological determinism)
- the influences of genetics, psychology, environment and social conditioning on moral choices
- the link between free will, determinism and moral responsibility.

Free will and determinism

7.1 Free as a bird?

In this topic you will learn about the ideas of free will and determinism.

We can all make choices. We can choose to get up in the morning or we can choose to run a marathon. We all have the freedom to make decisions about ourselves and about other people. To a certain extent we can seem to be totally free to do whatever we want to. We have the ability to exercise our **free will** in all manner of ways and make choices.

However an important question to examine is whether we always have free will? Can we always choose to do something? Is there anything that we don't have the freedom to do? How about these three choices?

- Open a window, jump out and fly in the sky.
- Grow a tail to help me climb trees.
- Become God and rule the universe.

Obviously we don't have the ability to do these things or the freedom to choose to do them, so therefore we can't truly be free at all. There are things that limit us and seem to stop us being free and using our free will. There are many factors that might assist in determining our actions and limiting our freedom:

- Family.
- Genetics.
- Society.
- Psychology.
- Natural laws.
- Religion.

Some philosophers believe that our ability to make free choices is an illusion – they believe we are not free at all. Others state that there is something else beyond our understanding that may cause our actions to be determined.

Determinism says that there are laws that exist outside of our control that cause the things that happen – laws such as gravity. Scientific laws determine all our actions based on what has happened before. Previous events have consequences that may be determined and which in turn will cause more consequences. Remember back to Aristotle's teaching concerning cause and effect – every action has some sort of cause and therefore an effect.

There are a variety of responses to dealing with the debate about free will and determinism, and on pages 132–135 we will explore three philosophical understandings of the debate.

ACTIVITY

Write your response to these statements:

'If I am forced against my will (with a gun to my head) to rob a bank, can I be held morally responsible?'

'I didn't mean to knock that man down: he just stepped into the road. But I still feel responsible. Should I?'

KEY WORDS

Free will: the ability to make free, unhindered choices.

Determinism: the idea that all actions are governed by laws outside of our control.

ACTIVITY

Watch two scenes from the film, *Matrix: Reloaded*. What do they tell us about free will and determinism?

Scene 1 = Neo's conversation with the Oracle.

Scene 2 = Neo's confrontation with the Architect.

Free will and determinism

7.2 Hard determinism and libertarianism

In this topic you will look at the contrasting philosophies of hard determinism and libertarianism.

KEY WORD

Hard determinism: the teaching that denies that humanity has free will and believes that all actions have a prior cause. It removes moral responsibility for actions.

ACTIVITY

In groups, discuss these questions and then report back to the class:

Would you like to be controlled like a puppet by a puppeteer?

In what ways do you believe that you are controlled or that your choices are already determined?

Is it morally wrong not to be able to make free choices?

FOR DEBATE

Psychological determinists believe they have made some progress in isolating physiological abnormalities in the brain that may cause people to murder without having made a choice to do so. Could it have been 'determined' that these people would murder because of a genetic defect?

Hard determinism

Hard determinism is the view that all choices are determined by other events or actions prior to the choice. Therefore they are caused by other events or actions that were themselves choices in the past – so when you 'decided' to take A level Philosophy and Ethics, this wasn't a product of free will but a choice determined by other events and actions going right back beyond your birth. The concept of free will would then be an illusion.

> *...all our choices, decisions, intentions, other mental events and our actions are no more than effects of other equally necessitated events.*
>
> Ted Honderich

Imagine if you were just like this puppet being controlled by a puppet master. Some philosophers, psychologists and scientists believe that we are controlled by external forces around us.

Humans may make a choice believing it was made using free will, however every event that went before has led up to this 'apparent' free choice, so therefore it had already been determined.

Hard determinism relies heavily on the work of Sir Isaac Newton (1643–1727). He said that all physical beings and things are governed by a series of unchangeable natural laws such as gravity or motion. These laws assist in forming the basis for the cause and effect that fills the discussion of hard determinism.

Hard determinists are very strict and rigid in their beliefs. If everything is determined and we are not free at all to act in any different way, then we cannot be held morally responsible for our actions, as we didn't choose to perform or commit these actions.

Modern hard determinists, such as John Hospers (1918–), claim that there is always something that is within us that urges us to make a choice that we believe was the result of our free will. We aren't always aware of any 'urging' in our choice making, however we have all probably made choices and not remembered why and how we made them.

Libertarianism

In the way that hard determinism says that everything is already determined and we have no free will, **libertarianism** says the complete opposite. We are completely free and nothing is determined in any way.

This approach arose because some philosophers rejected the idea of determinism as it ruled out any individual moral responsibility and also because people feel they have got the freedom to act and to be self-determining. This approach is also called **incompatabilism**, because it is incompatible with determinism.

Libertarians believe that cause and effect is not relevant, as determinists suggest, because moral actions are the result of individual character and values being applied to ethical concerns. Hume's description of liberty is quite useful:

> *By liberty, then, we can only mean a power of acting or not acting, according to the determinations of the will; that is, if we choose to remain at rest, we may; if we choose to move, we also may.*

For libertarians there is no compulsion to act, so every choice is free and therefore we must be responsible for performing or committing these free acts.

Sometimes we have to make a decision and we are torn between two different solutions that would both supposedly work. We may take time to think the decision through, we may be uncertain about either solution, yet we choose. After we have chosen we may discover we made the right choice or the wrong one, yet we chose a course of action. As we chose that course of action we must, by consequence, be morally responsible for the action and the choice.

There are stories of people who have grown up in abject poverty, surrounded by gang and drug cultures, who have been destined to follow in the footsteps of those around them. Yet, from within these people, some choose to be different and not do drugs, not join gangs and not do what everyone around them does. Libertarianism says that they had a choice, and we all have a choice that is free and not hindered or influenced by any determinism.

ACTIVITY

Explain the Ted Honderich quotation on page 132 to the rest of the group. Ask them what the implications might be and decide as a group how this would affect our society.

KEY WORD

Libertarianism (incompatibilism): this theory claims that we are morally responsible for all our actions and are free to make choices.

ACTIVITY

Produce a diagram summarising libertarianism and hard determinism and showing the strengths and weaknesses of each one.

FOR DEBATE

If a human child were raised by wolves in the wild, how would the child make decisions? Would they be based on genetic determinism or on upbringing? Could the child choose to not be a wolf or a human child?

FOR DEBATE

Does Prince William's life prove hard determinism is fact?

Free will and determinism

7.3 Soft determinism

In this topic you will explore an alternative to the two extremes of hard determinism and libertarianism called soft determinism.

KEY WORD

Soft determinism (compatibilism): the teaching that says we can be both determined and free, as some of our moral choices are free but aspects of our nature are determined.

ACTIVITY

Explain the point that Rachels is making. Do you agree?

FOR DEBATE

A paedophile in court claims that his abusive childhood and upbringing are justification for his actions and that he is not morally responsible. In groups, prepare arguments for both prosecution and defence solicitors using the three different approaches to free will and determinism.

With both of the previous theories we have got two extremes of belief:

1. Hard determinism says that everything is determined and we are not morally responsible for our actions.
2. Libertarianism says that nothing is determined, we are totally free and we are morally responsible for our actions.

To a certain extent, **soft determinism** is an attempt to combine the opposing theories of libertarianism and hard determinism. It is important to note that soft determinism is not a compromise between the other two approaches; it seeks to bring freedom and accountability together with the sense that choices are predetermined by prior choices.

Soft determinists believe that determinism and free will are compatible with each other, hence why this theory is also called **compatibilism**. They say that freedom to act is doing what you want to do, without any external interference or coercion, and completely voluntarily. They also say that our own values, desires and prior choices can determine how we will act in certain situations, however these 'causes' of our actions are so complex and numerous that they are almost completely random in their effects and may not determine a precise or specific action. So they are determined, yet they are also free because there is no external coercion involved.

> *...whether your behaviour is free just depends on how it is caused. Your act is free if it is caused by your own desires, rather than being caused by a mental disease, or by someone forcing you or tricking you, or the like.*
>
> James Rachels, *Dialogue*, Issue 19

If a man has had to deal with the experience of his wife being raped, and then at some later time witnesses another woman being raped, he will intervene and stop the attack that is somewhat similar to what his wife endured. His previous experience has determined that he will intervene to stop the rape, however he still had to make the choice to actually intervene. In this situation he had a choice, however prior events and the values that developed necessitated him to intervene. Therefore to some extent it was determined that he would intervene.

What about moral responsibility?

The other important aspect of soft determinism is that it emphasises the moral responsibility for actions that we perform. Therefore we are responsible for all our moral actions regardless of whether they could have been determined by our values or choices.

This idea of moral responsibility, combined with the idea of determined actions, is one that many people struggle with. If in fact we are responsible, then surely we 'ought' to have been totally free to perform the action to truly accept the responsibility?

In many ways this approach is one that seeks to balance the arguments against other approaches, like libertarianism or hard determinism, and relies very centrally on the idea of free will, but also on a reality of determining influences and forces.

In August 1945 the aircraft *Enola Gay* dropped the first atomic bomb on Hiroshima and changed the course of human history. Was the dropping of this bomb determined? Could a different choice have been made that would have achieved the same primary objective of a rapid Allied victory over Japan?

FOR DEBATE

'The fundamentalist who believes it is her religious duty to detonate an explosive device in a shopping mall bears no responsibility for her actions.'

ACTIVITY

Write down six actions from last week where you believe your actions were in some way determined. How much free choice did you have? What other action could you have chosen? What prior events influenced your action?

MAKING LINKS

Look back at the work you did on the problem of evil. Are there similarities with what you learned there? Create a mind map exploring the problem of evil and annotate it with perspectives from libertarianism, hard and soft determinism.

STRETCH & CHALLENGE

If we are to some extent determined by genetics, upbringing, etc. and also held morally responsible for our actions, then how can we explain and justify murderers who plead 'Not Guilty by Reason of Insanity' or 'Extenuating Circumstances' not being punished like other murderers in prison?

Free will and determinism

7.4 Approaches from key speakers 

In this topic you will discover the perspectives of important scholars who have taught about free will and determinism.

ACTIVITY

Look at the opinions from thinkers on these pages and make a bullet point list of each of their arguments. Their understanding of freedom is central to our appreciation of the whole subject. Do you agree with any of these ideas and statements? Explore these approaches and provide an evaluation of approximately 250 words debating the truthfulness of these statements using the teachings of hard and soft determinism and libertarianism.

Clarence Darrow (1857–1938)

I defended two young men who were accused of the murder of 14-year-old Bobby Franks in 1924. The two accused, Nathan Leopold and Richard Loeb, were rich and intelligent young men, who believed that they were superior to the rest of society and could commit the perfect crime. The crime didn't go to plan, the two men were caught, brought to trial and faced the death penalty if convicted. I argued that the two murderers were the product of their wealthy upbringing and therefore couldn't be held morally responsible for their actions – they weren't free to choose. I succeeded and their sentence was commuted to life imprisonment.

I believe that everything is determined, both externally and internally. There is no choice and therefore there cannot be moral responsibility. I can see no room for moral blame and subsequently no point in punishing someone just for the sake of punishing them. I argue against both compatibilism and incompatibilism; to me they are incoherent and by definition meaningless.

Ted Honderich (1933–)

Gottfried Leibniz (1646–1716)

I was a proponent of theological determinism. For me, God pre-ordained all things in the universe to be reliant and to be caused by each other. If it was determined that we should stand up, then when we stand up. God is actually causing us to stand up. I believe that the determinism of God works despite our experience of freedom and choice, and it harmonises to fit in with our choices.

I taught that we are free within our own will to perform unimpeded acts, whilst I believed that anything that was the object of knowledge was determined. I thought that to look for the causes of our actions outside of knowing and understanding our own will was not rational. Our understanding of the world around us and of our self-awareness says that we must be free. If we claim to not be free then we face a self-awareness problem of who originates our actions? My teachings followed a soft-determinist way of looking at the debate.

Immanuel Kant (1724–1804)

FOR DEBATE 

Is it possible for everything to be fully determined (as Honderich suggests) and to still be morally responsible?

ACTIVITY

7.2

Using all the teachings of the philosophers on these pages, draw a spider diagram of the perspectives, splitting them into hard determinism, soft determinism and libertarianism.

David Hume (1711–76)

My understanding of the debate is that we can choose to do something, or we can choose not to do this something. I believed that this was down to the power and determinations of the individual human will.

My ideas were that if Act B is observed to always follow Act A, then it is not correct to say that Act A causes Act B. We cannot say this, as it is not determined, it is merely our interpretation of what we have observed. People claim that I provided some excellent arguments for the compatibilist approach; I said 'moral responsibility requires determinism'.

I said that the phrase 'free will' did not make any sense and that to a certain extent it was an 'illusion'. I taught that the defining part of voluntary behaviour was that you could pause and reflect before you made a choice, therefore deciding what the consequences of the action would be. I illustrated this with the example of a man sleeping in a locked room. The man wakes up and chooses to remain there, not knowing that he is locked in. The man believes he made a free choice to remain in the room, however in reality he had no choice. Therefore he is determined.

John Locke (1632–1704)

John-Paul Sartre (1905–80)

I believed that, 'A choice is said to be free if it is such that it could have been other than what it is'. I also thought that with absolute freedom came unlimited moral responsibility, so if you want complete freedom the consequence of that was to be 100% morally responsible for all actions. One of my ideas was that intrinsically 'man is not free not to be free.' It didn't matter what you chose, as moral responsibility dealt with that, but rather that you were free to choose at all.

Baron D'Holbach (1723–89)

I believed strongly that determinism was universal, as directed by the Newtonian laws of cause and effect. I claimed that free will was an illusion and suffered from incoherency.

Reinhold Niebuhr (1892–1971)

I said that after an event it is easy to claim that it was determined due to the series of events that preceded it. It is a mistake to say that events were determined because they were inevitable. The biblical idea of divine providence over human destiny doesn't remove human freedom, but gives some element of meaning to it. I also argued that God respects and honours the free will that he has given mankind, despite the consequences.

STRETCH & CHALLENGE

Explore further the teachings of Kant and Honderich on the free will and determinism issue. Compare and contrast these opposing scholars and use this information to assist your understanding of the topic.

FURTHER RESEARCH

Investigate what Henry Sidgwick (1838–1900) contributes to the understanding of this topic and contrast his approaches with those of Kant, Hume and Locke. Useful material can be found online in the *Catholic Encyclopedia*'s article on free will – go to www.heinemann.co.uk and enter the express code 3587P.

STRETCH & CHALLENGE

Research the ideas of 'Liberty of Spontaneity' and 'Liberty of Indifference'. Present your findings to the group and suggest what they could add to their spider diagrams that they produced on the different thinkers' approaches to the issues of free will and determinism.

Free will and determinism

7.5 Predestination

In this topic you will look at Christian ideas about free will and a form of determinism called predestination.

KEY WORD

Predestination: also known as theological determinism. This is the belief that God already knew before all time began who would be 'saved' and go to heaven. Therefore there is no choice.

If God is omniscient, is he then not just a puppeteer controlling our actions and our destinies?

Many of the world religions have specific beliefs about how all things are determined by a God or through the actions and events that surround us.

There are within Christianity, specifically Protestant Christians, those who believe that God has already determined all things, including those who will be 'saved' at the end of all time and will live in heaven with God for eternity and those who will not be 'saved' and will live for eternity separated from God. In other words, no matter what we do and how good and committed we are, we can never change the fact that God has already decided whether we will be saved and go to heaven or whether we will not be saved and spend eternity separated from him. This teaching is called **predestination** and originated from the teaching of St Paul:

> *For those God foreknew he also predestined to be conformed to the likeness of his Son, that he might be the firstborn among all brothers. And those he predestined, he also called; those he called, he also put right with himself; those he put right with himself, he also glorified.*
>
> Romans 8:29–30

Augustine of Hippo (354–430) taught that in order for us to be good we need God's grace and his mercy, therefore as these are free undeserved gifts from God only he can choose who will receive the grace that is required for salvation.

> *The potter has authority over the clay from the same lump to make one vessel for honour and another for contempt.*
>
> Augustine Sermon 26: 12–13

FOR DEBATE

'If God has already decided who will go to heaven, through the theory of predestination, then I can't be free to choose to go to heaven.' How can a loving God choose to send so many people to eternal separation from him? (Draw links with the arguments from classical theism).

ACTIVITY

Use all the quotations from this topic and write them out on a sheet of paper. Then link together what they say and how each perspective/belief can be refuted and answered by the opposite perspective.

John Calvin (1509–64) taught that man is inherently evil and is not capable of good as his free will chooses to reject God. Therefore God has predestined those who will be saved, otherwise no one could be saved because of their sin and rebellion. In other words, Calvin is saying that man is so full of sin that he cannot do anything but reject God. However God, through his gift of grace, has predestined those who will be saved because otherwise no one would be capable of being saved.

If God decided at creation who would and would not gain salvation, then this means that no one has free will in their ethical or religious actions. If man isn't free to do this, is it possible for him to be morally responsible and to be rewarded or punished for the actions he performs? It could be possible to suggest that people only do good things because that is what God determined that they would do, and those who do sinful acts only perform these because God determined at creation that this is what they would do.

Religious understandings of free will

The claims of predestination say that God has not given humankind free will, however the Bible is very specific in other places that free will has been given to all people. The book of Genesis clearly teaches that Adam and Eve used their free will (God given) in choosing to eat from the Tree of Knowledge and in no way were compelled to do it. Aquinas stated that they were free because God created them with free will:

> *...man chose not of necessity but freely.*
>
> *Summa Theologica* 1:1:13:6

Traditional theism teaches that the Christian God is omniscient (all-knowing) and must, as a consequence, be knowledgeable of all that is in the past, happening in the present and going to happen in the future. He knows everything before it happens!

This causes a slight problem for those Christians who believe that God gave humankind the gift of free will. If God knows all things in the future, then he can know what choices we will make. This means we can't have free will, because God must have determined our choice in the past. If God knows that I will save a puppy from drowning the day before my next birthday, then that is what I will do as I cannot choose to do otherwise because God is omniscient!

It could be argued that free will is just an illusion for religious believers who believe in an omniscient God. However, this isn't necessarily true if we believe that we can still make free choices even if God knows what we will choose to do. Belief in a God who knows what choices we will make doesn't have to mean that he causes us to make these choices. It is suggested by several church denominations that he had to give humankind free will, even though he knew the choices they would make. This free will is essential to Christian beliefs about salvation, as humankind has to be able to make free moral choices of whether to obey or disobey God and accept the grace that saves them.

MAKING LINKS

Look back at the work that you did on knowledge of God and the arguments from classical theism. Link them with this work on predestination and religious ideas of free will.

STRETCH & CHALLENGE

Make out the case an omniscient God might put for being a puppeteer of humanity. Or offer the case God might give along Calvinist lines of predestination.

STRETCH & CHALLENGE

'God is like a spectator at a chariot race; he watches the actions the charioteers perform, but this does not cause them.' (Boethius, *The Consolation of Philosophy*)

Look at the quotation from Boethius and, using your knowledge from this topic and the theories on pages 78–81, write an extended piece of work on 'God cannot know all things, if he had predestined all things then he would have to have caused them, which would therefore make him non-benevolent.'

7.6 Influences on free will and determinism

In this topic you will explore other factors that may cause us to be determined.

Within the whole debate concerning free will and determinism there are other factors that need to be looked at that exist to a certain extent outside of normal religious philosophical debate. These factors are generally secular approaches and look at the area of personal freedom in light of psychology, genetics, environmental issues and social conditioning.

Psychology

Psychology seeks to understand how our mind works and how it influences our behaviour, attitudes and thinking. One area of psychology that links to determinism is that of behaviourism. This theory suggests that our behaviour can be predicted, as it is based on prior experiences and causes. J.B. Watson (1878–1958) said that human behaviour could be controlled because we live in a deterministic universe that doesn't leave anything up to choice. He includes all areas of ethics and moral decision making in this belief because these are all known and determinable in a universe that can be nothing but determined. In the psychological debate of Nature versus Nurture, Watson is convinced that heredity (nature) and environment (nurture) can be useful tools to change or reinforce forms of behaviour. That is, change the environment that a drug addict lives in and you can change the addictive behaviour.

B.F. Skinner (1904–90) believed that this approach wasn't the only one that was able to determine us. He saw behaviour as something that could be modified using punishment and reward. His belief was that our actions probably are determined if it is possible for scientists and psychologists to observe and control human behaviour. The primary implication of this is if our behaviour is determined by our psychological makeup, then we cannot be held morally responsible for actions if we could not have chosen to act any other way.

Sigmund Freud (1856–1939) taught that our early years have an immense impact on our actions in the future. In a similar way to behaviourism, his theories suggest that prior causes determine our moral development and therefore our actions in the future. His main theory in this area was that all actions, moral or non-moral, are caused by 'repressed' or 'subconscious' memories or feelings that stem back to our childhood. These are what determine our actions.

Social conditioning

This approach believes that people think and act in line with their social conditioning rather than through genetic determined factors or a real

ACTIVITY

Find out about the work of Ivan Pavlov and the dogs that he conditioned. Then answer the following:

- What was the purpose of his experiment?
- What does it tell us about determinism?
- Write up your own psychological explanations, using the examples of Pavlov and Skinner.

STRETCH & CHALLENGE

Find out about the psychological study of murderers in a psychiatric hospital investigated by Raine in 1997. Create a mind map making links between this psychological study and the types of determinism on these pages.

freedom of choice, therefore human action must have a distinct *social* cause. If we are socially determined, then all our actions are caused by something within society. The philosopher Thomas Sowell (1930–) said that social conditioning is 'the idea that the human self is infinitely plastic, allowing humanity to be changed and ultimately, perfected'. Actions are determined by society, by our upbringing, by our education or by whatever social setting we are in. This theory suggests that our social learning and placement is what determines our actions and we can do nothing else except follow the sociologically determined path.

FOR DEBATE

'Watching violent films creates a culture of violence.'

Genetics

Genetic determinism claims that almost all physical and behavioural aspects of humanity are determined by genetics. Some biologists would say that other influences may play a part, such as upbringing (nurture), however for most it is difficult to escape the fact that genes control so much of what we are and what we do. If it is true that genes can determine our actions, then once again is it possible to be morally responsible if we are only acting according to our genes?

FOR DEBATE

If we accept genetic determinism, would it not be possible with the assistance of scientific tests to know who would be the people who would murder or rape? Therefore we could stop them reproducing.

Evolutionary ideas in psychology suggest that we have evolved in certain ways to survive and part of this procedure is being partially determined or controlled by our genes. Steven Pinker developed the idea that moral reasoning is a result of natural selection, as ideas such as love, jealousy and guilt all have a basis in human biological evolution. He still maintains that humans have moral responsibility, as we all have an evolved, yet innate, sense of morality. This is based upon studies into the Environment of Evolutionary Adaptation, where humans first developed the first moral sense.

Environmental

Environmental determinism suggests that geography and climate influence individuals much more than social conditions do. It suggests that historically our climate contributes to our actions as it affects the behaviour of society. For example, tropical climates supposedly cause laziness and promiscuity and the less regular weather of Europe brings about a more determined attitude towards work and working. If this approach is true, then the weather and environment can affect our actions and possibly determine them.

Can environmental events really determine our actions? Does this once again remove human moral responsibility for actions if the looters say, 'The hurricane made me do it'?

STRETCH & CHALLENGE

If we accept that all the issues on these two pages determine us in some way, is there any way that we can remain convinced that we have freedom over any part of our lives? Do some internet research on the beliefs of Ted Honderich.

Free will and determinism

7.7 Free will and determinism – advantages and disadvantages

In this topic you will explore some of the strengths and weaknesses of the various approaches to free will and determinism.

Determinism

Determinism says that it is wrong to praise someone for doing something that is good or to reprimand someone for doing something wrong. They didn't choose to do it; it was determined so no responsibility lies with the person. The rational act cannot be made if the actions are determined. If this is right, then a murderer cannot be held morally responsible for his actions or receive any punishment. Libertarians say that determinists muddle things that are contingently true (dependent on circumstances with those that are only necessarily true).

MAKING LINKS

Look back at the theories of Hume on causation, on pages 60–61. If a cause does not exist then some of the tenets of determinism would seem to fall, i.e. if all events are caused according to determinism, and we deduce that cause doesn't exist then determinism isn't workable. We can't assume that A follows B every time, even though it always has done before. For Hume, cause is just a 'statistical' matter and, as a result, it is not intrinsic to events in the world and whether they actually occur or not.

Libertarianism

Determinists maintain that freedom is just an illusion, whilst libertarians' stance is that it is real. If we consider Locke's example of the man in the locked room (see page 137), the freedom that the man believes he has is only an illusion; he is unable to leave the locked room. The libertarian idea is that there is total freedom and total moral responsibility, yet there must be factors that we cannot control and cannot alter, such as genetics or psychology. Even if we spend time making the right decision and believe we are free, the fact is that our background and prior experiences determined that we would make that very decision. When making any moral decisions other issues always factor in our decisions, for example emotions and values, therefore the libertarian ideal of total freedom must be flawed as the decisions would be partially determined by these other factors.

MAKING LINKS

Look back at the work you have done on ethical theories at AS. Try to link each theory with the various approaches to free will and determinism. Explore and write up in your notes how each of the ethical theories views moral responsibility.

Soft determinism

The principal problem with the soft determinism approach is that it doesn't give specific guidelines as to which things are determined and which ones aren't. Human decision making can be influenced by so many factors, so which are the deterministic ones and which are not? Soft determinism can't decide which actions are determined as psychology, social conditioning and genetics make decision making so much more complex.

Moral responsibility

This phrase 'moral responsibility' is one that is mentioned frequently in this chapter and is central to the whole topic. Consider these statements:

- 'I can make choices freely, therefore I can be morally responsible.'
- 'I can make free choices, but I am not morally responsible for my choices.'
- 'I can make no free choices and so I cannot be held morally responsible.'
- 'I cannot make free choices, but still must be capable of being morally responsible.'

Which statement would the various approaches agree with? What one do you personally agree with? In light of the various approaches, it is difficult to fully settle on one statement as correct.

If a man, in an attempt to save 50 lives including his wife's life, was to deliberately kill one of the terrorists holding them hostage, would he be morally responsible for what he had done? He chose and maybe planned to kill this terrorist, therefore he made a free choice. However we could also say that his emotions were blurred because his wife was involved, or even that current social biases towards terrorists, due largely to 9/11, determined that the man would kill this terrorist. Is he morally responsible? Absolutists and deontologists would say that he is fully responsible, whilst relativists and teleologists would disagree.

The trial of Loeb and Leopold

This leads us back to Darrow's defence of Bobby Frank's two killers (see page 136) and his claim that they could not be held morally responsible as their actions had been determined by prior caused events in their upbringing. The question that this raises concerns whether someone who is found not morally responsible for a crime should still be punished for that crime.

Determinists would argue that there should be no punishment for the crime as the person was not morally responsible, but was probably legally responsible (their action led to the crime) and causally responsible (they caused the action). For this reason, Darrow did not ask that Loeb and Leopold be found not guilty and released, but had them imprisoned to protect society.

Libertarians believe that moral responsibility is a consequence of our freedom (and also a burden according to Sartre); if we act, we do it freely and must take the consequences.

Soft determinists would agree with the libertarian approach but would add that, even if an action is partially determined, we still have the choice whether or not to do it.

ACTIVITY 7.4

If a mentally-ill teenager kidnaps and murders a four-year-old boy, can she be held morally responsible for her actions? In which circumstances was she determined? Did she still choose to do it? Take on the role of a barrister defending the teenager in court and write a defence for her actions using one of the theories you have studied.

STRETCH & CHALLENGE

Apply all you have learned in this chapter to the plane hijackers on 9/11. Were they free or determined? Look at both sides of the debate and be objective. You will also need to explore moral responsibility. Write your findings up as a newspaper/journal article. Read your conclusions out to each other and see what agreement there is in the group.

Exam Café

Relax, refresh, result!

Relax and prepare

Hot tips

Sasha

Remember the key question with this topic is 'Am I morally responsible for my actions?' and there are three answers, yes, no and sort of!

Arthur

Make yourself a glossary with the key terms such as: determinism, hard determinism, soft determinism, compatiblism, non-compatiblism, libertarianism, free will, predestination, behaviourism and conditioning.

Leonie

Most textbooks contain lots of different scholars and it is really tempting to try and learn what all of them have to say. Instead I tried to concentrate on one scholar for each concept, for example: predestination = Calvin, hard determinism = Locke, soft determinism = Kant, libertarianism = Sartre, conditioning = Pavlov. My friends preferred to use Darrow and Honderich for hard determinism, and used Hume with libertarianism.

Isaac

I found this topic really easy until my teacher asked if God knows what decision I am going to make. Then all the rules changed and I had to start thinking all over again. Is God really omniscient? I wish I was, then I would know the exam questions and the answers!

Refresh your memory

Revision checklist for free will and determinism

Candidates should be able to demonstrate knowledge and understanding of:

- Hard determinism, soft determinism, and libertarianism.
- The views of Darrow, Honderich, Hume and Locke.
- Theological determinism (predestination) and religious ideas of free will.
- The influences of genetics, psychology, environment or social conditioning on moral choices.
- The implications of these views for moral responsibility.
- The link between free will, determinism and moral responsibility.

Candidates should be able to discuss these areas critically and their strengths and weaknesses.

Examiner's tips

Make sure that your notes and revision cover everything on the specification because questions on this topic will expect you to be able to draw on ideas from all aspects of the topic without specifically asking for it. You will not get a simplistic question such as 'Hard determinism is better than soft determinism'. Discuss. Instead you will be expected to discuss a variety of different aspects of the topic. For example 'God knows the ethical decision we will make'. Discuss. This essay will require you to both explain and evaluate. Therefore you will need to include both the AO1 explanation element and the AO2 discussion element in the same answer. You could explain and discuss each idea in turn, or define each term first and then spend time discussing them.

Get the result!

Sample answers

'God will know what ethical decisions we will make.' Discuss. (35 marks)

Danielle's answer

Libertarianism is the belief that people are free to make moral choices and so are responsible for their actions. Hume explained this idea of being free to act as 'a power of acting or not acting, according to the demonstrations of the will'. Hume and other libertarians are therefore suggesting that people are not forced to act by anything other than their own wills and desires. They are able to choose how to proceed in a certain situation without being compelled to behave in a set way. Because this view suggests that nothing but our own wants, desires or reasoning determines our actions, then it must follow that we would have to take full responsibility for the consequences of our actions. Sartre sees this freedom as the measure and goal of human existence. He suggests that if we do not choose for ourselves but conform to what others want from us, then our lives are absurd and meaningless.

However, not everyone agrees that the freedom and deliberation we feel we have is actually a sign of free will. Spinoza commented that 'men think themselves free on account of this alone, that they are conscious of their actions and ignorant of the causes of them'. Hume counters this view by suggesting that we cannot say that X causes Y, just because on every observed occasion of Y happening X always preceded it. This goes beyond observation and into the realms of interpretation therefore suggesting that an action is not necessarily caused by preceding events.

Examiner says

This answer shows a high level of understanding of the topic and a good grasp of the different scholars connected to it. Danielle explained the Libertarian point of view first and then discussed it by showing a contradictory view and how that contradictory view can be countered. What it lacked was any meaningful discussion about moral responsibility.

Examiner's tips

Write your own answer to this question using the tips below.

AO1	Candidates are likely to show knowledge and understanding of a range of approaches to the topic of free will and determinism. They are likely to show understanding of the links between free will, determinism and moral responsibility. Candidates could link the ideas of hard and soft determinism and libertarianism with the omniscience of God. This may well lead on to an explanation of the idea of predestination and religious ideas of free will. Candidates may explain the view that if God knows all our actions we cannot possibly be free, and we are not morally responsible for our actions. Candidates may explain the idea that freedom is an illusion.
AO2	Candidates could explore the implications for ethics if we are not free in terms of human accountability and responsibility. They may argue that moral responsibility is only possible with free will and look at the teaching of Kant. Better responses may consider whether our freedom to make ethical decisions takes away God's omniscience, or whether his foreknowledge does, in fact, take away our freedom.

8 Conscience

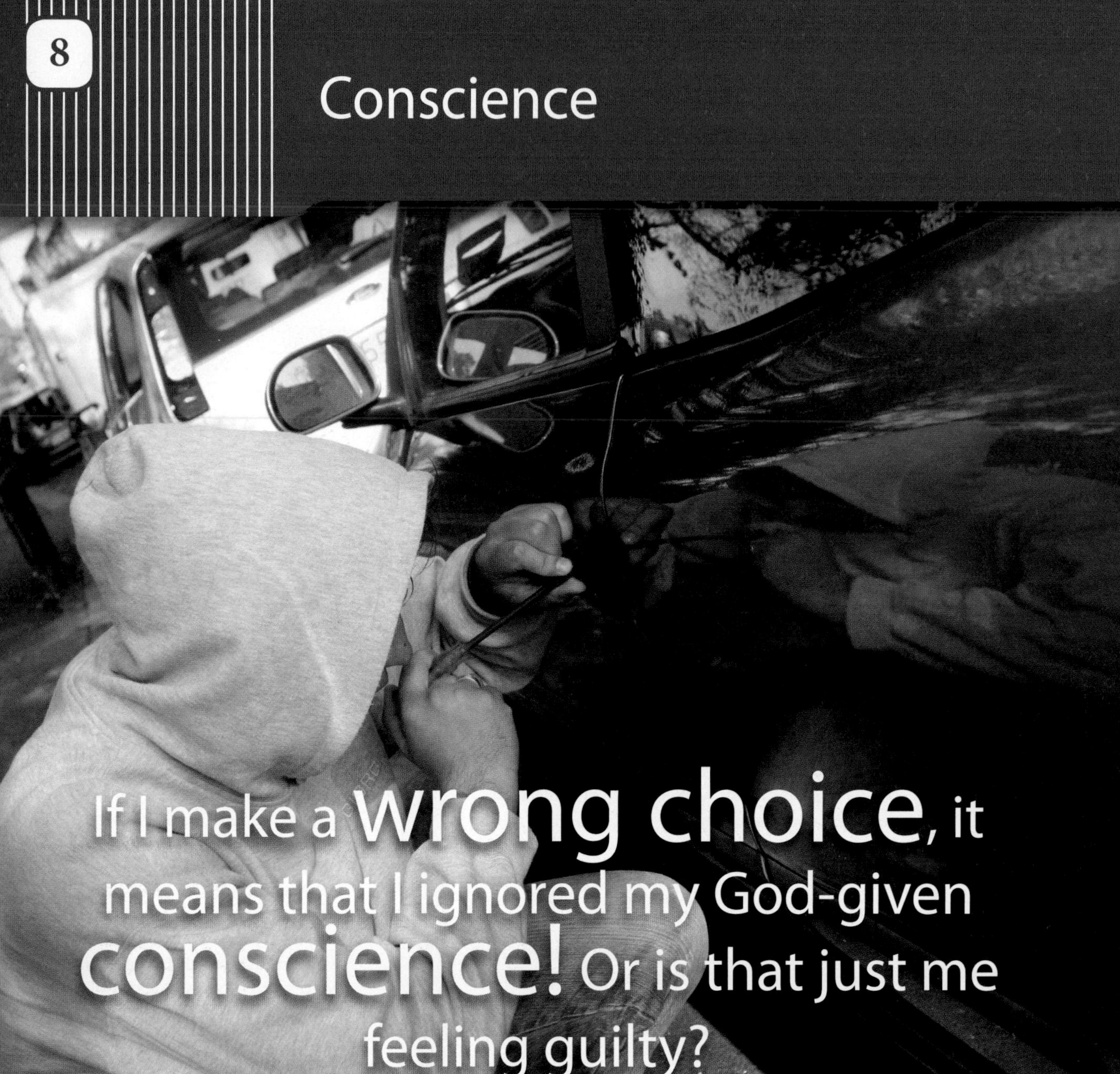

In this chapter you will learn about:

- the different views of the conscience as God-given, innate or the voice of reason or instilled by society, parents and authority figures
- whether conscience is a reliable guide to ethical decision making
- the views of Augustine, Aquinas, Butler, Newman, Freud, Fromm and Piaget
- the strengths and weaknesses of these views.

Conscience

8.1 Introduction to conscience

In this topic you will explore the idea and concept of the conscience.

We always talk about what our conscience says when we are making moral choices, but many people never really think about what this inner voice really is. Is it God speaking to us? Or is it just memories of our elderly relatives telling us off for doing something wrong?

Mark Twain famously said:

> *I have noticed my conscience for many years, and I know it is more trouble and bother to me than anything else I started with.*

For some people it takes the form of guilty feelings for contemplating or performing wrong actions. For others it is something different, as this quote from the actor Christopher Reeve explains:

> *I think we all have a little voice inside us that will guide us. It may be God, I don't know. But I think that if we shut out all the noise and clutter from our lives and listen to that voice, it will tell us the right thing to do.*

Conscience is something that is intrinsic to our everyday lives. Regardless of what we believe its nature is, we all use it for making decisions. Individual consciences can choose very different actions and have very different effects. Two people may be led by their conscience to very different courses of action, for example one person may be led by conscience to support the right to choose to have an abortion, whilst another person is led to support the pro-life position that abortion is wrong.

The origin and role of the conscience is something that divides people and something that has been used to justify some very terrible acts, including the Holocaust and genocides in Rwanda and Darfur. People have different interpretations of what is morally right and in many cases they justify their actions and motivations in this idea of the conscience.

The *Oxford English Dictionary* defines conscience as:

> *a moral sense of right and wrong, especially as felt by a person and affecting behaviour or an inner feeling as to the goodness or otherwise of one's behaviour.*

Approaches to conscience vary, there are religious theories and there are secular theories that base themselves in psychology, sociology and genetics. All provide an insight into what this idea of the conscience is.

ACTIVITY

Write down a list of all the possible things that you think might explain what the conscience is. When you have done this, list evidence that you think might support this viewpoint and also evidence that would disagree with it. Finally write down what you believe conscience is and how you use it yourself, including feelings and examples.

FOR DEBATE

Some people claim that their conscience permitted them to be prison guards in concentration camps during the Second World War. How could they have stood back and watched what was happening or even participated in such atrocities?

STRETCH & CHALLENGE

Look at the quotation from Mark Twain again. How could you link his idea about being born with conscience to some of the ethical teachings you looked at during the AS course, (e.g. Natural Law, religious ethics)?

Conscience

8.2 Views of conscience

In this topic you will learn about the different views of what conscience is, and about specifically religious approaches to understanding the conscience.

For many people, their idea about the conscience is having an angel on one shoulder 'urging' them to do a good moral action and a devil on the other shoulder 'urging' them to ignore the angel and perform an immoral action.

Philosophers, psychologists and theologians are divided over what conscience truly is and where it comes from. Some religious philosophers and theologians believe that in some way it originates from God or a higher power, whilst psychologists will claim that it is innate within us at birth or that it develops as we learn and move towards adulthood. It is therefore important to explore these ideas individually and then to look more closely at the specific beliefs or claims of each philosopher and psychologist.

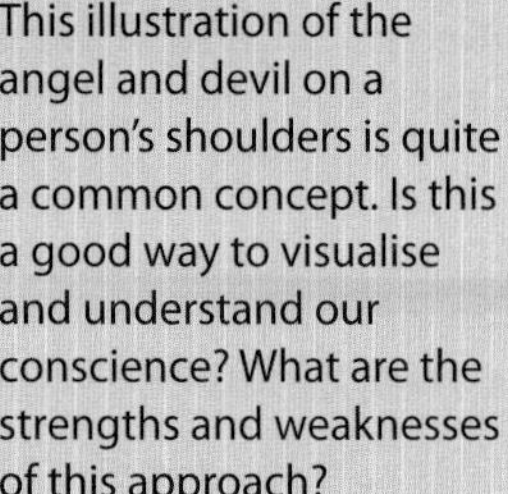

FOR DEBATE

This illustration of the angel and devil on a person's shoulders is quite a common concept. Is this a good way to visualise and understand our conscience? What are the strengths and weaknesses of this approach?

A God-given conscience?

This is the belief that either at conception God gave each person a conscience or that it is imparted to us at some stage to enable us to discern morally correct and incorrect actions. For some philosophers, it is the actual voice of God that speaks to them through their conscience (Butler, Newman, St Augustine) and for others it is the ability to reason and determine right and wrong that comes from God and which is our conscience (Aquinas, St Jerome, St Paul). Central to this approach is the concept that conscience is a gift that is required in order for humans to be moral. Therefore, as it comes from God, it is implied that we have to reason using our consciences in order to understand and know what the right or wrong action will be.

Innate within us?

The idea that the conscience is innate within us means that it doesn't depend on our experiences or any sort of social conditioning or learning. Instead, within each one of us there is a conscience that was either part of us when we were created or is part of how our brain is wired by genetics due to previous human evolutionary design or development. Some religious and secular approaches could accept this approach in some form, as it provides a framework to explain the need to be moral that is evident in all of us. It would seem that it is normal to have a conscience of some sort, which would suggest that everyone must have an innate skill, which we refer to as conscience.

However this idea may lead us to believe that, if we all have the same innate conscience, we should all therefore follow the same principles. Aquinas believed that though the conscience may be innate, it still requires instruction and training, whilst some sociologists and psychologists may suggest that this innate idea is the human need to be accepted, which in turn must be justified with the conscience. (See pages 154–155 for more on this.)

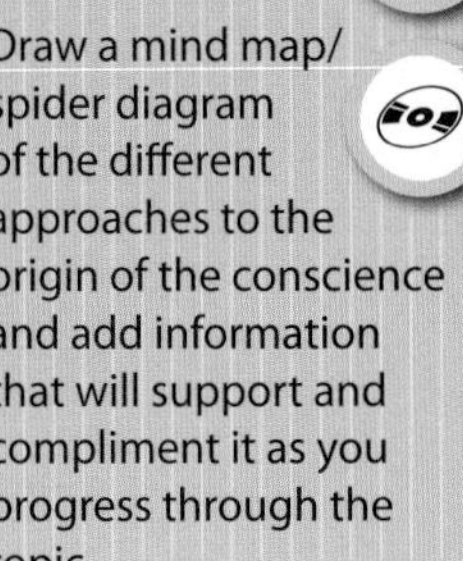

ACTIVITY

Draw a mind map/ spider diagram of the different approaches to the origin of the conscience and add information that will support and compliment it as you progress through the topic.

FOR DEBATE

If we accept the idea that conscience is instilled by external influences such as parents or other authority figures, then does that not mean that the negative actions that people perform can be attributed and blamed on these authority figures?

Instilled by society?

Some secular approaches suggest that the conscience is really a result of society's expectations upon us. Something is acceptable if society in general accepts it, therefore our conscience will generally accept these ideas of morality that are a reflection of society's values and rules. The culture in which we are raised plays a large part in the development of our moral reasoning. Georg Hegel (1780–1831) referred to the idea of 'the spirit' of each age that not only defined cultural awareness but moral awareness as well. He would suggest that we make our judgements according to the conscience that society has formed.

Instilled by our parents?

For the majority of us, our values and morals originate in our upbringing. In many ways we are the products of our parents' example as moral teachers. We accept the morality of what our parents teach us, at least to around the age of ten, if Piaget's developmental theories are correct (see page 154). Even after this point, when we make our own morally reasoned decisions, we will still be influenced by the moral awareness that was instilled by our parents. Sociologists also propose that the concept of conscience is significantly reinforced by the upbringing and influences we have in our early years.

Instilled by authority figures?

Another approach suggests that our conscience is formed and moulded by the authority figures we have around us, such as police officers, teachers, parents or politicians. They provide role models for us concerning what is right and what is wrong. This influence can be both negative and positive, yet these figures would seem to be essential to explaining who we are as adults. Many serial killers or paedophiles would claim that their reasoning and motivation for their horrendous acts and for who they have become were due to negative authority figures in their early years.

8

Conscience

8.3 Religious perspectives of conscience

In this topic you will learn about specifically religious approaches to understanding the conscience using religious philosophers.

Early Christian ideas about conscience

The teaching of the Christian Bible would suggest that the conscience is something that is given by God.

The apostle Paul (1st century CE) outlined this idea in his letter to the Romans when he talks about the Gentiles:

> *...who do not have the law, do by nature things required by the law...since they show that the requirements of the law are written on their hearts, their consciences also being witness...*
>
> Romans 2:14–15

If God speaks to people through their conscience and tells them what to do, would it not be more accurate to just use an audible voice?

Paul's other major contribution was to say that conscience was an awareness of good and bad, but that it can sometimes be weak and therefore mistaken.

Saint Jerome (147–240 CE) had the idea that it enabled us to distinguish good from evil:

> *...the spark of conscience...with which we discern that we sin.*

He saw it as intrinsically important for our moral well-being and for our relationship with God to be able to discern the leading of the moral away from the immoral (sin).

Saint Augustine of Hippo (334–430 CE) saw conscience as the voice of God speaking to us from within. It is the law of God in our hearts that we use to understand right and wrong actions. This behaviour helps us to become closer to God, as we listen to the voice that guides our moral reasoning. For Augustine the conscience must always be in every circumstance turned towards the good and away from all that is evil.

FOR DEBATE

If conscience is the voice of God speaking to and guiding us, then would it not mean that everyone hears the same voice and should do the same actions?

Thomas Aquinas and reason

Thomas Aquinas (1224–74 CE) saw conscience as 'right reason' – *recta ratio*. For him, reason was central to the moral life and to understanding the differences between right and wrong. He did not agree that the conscience was an inner voice telling us what is right and what is wrong; he believed that it was 'reason making right decisions' and used correctly it helps us to understand what God sees as good and right.

His belief was that people try to do good and to avoid what is evil – he called this the **Synderesis** Rule. In all situations our subconscious actions are to do good, however he said that due to faulty reasoning or weakness of will some people perform bad actions thinking that they are good, and therefore commit sinful acts. Aquinas said that they had followed an apparent good, rather than a real good – therefore their conscience was mistaken.

This idea of faulty reasoning is how Aquinas explains when people do things that are viewed as wrong, bad or sinful. He used the example of a man who slept with another man's wife and claimed that doing this is based on faulty reasoning and therefore evil. However if the man did it because he believed that she was his own wife and that she wanted him, then he is free from any fault. He is also free from fault if he could not have been expected to know otherwise.

Aquinas divided his understanding of conscience into two essential parts:

1. Synderesis – right reason.
2. **Conscientia** – distinguishing between right and wrong and making appropriate decisions.

The two parts are vital for making moral decisions.

The synderesis enables us to develop the knowledge of some moral principles and guides us towards the things that are good and away from those that are bad.

The conscientia is the actual choice to follow an action based upon the principles and right reasoning of the synderesis.

Both parts enable us to deliberate between good and evil and then use 'right reason' to make the moral decision that is morally correct.

Aquinas didn't believe that the actions of the conscience were always correct. He said that as long as you apply the moral principles that your conscience has shown you, then you are following the correct course of action. However, if your principles are flawed or incorrect, then your conscience must be too.

For many Christians, Aquinas' rationalistic approach doesn't sit very well with their beliefs in God's divine revelation. If God was to speak to us, Aquinas' approach may not allow us to accept it as God because of Aquinas' rationalistic outlook on conscience.

ACTIVITY

Look at Aquinas' understanding of the conscience, especially synderesis and conscientia. List the problems of this approach and then list the strengths. Is an approach from reason really practical? Write up an evaluation of Aquinas' teachings on conscience.

KEY WORDS

Synderesis: the innate 'right reason' that gives knowledge of the basic principles of morality.

Conscientia: using the principles of synderesis, this is the ethical judgement which leads to a specific action.

FOR DEBATE

If decisions are left to our reasoning, then we can make any decision and claim that we have reasoned that it is morally correct! Why is this a dangerous approach? Consider Adolf Hitler's approach to racial purity and equality.

Conscience

8.4 Further religious perspectives

In this topic you will learn about two more specifically religious approaches to understanding the conscience using religious philosophers.

Joseph Butler and intuition 

Joseph Butler (1692–1752) was a Church of England bishop and theologian who saw conscience as the final moral decision-maker. He believed that what made humanity different from all other animals was our ability to reason and to rationalise, which he claimed was the evidence for the existence of the conscience.

> *There is a principle of reflection in men by which they distinguish between approval and disapproval of their own actions...this principle in man...is conscience.*
>
> Sermon I.8, Joseph Butler

According to Butler, humans are motivated by two basic principles:

1. Self-love – only interested in our well-being.
2. Benevolence – actively seeking the well-being of others.

Conscience encourages humankind away from selfish love towards focusing on the interests and happiness of other people.

Similarly to Aquinas, Butler held that conscience enables us to judge and determine the rightness or wrongness of our actions. His belief was that it is given to us intuitively and it exerts itself at the correct time without being called upon. For Butler it was the ultimate authority in moral judgements.

This approach would seem to be an innate sense and knowledge of right and wrong that comes directly from God as our conscience. Butler referred to it as 'our natural guide, the guide assigned to us by the Author of our nature'. For him, it was the final judge of right and wrong that must be obeyed.

If your conscience says to do it, then you must do it! Butler gives the moral judgements that come from this intuitive conscience ultimate and binding authority, as he believed that they originated from God. His idea was that God guides humanity through their conscience and the understanding that it gives them towards their morality. Butler really didn't seem very concerned whether the conscience was based on reasoning or on feelings – the important point for him was that it comes from God and therefore must be obeyed.

To a certain extent many people could use Butler's approach and understanding of conscience to justify almost any action. However, it is important to note that Butler believed that people will know intuitively what

MAKING LINKS

Look at how Butler's approach to the conscience can be linked with G.E. Moore's ideas about meta-ethics and moral statements.

STRETCH & CHALLENGE

How can Butler's perspective be taken seriously as an academic approach if it requires a belief in a God who intuitively speaks to humanity and tells them definitively the correct action to pursue? Try to give an evaluation of this theory, using your knowledge of situation ethics, Natural Law and the teachings of Aquinas.

is the right thing to do in each situation; therefore not every action could be justified and mistakes of conscience will not be made. He was also quick to condemn people who convinced themselves that a wrong action was a correct and good one and claim that their conscience told them it was acceptable. He said that this was deluded self-deception that interferes with the purpose and purity of God.

Can conscience really be like having the voice of God speaking to you like a voice on the telephone?

Cardinal Newman and the voice of God

Cardinal John Henry Newman (1801–90) was a Roman Catholic who agreed with Aquinas that conscience is the ability to appreciate and apply moral principles, however his approach was more intuitive like Butler than rational like Aquinas. He believed that when someone is following their conscience they are to an extent following a divine law as given by God. When our conscience speaks to us, Newman believes that it is God's voice giving us moral direction and that it is more than just a sense of reason. He said that conscience does not create truth, but it does detect truth that already exists. It is the responsibility of a person to intuitively decide what truth God is guiding them towards.

Therefore for Newman following conscience was following divine law and one that must be followed at all times. This can be seen in a statement that is attributed to him, 'I toast the Pope, but I toast conscience first'. Roman Catholic teaching on the conscience reflects both Aquinas and Butler and states that it is the law that speaks to the human heart, a law written by God. The guilt and shame that they feel when they have made an incorrect choice by ignoring the conscience is the consequence of not obeying the voice of God.

ACTIVITY

Look at the three religious approaches included on the previous pages. Make a chart outlining the main propositions, the philosophical differences, the strengths, weaknesses and practical use.

FOR DEBATE

Can a religious approach to conscience really explain how moral decisions are made? Butler and Newman have quite 'fixed' and absolute views, whilst Aquinas seems to present a more realistic teaching.

STRETCH & CHALLENGE

How could the religious approaches be developed, amended, combined or restructured to make them more effective, whilst still retaining their basis in Christianity's truths?

Conscience

8.5 Secular perspectives of conscience

In this topic you will learn about specifically non-religious or secular approaches to understanding the conscience using philosophers and psychologists.

KEY WORDS

Id: part of the unconscious personality that is driven by impulses to seek pleasure and satisfaction.

Ego: part of the personality that experiences and reacts to the world, as well as mediating between the drives of the id and superego.

Superego: part of the personality that seeks to censor and restrain the ego. Often associated with feelings of guilt.

Heteronymous morality: occurs when the conscience is immature and the consequences of the actions determine whether it is right or wrong (usually between the ages of five and ten years old).

Autonomous morality: when someone is less reliant on the moral authority of people around them and is able to develop their own perspectives (usually occurs after the age of ten years old).

ACTIVITY

List reasons why Freud's understanding of conscience seems good and why his approach may be too simplistic.

Sigmund Freud and guilt

Sigmund Freud (1856–1939) developed several theories concerning the human personality and how it deals with issues of conflict or disorder. He believed that conscience was a construct of the mind that sought to make sense of disorder and to deal with the conflict that guilt brought.

Freud believed that during our early upbringing we accept certain values and beliefs about morality and society, which may at some stage be rejected by our moral reasoning. However these early formed values and beliefs still continue to influence our morality through the conscience that seeks to deal with the conflict that the early beliefs and the later beliefs bring.

Freud believed that the human personality consisted of three areas. These are now commonly called the **id**, the **ego** and the **superego**.

The super-ego is the part that is most closely linked with the feeling of guilt that conscience brings. The guilty conscience is an internalisation of anger and disapproval of others that causes the conflict and must be addressed.

Freud believed that the feeling of guilt that humans feel was intrinsically linked to the third stage of his theory of psycho-sexual development and the development of what is referred to as the Oedipus Complex. This is the theory that all young boys are sexually attracted to their mother and resent their father, who they believe will castrate them out of revenge for these feelings. Freud taught that these feelings are eventually repressed into the unconscious and then form the basis for neuroses that lead to the concept of guilt, as illustrated by the construct of the super-ego.

Freud believed that in religious people this was in response to ideas about God and the values of the Bible. In non-religious people this construct was in response to another source of external authority, like government, family or societal values.

Freud believed that our experiences are what make us who we are; they decide our path. There can't be any definite moral code of conduct or absolute moral law as our individual consciences are shaped by our own experiences. That is why there are so many ethical codes within societies; they are all part of these external constructs of authority that are determined by our individual experiences.

Piaget and the developmental conscience

Jean Piaget (1896–1980) believed that before the age of ten children take their morality from their parents/carers (**heteronymous morality**), but that after this stage their own moral reasoning becomes more prominent due to increasing awareness of morality and society around them (**autonomous morality**).

This development is essentially due to a child's cognitive development. Piaget's approach suggests that the development of conscience is something that is learned from external influences but also that it is naturally occurring.

Erich Fromm and his two consciences

Erich Fromm (1900–80) believed that our moral centre came from those around us who exert their authority over us, e.g. parents, teachers, religious leaders, etc. Their authority involves reward and punishment for our actions, and over time these authorities that we have internalised become central to our understanding of morality.

Fromm believed that the guilty conscience was a result of displeasing those in authority, therefore we fear some sort of rejection from them and the influence that this has over us is what Fromm called the **authoritarian conscience**.

A good authoritarian conscience provides a sense of security and well-being, as it provides a structure that we can work within to ensure that both society and we are moral.

A negative authoritarian conscience can be seen from Fromm's own experiences in Nazi Germany. The German people would feel guilt if they disobeyed their government and this weakened their power and made them submissive to the demands of the Nazi party. The government manipulated their weakened consciences to make them feel guilty about helping or supporting Jews during the 1930s, and it is suggested that this may be a reason why so many Germans were willing to participate in the atrocities of the Holocaust.

Fromm's perspectives on the conscience evolved and developed over the years and he began to develop another healthier perspective of conscience. This conscience he saw as the **humanistic conscience**.

He said that our conscience enables us to assess our success as a human by evaluating our behaviour. In this way we moderate our behaviour according to the examples of others, by developing our integrity and honesty to become moral people. This approach has many similarities with the ideas of virtue ethics in attempting to become a better person by developing virtues (see page 163).

This approach to conscience is very different from the ideas of the authoritarian conscience as it seeks to understand humanity and morality from a much more positive and hopeful angle. It is sometimes referred to by Fromm as 'the real conscience' and is 'a reaction of ourselves to ourselves; the voice of our true selves' that guides us to achieve our potential.

FOR DEBATE

Using the Freudian approach to conscience, discuss how issues such as racism and discrimination can be explained and approached.

STRETCH & CHALLENGE

Why do you think Fromm's perspective changed from authoritarian conscience to humanistic conscience? Could they be two sides of the same approach or are they completely opposing views?

FOR DEBATE

'Fromm's humanistic conscience is too idealistic, the authoritarian conscience is more likely to be true.'

FURTHER RESEARCH

Investigate how Laurence Kohlberg (1927–87) built upon Piaget and Freud's work, and how it is relevant to our understanding of moral responsibility.

FOR DEBATE

'Secular approaches to explaining the conscience are much more realistic.' Discuss.

Conscience

8.6 Conscience as an ethical and moral guide

In this topic you will learn about how conscience enables us to make ethical decisions.

Cicero once famously said 'If conscience goes, then everything collapses around us'. He saw the importance and the value of the human conscience and his belief is mirrored in the teachings of the Christian New Testament. Here it is taught that conscience is a moral guardian that impels followers to perform morally good actions by causing them to feel peace of mind or guilt.

If the conscience is so central to our identity as moral beings, is it possible to rely upon it? Roman Catholics are encouraged to inform their conscience before acting upon it, so as not to make the wrong decision. However it raises the question of what should be done if the informed conscience disagrees with the teaching of the Roman Catholic Church. The Church teaches that if we fail to follow our conscience, it is at this point that we sin, even if the conscience is objectively wrong. The quandary for Roman Catholics is concerned with understanding whether conscience is adequately informed for us to make morally correct decisions.

Christian approaches give conscience a large role in moral decision making, and expect that people should follow the urging of their conscience. This seems to put a lot of faith in the individual consciences of human beings; what if their reasoning is flawed due to subjectivity or inaccurate training? Aquinas believed that it was wrong to not follow your conscience, as he believed it was denying what you knew to be true. Even if your conscience is misinformed, it is essential to follow your conscience in order to be true to yourself and your creator.

Secular approaches suggest more caution is required before using conscience and following its directions unquestioningly. If the various psychological approaches are correct, then our conscience can't be an accurate moral guide to be followed without question or reasoned thought because it may be repressed guilt or emotional reasoning or social conditioning that is guiding us.

ACTIVITY

Using your knowledge of the various theories or perspective on conscience, produce a chart showing how each of the approaches show conscience as a moral guide. Include another column that can be filled with advantages and disadvantages of these views.

If conscience is to be used as a moral guide, it is necessary to ascertain how accurate it is in the situation. How many times do we as humans make errors of judgement because our conscience leads us in a certain direction? People suggest that if you follow your conscience properly, it will stop you breaking laws. Yet is this always true? Consider this quotation from Martin Luther King:

> *I submit that an individual who breaks a law that conscience tells him is unjust, and who willingly accepts the penalty of imprisonment in order to arouse the conscience of the community over its injustice, is in reality expressing the highest respect for the law.*

If our conscience is the voice of God or the experience of our upbringing or authoritarian pressure, then why do different people make different decisions and claim that it is based on conscience? If we have different beliefs concerning actions based on our individual consciences, then perhaps allowing individual conscience to make moral and ethical decisions and choices is perhaps too subjective a venture and one that really ought to be stopped.

Corporate or collective consciences as ethical decision makers also have their drawbacks. How many does it take to make a decision, and is that decision always moral? It is possible for a society to make collective moral decisions and end up performing immoral acts that are obviously morally wrong.

The example of the Rwandese Genocide in 1994 shows how a collective conscience of Hutu people led to the massacre of nearly one million Tutsi people in three months. Is there a safeguard against collective conscience and avoiding situations like the Rwandan one?

If conscience is to be educated and informed, then how can we ensure that the decisions we are making are the correct ones? If we take Butler's approach and use our conscience as the guidance of God, then every action ought to be a moral one. However, in this world it is very apparent that this is not the case.

Perhaps the most sensible approach is to use Aquinas' idea of reason informing our conscience, and qualifying this with a basis in some other sort of traditional ethical theory.

ACTIVITY

Look at the history of the Civil Rights Movement in the United States. Specifically look at the incident with Rosa Parks and the Bus Boycott. Write an evaluation of whether she was justified in using her conscience in this situation. (Remember you can also consider the use of conscience in relation to teleology and deontology.)

FOR DEBATE

The soldiers during the First World War who deserted or refused to fight due to their conscience's objection to war were usually executed. Was this justified or do ethical considerations come above their duty to their country?

STRETCH & CHALLENGE

Is using conscience as a moral guide not too difficult to reconcile with objective moral truths such as the Ten Commandments or the law of the land? Is it not just an excuse to follow any course of action that you choose?

8.7 The strengths and weaknesses of the arguments for conscience

In this topic you will learn about the critical strengths and weaknesses of the various approaches to conscience.

FOR DEBATE 

How would you make the right decision in the dilemma described opposite if both Christians have different perspectives? Is there a definitive right answer?

The dilemma

Linking conscience with the idea of it being the voice of God provides some problems. For instance, consider the case where two Christians are faced with a moral dilemma of how to deal with the situation of a 12-year-old girl who has been raped and now is found to be pregnant. Christian A's conscience says that the girl should have the child and then either keep it or give it up for adoption, whilst Christian B's conscience says that the correct thing to do is to allow her to have the foetus aborted. Whose conscience is correct, if both Christians are hearing the voice of the same God?

If God's voice is everyone's conscience, then how can we reconcile this with the different moral beliefs and convictions of people all over the world? Butler and Newman gave complete authority to conscience, so therefore their theories are somewhat lacking in substance when faced with this criticism. However Aquinas' belief that sometimes conscience is misinformed or misled could explain the disparity in different people's conscience. Other approaches are that we are mishearing God's voice and therefore it is due to human error, rather than conscience not being the guidance from God.

The views of different religions

Different religious denominations within the religions disagree over moral issues such as euthanasia and sex. If they are hearing the voice of God, then why do they differ in their beliefs? It is clear that claiming conscience is the voice of God is not quite as accurate in the form that Butler and Newman have expressed it.

Atheists and humanists

Atheists and humanists generally believe in the concept of the conscience and don't require a supernatural intervention of God to explain the origin of this moral guide. In many ways the religious approach is quite narrow-minded as it assumes the existence of and a belief in God. Atheists and humanists are content to accept that it is due to psychological development or to genetic determinism of evolutionary history. They see it as an essential part of humans and therefore what guides humanity in its moral living.

The superiority of conscience?

Another criticism that is levelled against the various teachings on conscience is the superiority that seems to be given to conscience. The actions and leadings of the conscience can be very wrong and its unconditional use can lead to wrong decisions being made. Aquinas' approach provides us with the tools to make decisions, but it doesn't give us a foolproof answer as to what to do. His reliance on reasoning is good, especially the distinction between the conscientia and synderesis, however he does say that the closer we are to a situation the more we need to enquire and vary our decisions or actions. He does not believe that conscience will give us a definitive answer but will, by the use of conscientia and synderesis, lead us towards the correct moral path.

The weakness of the secular approaches

The secular approaches also seem to fail in this way, they explain where conscience might come from and how it influences decisions but they don't provide an accurate method of understanding what is the correct approach. The teachings of Butler are based on an intuitive understanding of what is right, perhaps this approach might be a better explanation of the conscience as we all have a sense of intuition. The problem with his theory is the origin of the intuition. If conscience was explained using the idea of a genetic intuition instead, then perhaps a new understanding of conscience could be proposed; one that is intuitive in nature but expressed through the ideas of religion or psychology or sociology.

Conscience and our emotions

Conscience can also be influenced by our emotions or emotional attachments. It is very easy to make a decision based on conscience when he have an emotional interest in the situation; in some ways this can be beneficial, however, it can also cause us to make decisions that are subjective and possibly morally dubious.

It may be necessary to detach our emotions when making decisions according to conscience, otherwise what we do will merely be what we think is right. When people are torn about what is the correct thing to do, the emotional influence, whether guilt or altruism, will sometimes be the easier decision to make, but not necessarily the morally correct one.

Those without conscience

Despite all of the approaches discussed in this chapter, there are suggestions by psychologists that there may be people who seem to have no conscience at all. As philosophers, how can we explain actions that we may call 'unconscienciable'? There are suggestions that the infamous Moors Murderers or the young James Bulger killers did not have any conscience. None of the approaches mentioned provide an adequate explanation. If conscience comes from God, why do some not appear to have one? If the conscience is developed through childhood, why do some not possess this inner moral sense?

ACTIVITY

Look at the religious and secular approaches to conscience again. Decide which one you agree is the most convincing theory. Write down your reasons for choosing it and then evaluate why you believe the others are less likely. This will involve you looking at all the approaches critically.

FOR DEBATE

If conscience is God-given, then we must be born with it, however the psychological approaches believe it is learned. Does it have to be one or the other? Could there be a mix of the two ideas of nature and nurture?

STRETCH & CHALLENGE

If conscience should be our guide to moral decision making, then how do we apply the theories to someone who suffers from a psychiatric or learning disorder? If they use their conscience to make decisions, can they be held responsible if they get it wrong?

Exam Café

Relax, refresh, result!

Relax and prepare

Hot tips

David

I did not learn all the different philosophers' views and I found it really difficult to get a good grade. Now that I have learnt their different views my grades have improved.

Lisa

I stuck to Freud and Aquinas because these views contradict each other nicely and really help when writing the discussion part of the essay. But I did not ignore the other views because I needed these to show that I know what I am talking about in the explanation part. I also tried to balance my arguments so that I gave the same time and detail to both sides of the argument.

Kam

I tried to write the same essay in two different ways. Firstly I wrote the explanation part, then I wrote the discussion element. This took a long time and I repeated myself but I got a good grade because I covered everything. The second way was to have two sides to the argument and explain the ideas as I went. This stopped me repeating myself but I found it harder to write. My grades were exactly the same for both!

Refresh your memory

Revision checklist for conscience

You should be able to demonstrate knowledge and understanding of:

- The different views of the conscience as God-given, innate or the voice of reason or instilled by society, parents and authority figures.
- Whether conscience is a reliable guide to ethical decision making.
- The views of St Paul, Augustine, Aquinas, Butler, Newman, Freud, Fromm, Piaget and Kohlberg.
- The strengths and weaknesses of each approach and be able to discuss these critically.

Get the result!

Exam question

Evaluate the claim that conscience is the voice of God. (35 marks)

Examiner's tips

Write a response to this question using the tips below.

AO1	You should show knowledge and understanding of the views of a range of scholars; if you can address these views specifically to the question, you will achieve higher levels. You may wish to include an explanation of the views of scholars such as Aquinas, Butler and Newman and you may wish to connect these views with the concept of innateness in order to defend the proposition in the question. You might also what to explain the influence of sociologists such as Freud, Fromm, Piaget and Kohlberg to argue against the statement. Good responses may question the concept of 'conscience', and argue that there is no substance to it.
AO2	The proposition in the question can be argued either way and the conclusion reached is less important than the quality of your discussion. You may wish to argue that the conscience is God-given, but not infallible and requires training. Or you might want to argue that the conscience is related to revelation and the idea of 'synderesis' may be introduced to defend the case that it is a divine voice.

Sample answers

Exam question

Is conscience innate? Discuss. (35 marks)

Examiner says

Not a good introduction. It does not show that they have read our understood the question. Try writing a better introduction than this.

Beth's introduction

Aquinas' view on conscience is the traditional idea that the Catholic Church upholds. As Aquinas' view is an interpretation of the Bible, he began with the statement by St Paul that 'they show that what the law requires is written on their hearts'. (Romans 2:14)

9

Virtue ethics

In this chapter you will learn about:

- the principles of virtue ethics from Aristotle
- the 'agent-centred' nature of virtue ethics
- the concepts of eudaimonia and the doctrine of the mean (the Golden Mean)
- the importance of practising the virtues and the example of virtuous people
- the modern approaches to virtue ethics
- the critical strengths and weaknesses.

Virtue ethics

9.1 Introduction to virtue ethics

In this topic you will learn how virtue ethics is different from other ethical theories.

We all desire to be the best in some way. We only have to look at the television to see people on a reality television show desiring to be the winner or to have their 15 minutes of fame. We all aspire to many things, some of which may just be dreams and others may become a reality.

In moral decisions we may want to be good and do the right thing, but like most people we make the wrong decisions or get into trouble with our friends. The way that we feel and understand right and wrong generally comes from moral rules and guidelines found in traditional ethical theories (e.g. Natural Law or situation ethics) that are either deontological or teleological. We all get it wrong and manage to go against these moral theories. As a consequence we feel like failures and are disappointed with ourselves.

What is it about shows such as *Big Brother* that encourage people to compete? Are the participants any better than the rest of us?

What is virtue ethics?

Virtue ethics suggests that we should not focus on following guidelines about what types of things are right and wrong and what we should and should not do. Instead we should aim to become better people by developing positive character traits called virtues.

Therefore, whether our actions are right or wrong should not be our *sole* focus. Instead, as we aspire to become better people by developing and using these virtues, we will do the morally correct actions that develop our character.

Virtue ethics aims to provide an alternative approach to morality that enables people to achieve their potential as human beings and not to have to focus solely on the rightness or wrongness of their actions. Instead it provides a way to develop character and to flourish as a person, and this is achieved without persistent rule-following, but rather by pursuing just actions that encourage character development which make us just people.

KEY WORD

Virtue: a positive characteristic that suggests moral excellence or goodness.

ACTIVITY

Write down what you desire most as a person. Does being the best or excelling in some area come into your desires? Write down what you believe are your biggest character flaws and why, using examples. If you could change these would you?

FOR DEBATE

Some people say that you should just be yourself and not try to better yourself. Do you agree?

Virtue ethics

9.2 Aristotle 

In this topic you will learn about the principles of virtue ethics from the teachings of Aristotle (384–322 BCE).

KEY WORD

Eudaimonia: a contented state of being happy, healthy and prosperous.

ACTIVITY

List what you believe personally brings happiness. Do you agree with Aristotle about what eudaimonia is and about the goal of life? Write down your ideas and discuss them objectively.

MAKING LINKS

Look at the teachings of Aristotle as used by Thomas Aquinas in his Natural Law theory. How are they similar to his teachings on the virtues and developing life filled with eudaimonia?

FOR DEBATE 

Do you think that moral actions are not right or wrong, and that being a good or virtuous person is sufficient?

Aristotle's belief was that every action is focused on an aim or outcome. This places his theory amongst teleological ethics. He believed that in everything that we do we have an end or outcome in our minds. This, he then said, could be seen as the ultimate end of ends, which is the greatest good.

Take the following example. When you get up in the morning, you do so because you want to go to school. You go to school because you want a good education. You get a good education because you want a good job and good earnings. You want a good job and good earnings so that you can live well and be happy.

Aristotle believed that we did these things for a greater reason, as shown in the example above. The superior aim is to achieve the supreme good, which is happiness. For Aristotle, happiness or fulfilment was the goal and purpose of life. In this understanding he meant more than just pleasure, he understood it in three different ways:

1. Happiness as a life of enjoyment of pleasure.
2. Happiness as a free member of society.
3. Happiness as a philosopher.

For Aristotle, living a life of pleasure wasn't enough, there was a responsibility to live a good life and to show and use qualities that enabled people to live together in society.

In order to achieve this happiness or **eudaimonia** (see page 168 later in this chapter), he believed that you had to practise skills or virtues to achieve happiness and live good lives.

For Aristotle, the basis of morality is to have a firm foundation of good and positive character traits. Therefore, a person is morally good if they have these positive traits or virtues and do not have negative traits or vices. This understanding of Aristotle formed the basis of his virtue theory or aretaic ethics.

The virtues

Aristotle distinguished between two types of virtues:

1. Intellectual virtues are developed by training yourself and being educated, e.g. learning to play the piano takes time, commitment and sometimes sheer will power.
2. Moral virtues are developed by practice and habit, e.g. being compassionate towards less fortunate people helps to develop the moral virtue of compassion.

A musician has to commit a lot of time in order to perfect their instrument. If we follow Aristotle's approach, then this intellectual virtue is not as highly valued as a moral virtue. Is this a fair approach?

ACTIVITY

In groups make a list of what you believe are the virtues that we should aim to develop and practise. Share your ideas with others and see if they agree with all the things that you believe are virtuous.

Aristotle believed that friendship was an important social virtue that needed to be developed within society as a whole to encourage personal, as well as societal and altruistic flourishing. Friendship as a virtue will develop the person, but will also by nature develop the friend, as long as both continue to cultivate and develop the virtues. Aristotle believed that we ought to develop 'Friendships of the Good' (based upon enjoyment of each other's character) as a means to developing eudaimonia, rather than merely focusing on 'Friendships of Utility' (based on necessity and usefulness) or 'Friendships of Pleasure' (those based on common interests or enjoyment). For Aristotle friendship is key to our achievement of eudaimonia and therefore of modelling the virtues.

FOR DEBATE

Are the four cardinal virtues all that we should develop? Do they cover and encompass all other virtuous acts?

Aristotle, and others since, believed that there were four cardinal virtues that were to be favoured and achieved:

1. Temperance/Moderation, e.g. family members who live life in moderation try not to get into debt or to be too thrifty with their money and enjoy life in the fullest way that they can.
2. Justice, e.g. a teacher who ensures that students are treated equally and get what they deserve, whether they are rewarded or punished.
3. Courage, e.g. a man who has a phobia of snakes who attends counselling sessions to help him deal with his fear and then confronts his fear by handling a snake.
4. Prudence/Practical Wisdom, e.g. if a man knows that he should be honest, he must know how to apply honesty in balance with other considerations, and this requires practical wisdom or prudence.

STRETCH & CHALLENGE

If people who were following the virtues were to focus on them rather than, as Aristotle intended, on the actions and their consequences, how would this affect society if everyone were to do the same?

To practise these was considered to be the way to live a life that flourished. In other words, Aristotle believed that if you cultivate these virtues and put them into practice as actions, then your life and outlook would be happy ones and that you would be closer to achieving eudaimonia. Other virtues such as sincerity or comradeship can also assist in helping us to live the fulfilled life that Aristotle referred to.

Virtue ethics

9.3 Exploring the concept of virtue ethics

In this topic you will learn about how virtue ethics is concerned with becoming a good person and therefore **agent-centred**, and about why using the virtues and aiming to perfect them is important to having a life that flourishes.

KEY WORD

Agent-centred: ethical approaches that are focused on the development of the person rather than on the morality of what they are doing.

Agent-centred

Virtue ethics is an ethical approach that focuses on the person performing the actions themselves, rather than the actions that they perform.

The moral actions that are performed may be right or wrong in themselves, so too may the consequences of the actions be viewed as right or wrong. It is the moral development of the person performing the acts that is central, although they can still be held morally blameworthy for the actions that they have performed even though it theoretically leads them forward in developing a virtuous life. This makes the nature of virtue ethics agent-centred rather than action- or consequence-centred.

The purpose of doing the moral actions is to become a better person by developing the virtues. If we aim to develop a certain virtue and in the process of practising it we perform a moral action, then this would be seen as a good outcome for the development of our virtue. For example, a woman who wishes to develop courage performs a courageous act by stopping a mugger in his attack on an elderly woman. This act has helped her in her desire to develop courage, but in doing so she has also performed a morally good act.

ACTIVITY

Think back over the last seven days and list things that you have done that may have helped you develop or perfect virtues. Write down why this approach and your actions over the last week would be opposed by a Kantian approach.

The way that virtue ethics is understood as an agent-centred theory is that as we develop virtues we will do morally correct actions, which will in the end benefit society. Therefore if everyone develops virtues, then they will perform virtuous acts, which are morally good and society benefits as the outcome. If everyone developed courage like the woman in the example above, then they would all act in the same way that she did and therefore society would become better because there would be fewer successful muggings. It is important to note that in order for the virtues to develop, it is essential that just acts are performed, otherwise no virtues can ever be cultivated or developed.

To many observers the approach of virtue ethics may seem subjective and selfish, as it does not focus on a specific action or outcome being correct, but rather on a person developing their own virtues. However, it is crucial to note that because this theory has as its intention the achievement of eudaimonia, that personal achievement is also a societal achievement as the virtues influence the world around us. After all, for Aristotle, we cannot be good persons without performing good acts.

FOR DEBATE

Is virtue ethics being 'agent-centred' not an excuse for being selfish and subjective?

The importance of practising the virtues

If you want to become a great athlete, you cannot just make the decision today to become that great athlete tomorrow. Practising will be vital;

If Mike Catt hadn't trained hard, he wouldn't have played in two Rugby World Cup finals. Is practice worth the glory of winning the top international prize?

dedication will be essential; perseverance also will be necessary. The list goes on, but it's clear what the message is. An Olympic swimmer in training will be practising on average 49 hours a week in the pool in the months leading up to the London Olympic Games in 2012. It is clear that a lot of work and perseverance is required to achieve this privilege in the first place.

When people are attempting to develop a new skill they need to invest time and it will not happen overnight. For many musicians their skill must be practised daily and if it isn't they risk losing their proficiency in their chosen instrument. Therefore it is clear that once a skill is acquired it is essential to practise to maintain it.

The same is true of the virtues, they must be:

- achieved through perseverance, practice and dedication
- practised to maintain proficiency in them.

Time is required to develop and perfect these positive character traits, but also time is required to maintain the virtues once they are achieved.

If someone wishes to develop one of Aristotle's other virtues, for example sincerity, it is likely that it will have to be worked at and practised. It may be a naturally-occurring trait, but even then the person will still need to put in effort to achieve, maintain and perfect it. The old belief that 'practice makes perfect' would seem to fit well with the overall idea of virtue ethics.

The impact on society

The other importance of practising is that it will have an impact upon society. As people are practising the virtues it will in turn cause society to become more moral. It is in the best interests of society for people to be practising the virtues as then society will progress morally, be more stable and therefore a much more virtuous and just place to live.

FOR DEBATE 

How many hours are required to develop a virtue? Is it possible to limit the time required or is it a life-long pursuit?

FOR DEBATE 

Is it possible to practise tirelessly all your life to develop a specific virtue and never come close to achieving it? What do you think would be Aristotle's response to this question?

STRETCH & CHALLENGE

Is saying that developing and practising virtues is a better approach than following traditional ethical theories not a recipe for disaster? Would this new system of morality not send society spiralling into subjective moral chaos?

9.4 Eudaimonia and the doctrine of the mean

In this topic you will learn about the ideas of eudaimonia and the doctrine of the mean (also referred to as the golden mean).

STRETCH & CHALLENGE

Is achieving what Aristotle called eudaimonia the ultimate goal that we can reach? Is there not some more altruistic goal that would be more important?

FOR DEBATE 

'Eudaimonia is unachievable, as it's too idealistic.'

ACTIVITY

Explain how eudaimonia has intrinsic value. Use examples to illustrate your answer and provide a critical evaluation of its worth.

Eudaimonia

Aristotle believed in humans flourishing and achieving the most that could be achieved in our lives. We ought to be aiming for happiness, not a happiness of just pleasure but something much more.

This idea of eudaimonia encompasses all aspects of happiness including political, emotional and philosophical happiness. It is also important to note that the idea of eudaimonia isn't just happiness or pleasure as we generally understand it, because in some ways the concept is not pleasurable or happy.

Eudaimonia also contains an element of justified and deserved happiness that ought to be the goal in life of everyone. In order to achieve it, eudaimonia must be a deserved happiness, rather than undeserved or ill gotten. It is emphasised by philosophers that eudaimonia is of intrinsic value and is never a means to another end, therefore it should be desired for its own sake by individuals and by society too. The only way to achieve eudaimonia is to truly deserve it and to have worked tirelessly to achieve it through the development of the virtuous character traits and avoiding the negative ones. For example, Mother Teresa spent all her life working with social outcasts in Calcutta showing many of Aristotle's virtues in her outlook towards people and could conceivably be said to have achieved eudaimonia and deserved it.

For Aristotle, living alongside other people encouraged the virtues to develop and the vices to disappear as the social context of acceptable behaviour would ensure that everyone would develop happiness or eudaimonia. Although virtue ethics does seem to be a very personal and subjective ethical system, it is also a political and social feature of life, as it must be developed in a social context that encourages all people to flourish.

This is an event that brought happiness and pleasure. Could this be characterised as eudaimonia?

The doctrine of the mean

Central to the ideas of virtue ethics are virtues that we should aim for and the vices that we should avoid. Aristotle taught about two different vices that accompanied every virtue:

- The vice of deficiency is the distinct lack of the virtues, e.g. the deficient vice of modesty is shamelessness.
- The vice of excess is entirely too much of the virtue, which leads to excess rather than moderation, e.g. the excessive vice of modesty is shyness.

Consider this example: Ben, Priya and Mabel are all going to do a parachute jump to show that they have been developing courage. They are all nervous but, to develop the virtue, they persevere. When it comes to making the jump the following happens:

- Ben won't jump as he is displaying cowardice (the deficient vice of courage).
- Priya cautiously jumps because she is showing courage (the virtue).
- Mabel decides to show her courage through jumping without a parachute, however she displays foolhardiness (the excessive vice of courage).

At some point between the two vices exists the virtue; this Aristotle referred to as the **doctrine of the mean** (golden mean). He believed that the virtue provided a balance of the extremes of the two vices. This golden mean removed the negative aspects of each vice (i.e. excess or deficiency) and provided a 'pure' virtue between them.

It is important to remember that this idea of the golden mean is also referring to the actions that follow when people practise the virtues. The motivation for following the virtue must be to produce a moral action. It is not possible to determine a virtue by placing it arithmetically half way between the two vices; it cannot be that exact. It will be different in different situations. Sometimes the brave thing to do is run away. It is also important to note that some actions do not have a mean and searching for one is pointless, e.g. rape.

The table below lists the virtuous means and their accompanying vices.

Vice of deficiency	Virtuous mean	Vice of excess
Cowardice	Courage	Rashness
Insensibility	Temperance	Self-indulgence
Meanness	Liberality	Prodigality
Pettiness	Magnificence	Vulgarity
Humble-mindedness	High-mindedness	Vanity
Unambitiousness	Right ambition	Over-ambition
Spiritlessness	Good temper	Irascibility
Surliness	Friendliness	Obsequiousness
Ironical deprecation	Sincerity	Boastfulness
Boorishness	Wittiness	Buffoonery
Shamelessness	Modesty	Bashfulness
Callousness	Just resentment	Spitefulness

ACTIVITY

Using the virtues listed on this page give an example for each virtue and its two vices. When you have done this discuss your examples with someone else in the class Then list other virtues that are missing from Aristotle's list along with their vices.

KEY WORD

Doctrine of the mean: the desirable middle between two extremes, one of excess and the other of deficiency.

FOR DEBATE

Can the idea of the 'golden mean' also be applied to the moral actions rather than just motivating them?

STRETCH & CHALLENGE

How can the true midpoint of the vices be definitively known? At what point do vices become virtues and at what point do the virtues become vices? Is it down to intuition or is there a definite point? Write a couple of paragraphs laying out your thoughts.

Virtue ethics

9.5 The examples of virtuous people 

In this topic you will learn about why it is important and valuable to look at the lives of other people who have shown an aspect of a virtuous life.

ACTIVITY

Use the principles of virtue ethics to examine the life and work of someone such as Angelina Jolie or David Beckham. List ways that they show and model examples of virtues.

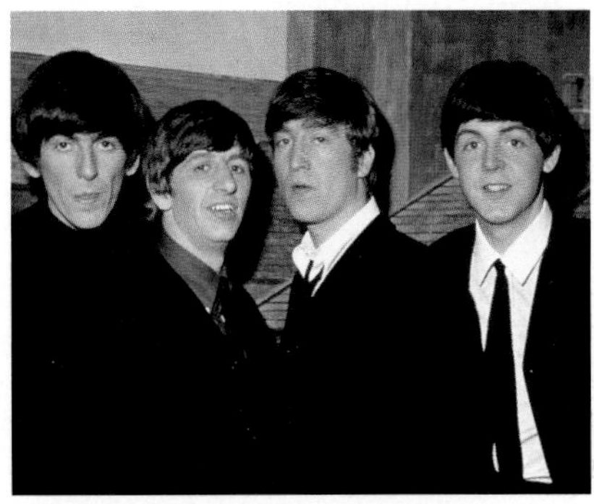

These famous people inspire thousands of others in some way. Should we look up to and admire these people just because they inspire us?

Another area that virtue ethics focuses on is the idea of modelling the behaviour and virtue of those people whom we consider virtuous. We should aim to imitate their example and become virtuous like they were and possibly do what they did or display the behaviour and attitudes that they showed.

In most areas of life there are people we want to be like, for example political idealists such as Che Guevara or musicians like U2 and Snow Patrol. We try to model our lives and beliefs on their lives and their examples.

If you are an aspiring rugby union player, who wants to reach the top of your game and represent your country at an international level, then you could look to the skills and expertise of Danny Cipriani, Johnny Wilkinson or Shane Geraghty. If you explore how they perfected their abilities and aim to use aspects of their skills and styles, then you could develop to become a better rugby player.

The list of virtuous people or people who showed virtues is probably endless. We can see moral excellence amongst people as diverse as Gandhi, Nelson Mandela, Bob Geldof, David Beckham and Angelina Jolie. They all have shown important character traits or virtues in some form and they provide an example for our own development and progression in attaining the virtues. These people's examples can provide inspiration and guidance in situations where difficult moral decisions need to be made.

FOR DEBATE 

If virtue theory encourages people to use virtuous people as role models, what if our role model is not really virtuous in the eyes of others? Adolf Hitler and Saddam Hussein inspired thousands of people, yet their actions and the consequences were horrendous and destroyed millions of lives.

Virtuous role models are not perfect

The examples of virtuous people are not expected to be illustrations of perfect people, but they are a challenge for us to aspire to greater moral heights and to become the best that we possibly can be.

One famous example of someone who showed the virtues of compassion and righteous anger in a large number and variety of situations was Diana, Princess of Wales. For example, take the work that she did with the children dying from HIV and AIDS, or her endless campaigning to end the use of anti-personnel landmines. However, despite showing these virtues, it is possible to look at her example in other parts of her life as less than virtuous and more in line with some of the vices. Despite this, people can look to the virtues that she did show – she can be an inspiration to people to become the best that they can be.

FOR DEBATE 

'Harry Potter is a more relevant role model for the 21st century than religious people from hundreds of years ago.' Discuss.

Virtuous role models in popular culture

Popular culture also provides role models for us who show great virtue and others who are an illustration of the vices that people have, e.g. Harry Potter, the virtuous young wizard and Voldemort, the vindictive villain. Some people look to the example of literary characters such as Frodo Baggins (Lord of the Rings) in a similar way to how others look to Mandela, Jesus or Mother Teresa for guidance, as they all encourage us towards behaviour and a lifestyle that is excellent and encourages flourishing.

STRETCH & CHALLENGE

In some ways it could be suggested that Jesus was not a virtuous role model. His actions and teachings have supposedly caused wars, death and persecution. Mother Teresa's support of Catholic teaching on the use of contraception is used as a reason for the spread of HIV/AIDS in parts of India and Africa. Is it possible that we have got it wrong about these supposedly virtuous people?

Jesus as a model of virtue

In the Christian Bible, Jesus encouraged his disciples that they should continue to do the things that he had done and to go on to do even greater things. Some Christians will even devote their whole lives to becoming more like the example that Jesus gave by entering Holy Orders as a monk or a nun.

Jesus' life was one that was virtuous; he showed compassion towards those who others rejected, he demonstrated righteous anger in the Temple courts, he showed great wisdom in dealing with the adulterous woman and great patience with his disciples. Most Christians desire to live their lives along the same principles by aiming to mirror Jesus' attitudes.

The teachings of the apostle Paul encourage Christians to model themselves on the characteristics of Jesus and the Holy Spirit.

> *But when the Holy Spirit controls our lives, he will produce this kind of fruit in us: love, joy, peace, kindness, goodness, faithfulness, gentleness and self-control. Here there is no conflict with the law.*
>
> Galatians 5: 22–23

Younger Christian believers sometimes wear a wristband or necklace that has the letters WWJD (What would Jesus do?) on them, to encourage them to consider the example and leadership of Jesus in an attempt to become more like him.

FOR DEBATE 

'Everyone, regardless of their religion or beliefs, should aim to develop the virtues of Jesus.' Discuss.

9.6 Modern perspectives on virtue theory 

In this topic you will learn about modern developments and perspectives on virtue ethics from the last century.

In the 17th and 18th centuries, virtue ethics was criticised as being too imprecise, and for not applying itself to the absolutes of right and wrong as traditional theories did. By the 20th century, teleological theories such as Utilitarianism, and deontological theories like those proposed by Immanuel Kant were popularly accepted as solid theories of ethical morality.

In the second half of the 20th century, virtue ethics went through a revival due to the declining basis of traditional morality from within religious teaching. Ideas swung away from thinking about principles and general rules towards questions about the values and qualities that characterise a good life.

STRETCH & CHALLENGE

Investigate the issues on these pages by looking at Herbert McCabe's *The Good Life*. Consider how this represents an advance or otherwise on Aristotle.

Elizabeth Anscombe

Elizabeth Anscombe (1919–2001) believed that other theories, whether act or consequence based, did not have the foundation to provide moral guidelines. She believed that they each relied on the idea of punishment and reward, either by a divine law-giver or by their consequences. Therefore Anscombe believed that the older systems couldn't provide a basis as guidelines for the moral life.

What was required was a return to the ideals of eudaimonia, outlined by Aristotle and to a morality that is based on the person (agent) rather than on the act or the outcome. She also believed that other ethical theories were too focused on autonomous actions, whilst disregarding the social aspect of morality that unites a community.

Philippa Foot

Philippa Foot (1920–) attempts to update virtue ethics whilst still maintaining its roots in Aristotle. She believes that virtues are a way for people to flourish by correcting tendencies that we naturally have towards the vices. She would say that there is a human inclination to self-interest, which ought to be corrected by becoming more compassionate or benevolent.

FOR DEBATE 

Modern approaches to virtue ethics provide an excellent alternative to religious teaching. Why is this too simplistic an approach?

Foot also believes that virtues don't necessarily guarantee happiness, but they do help in moving towards achieving it.

She also emphasises that virtues are only virtuous as long as they are used in the correct way to bring a good outcome, therefore someone who requires courage to rob a bank cannot be seen as virtuous.

Alasdair MacIntyre

Alasdair MacIntyre (1929–) believes that modern ethical morality has lost its way. Words such as good, right and wrong are purely subjective and don't mean anything and people disagree whether morality should be deontological or teleological.

MacIntyre says that morality should be focused on Aristotle's idea of developing your telos (purpose/end), as otherwise we are in danger of losing our 'moral wisdom.' A man's purpose is in what he does and therefore it is judged accordingly. For MacIntyre and Aristotle, virtues are something that is judged in a society by other people. They judge our actions and behaviour to decide whether it is a morally virtuous act or an example of human excellence.

Therefore MacIntyre encourages a return to the basis of Aristotle's understanding of virtue by encouraging society to assist in developing virtues that are relevant to the contemporary times. It would seem from MacIntyre's approach that the virtues that were expounded by Aristotle or Jesus are not necessarily the virtues that will help people in the 21st century to flourish.

Richard Taylor

Richard Taylor (1919–2003) was very outspoken against the influence that religion had upon morality. He believed that humans should flourish and achieve their eudaimonia, but that religious teachings undermine this and almost encourage the opposite idea.

He referred to the Christian teaching of 'Blessed are the meek, for they shall inherit the earth'. If the meek inherit the earth, what encouragement is there then to be a good person and to strive for moral excellence if all that you need to do is lie back and wait for the inheritance? Taylor's criticism is that Christianity emphasises equality and to a certain extent the status quo of a 'self-negating' equality, rather than encouraging people to strive to become greater and better people.

Rosalind Hursthouse

Rosalind Hursthouse's (1943–) main contribution to the understanding of ethics is to address the criticism levelled at virtue ethics that it doesn't provide moral guidance in dilemmas. She says that it doesn't explain how a person would or should act, but instead how a virtuous person would think about the moral dilemma. She is a strong believer in Aristotle's approach to morality – virtues are virtuous because they encourage humans to flourish and achieve eudaimonia.

Hursthouse says that the virtues assist our practical reasoning, enabling us to become better and, as a consequence, to respond to moral dilemmas in a totally virtuous way. Therefore, if we use the virtues, our reasoning will enable us to be virtuous people.

Michael Slote

Michael Slote (1941–) uses the words 'admirable' and 'deplorable' as alternatives to 'good' and 'bad', which he believed always required clarification. If something is either admirable or deplorable, then we know by definition what the right action to pursue is going to be, i.e. to do the admirable and to avoid the deplorable.

ACTIVITY

Draw a mind map or spider diagram outlining the different approaches to virtue from these modern philosophers. Provide advantages and disadvantages for each approach using other theories within this topic, or problems that you see other more traditional ethical theories deal with or could respond to.

FOR DEBATE 

Taylor's attitude towards Christianity and its teachings on morality is not supportive. Can it be argued that he is justified in levelling the accusations against them?

Virtue ethics

9.7 Strengths and weaknesses of virtue ethics

In this topic you will learn about the critical strengths and weaknesses that are part of virtue ethics.

ACTIVITY

Outline the theory of virtue ethics. Using different coloured pens, annotate it to show its advantages and disadvantages.

STRETCH & CHALLENGE

Consider the Nuremburg War Crimes Trial in 1948 of prominent Nazis and their supporters. Apply the principles of virtue ethics to the jobs of the defence and prosecuting lawyers. How they would argue their cases?

Strengths of virtue ethics

- *Virtue ethics appeals to both secular and religious morality. An atheist can aspire to be like Jesus without believing that he was the Son of God. Despite Taylor's belief that Christianity and the example of Jesus encourage weakness and mediocrity, it is apparent in Christian texts that weakness becomes a strength and that taking an altruistic attitude is a virtuous thing to aspire to. The example of Jesus is an inspiration to people of different faiths or those of no religious faith whatsoever.*
- *The principles of virtue ethics are compatible with religious beliefs. They can complement the moral guidelines outlined in religious writings, as the teachings on virtues are focused not on the moral actions but the agent's moral development.*
- *Virtue ethics doesn't have a set of rules that must be followed like other traditional ethical systems, such as Utilitarianism's 'greatest good for the greatest number' or Kant's concept of duty and the Categorical Imperative. It focuses on becoming a better person and providing a way for humans to develop into the type of person that they ought to be.*
- *It avoids the inequalities that absolutist ethical systems cause and the dubious morality of actions that relativism can justify. This is only true if human flourishing and good is promoted (eudaimonia).*
- *It is a logical theory, as it focuses on our practical reasoning and the traits that will help society prosper.*
- *Virtue ethics encourages us to become better people and improve ourselves by aspiring to the virtues of other people such as Martin Luther King or Simon Wiesenthal. For virtue ethicists, character is vitally important because as we develop these traits we will no longer require ethical theories to follow. Therefore we will make decisions based upon our virtues that are fully morally correct.*

Weaknesses of virtue ethics

- Susan Wolf (1952–) claims that if everyone is virtuous, then there will be no variety or excitement in the world. We need the negative traits so that we can admire the positive ones. If all people are virtuous, then possibly a sense of apathy or boredom would become apparent, as there would be no variety.
- If society is to develop along the lines of MacIntyre's beliefs, how can we decide which are the most important virtues to develop or what types of things are virtuous? It requires some sort of value judgement to be made about the importance of each virtue.
- Virtues sometimes will clash with each other. Which one is more important in each situation? Should pragmatism always come above courage?
- Some virtues can be incorrectly used to perform immoral actions. Certain people believe that specific values are actually immoral. So if you believe that the war in Iraq is unjust, can the action of courageous soldiers fighting there be seen as developing a virtue by doing something that is perceived as immoral?
- At what point does a virtue become a vice? Is there a definitive point where it crosses over or is it purely subjective? When does courage become foolhardiness? Aristotle said that it would depend on the situation and is not a fixed point. Yet this is still subjective and lacks precision.
- Virtue ethics is still seen by many people as a theory that encourages subjective moral actions through personal moral development. The actions, although important, are rarely considered as highly as the personal moral development that follows the virtues, despite Aristotle's teaching to the contrary.
- Aristotle's teachings on virtue were aimed at more masculine attributes such as bravery, honour and comradeship, rather than more feminine virtues like empathy, compassion and humility.
- Virtue ethics is very difficult to apply to moral problems because it doesn't provide a method for knowing what to do, except to be virtuous. It provides no answers, but instead encourages us to focus on the practical reasoning and wisdom given to us by the virtues to know what we ought to be doing.
- Robert Louden (1952–) believes that there are certain actions that are so intolerable, like rape, that they must be morally wrong. Virtue ethics' focus on becoming a better person through practising the virtues can lead some people to justify certain actions as appropriate to this end of personal development, despite Aristotle's teaching that the good of the polis (body of citizens) is a higher value than that of an individual.

FOR DEBATE 

Wolf claims that being virtuous can be dull and bland because being virtuous is 'so very, very nice'. Is there justification for her viewpoint? Would a virtuous society be boring and require negative character traits in order to flourish fully?

MAKING LINKS

List the criticisms of other ethical theories and approaches that you have studied (Natural Law, situation ethics, Utilitarianism, Kantian ethics, etc.), and then compare to see if virtue ethics can provide a more suitable approach that deals with these criticisms. After you have done this, reverse the procedure and see if the criticisms or problems of virtue theory can be addressed in a more traditional ethical approach.

Exam**Café**

Relax, refresh, result!

Relax and prepare

Hot tips

Ben

Virtue ethics asks three questions: Who am I? What sort of person should I become? How can I get there? It is all about agent-centred ethics which sounds really good.

Sanjiv

Eudaimonia is a word I can never spell correctly. I know it is the final goal of human activity and means happiness, well-being and human flourishing but I still can't spell it!

Lisa

I tried to show which virtues could be practised or developed when applying virtue ethics to situations. I have also looked at what modern philosophers have said about applying virtue ethics and they seem to suggest that it is about moderating harmful passions or temptations, evolving shared community virtues or looking at how a virtuous person would think about an ethical dilemma.

Fabienne

Knowing more than just 'courage is the golden mean between the excess of rashness and the deficiency of cowardice' is essential, especially when it comes to applying virtue ethics to ethical issues, which can be difficult.

Refresh your memory

Revision checklist for virtue ethics

You should be able to demonstrate knowledge and understanding of:

- The principles of virtue ethics from Aristotle.
- The 'agent-centred' nature of virtue ethics.
- The concepts of eudaimonia and the golden mean.
- The importance of practising the virtues and the example of virtuous people.
- More modern approaches to virtue ethics.
- The strengths and weaknesses of each approach and be able to discuss these areas critically.

Get the result!

Exam question

Apply virtue ethics to issues surrounding protecting the environment. (35 marks)

Rachel's original answer

Virtue ethics has nothing to do with environmental issues because it is all about people becoming better and flourishing and not about global warming. Therefore, virtue ethics is not a good ethical theory to use when discussing environmental issues.

Examiner says

This is not a good introduction. It has given a clear statement of intent but it does seem to have missed the obvious connection between human activity and global warming.

The golden mean between the excesses of vice and deficiency cannot help someone make a decision about environmental issues because these were not concerns in ancient Greece. This is especially true for Plato and Aristotle who were rich men with slaves, who cared little for the rights of women or slaves.

Examiner says

This is more of an anti-Greek philosopher's rant than a useful paragraph on applying virtue ethics to environmental issues. Try your hand at improving this paragraph of Rachel's answer.

Virtue ethics does not have a single view on environmental ethics but it does take into account the situation. This means that virtue ethics can be used to justify the destruction of the environment if the people think it is the right thing to do in their situation. Not having any absolute rules means that virtue ethics is not a good ethical theory to apply to environmental issues.

Examiner says

This paragraph is not very good because it is too general when discussing virtue ethics. It also concentrates too much on the relativistic nature of virtue ethics which is not entirely valid. It does, however, link its views back to the question, which is a good habit to get into. Try your hand at improving this paragraph of Rachel's answer.

Rachel's improved introduction

The issue of protecting the environment usually focuses on human activity and the destruction of habitats, whether it is rainforests or marine environments. This therefore concentrates on how humans ought to act towards the world in which they live. Virtue ethics is an agent-centred ethical theory which looks at what sort of person I ought to become. At first glance, there does not seem to be any correlation between the two. However, if you asked the question 'would a virtuous person knowingly damage the environment?' Then you can start to see how useful virtue ethics could be.

Examiner says

This is a better introduction because it already shows knowledge of specific environmental issues and key aspects of virtue ethics.

Examiner's tips

Virtue ethics is a difficult topic to apply if you do not know the basics. Give yourself a bit of thinking time to see how the key ideas suggest a virtuous person should consider or act in a situation. Being very specific is a much better way of applying virtue ethics. Being too general will only lead to incorrect conclusions.

10 Environmental and business ethics

In this chapter you will learn about:

- the issue of how humans should relate to the environment, its resources and species
- secular approaches towards the environment, for example the Gaia hypothesis
- issues in business ethics, including the relationship between business and consumers and the relationship between employers and employees
- the relationship between business and the environment and between business and globalisation
- the application and the different approaches of ethical theories to environmental and business ethics.

Environmental and business ethics

10.1 What are environmental and business ethics?

In this topic you will learn about the areas that business and environmental ethics deal with.

Environmental ethics

When you look at all the wonderful places in the world, you have to have some level of respect or awe. For example, you may go diving in the Maldives and see incredible creatures, or go hiking in the Alps and explore the beautiful mountains and glaciers. Yet some of these sites, such as the two listed above, are in danger of being permanently damaged due to environmental problems that have been attributed to humankind's negligence.

Environmental ethics seeks to explore what responsibility humans have towards the world in which they live. It also attempts to provide theories that suggest that perhaps humans are not the only intrinsically worthy and valuable creatures on the planet.

The purpose of environmental ethics is to understand more about the value of the environment as a whole (including non-rational and non-living parts) and to devise a solid moral basis through which to understand this. Religious perspectives on environmental responsibilities can be contrasted with secular or non-religious theories.

Business ethics

Most people don't consider business ethics in their daily lives, yet the principles are staring us in the face every day.

Imagine you are walking into the town centre and you see a new perfume or aftershave advertised using sexual imagery. This example touches on the ethics concerning business advertising and how companies have a duty to be truthful in their claims. The advert doesn't guarantee that by using the aftershave or perfume you will look like the model or even get a chance to date the model, but does it suggest it? This does raise the question about the practices of other companies who are less honest in their promotions.

Business ethics doesn't just deal with advertising – it looks at the rights of the consumer in relation to the business owner, and it explores the relationship between employers and employees. Businesses must take increasing notice of business ethics, especially in the light of health and safety issues and environmental concerns.

Business ethics also looks at the responsibilities that businesses have, for example when employing workers in foreign countries.

The purpose of business ethics is to provide moral justification for all practices that businesses undertake and to ensure that an ethical code of practice is implemented.

ACTIVITY

In groups, compile a list of what you believe are the ten most important environmental concerns facing the human race. Place them in order of importance. Then discuss your concerns and their order with the rest of the class. What makes them *ethically* important?

FOR DEBATE

'Humankind is the most important species on the planet; all other species are there for their use.' Discuss.

ACTIVITY

List all the businesses that you have purchased a service or goods from in the last week. For each one, state whether or not you were satisfied with the product or service.

ACTIVITY

Think of a time when you were dissatisfied with something you paid for. Did you return it or complain about it? Discuss what you think the ethical and the legal responsibilities of businesses are in this situation. Are they always the same?

10 Environmental and business ethics

10.2 Conservationism and libertarianism

In this topic you will learn about the ideas of **conservationism** (shallow ecology) and its human-centred approach, and the less human-centred approach of libertarianism (deep ecology).

KEY WORDS

Conservationism (shallow ecology): the theory that the environment's importance is related to its usefulness for humanity.

Instrumental value: belief that something is only valuable because of its importance to something else.

Anthropocentric: belief that humanity is central and more important.

Intrinsic value: belief that something is valuable in itself.

FOR DEBATE

Rainforests are being burned down in the Amazon to provide grazing for cattle, and new land for soya bean crops. Discuss as a class whether this destruction of a natural habitat serves the best interests of humanity and ought to be pursued.

FOR DEBATE

Look at La Bossiere's perspective on the environment and human responsibility to it again. Is his idea one that is ethical and one that is sustainable?

Conservationism

This approach looks at the value that the environment has to us as humans and how its welfare will affect us. If we need to reduce, reuse and recycle in order for humanity to survive, then this is a conservationist approach. Effectively the environment is only a means to an end – the end being the survival and well-being of humankind.

According to this approach plants and animals only have **instrumental value**, as their usefulness only lies in their usefulness to the human race. They are a means to an end, rather than being an end in themselves. If an animal or plant can provide ingredients for medicine or provide food, it has importance for humans and must be protected and preserved.

This approach is also called shallow ecology and is **anthropocentric** (meaning human-centred). Human beings are believed to have **intrinsic value**, and protection of their interests at the expense of other non-human entities is believed to be fully ethical. It is important to note that this approach also believes that only humans have true moral worth and standing.

Some approaches from philosophers, like Michael La Bossiere (1966–), suggest that an anthropocentric approach can be justified as part of the natural order of evolution, i.e. if an animal becomes extinct due to human activities, this can be deemed as nature taking its course. La Bossiere is not suggesting that humans should try to wipe out a specific species, however, if it becomes extinct naturally as a consequence of humanity's actions, this is acceptable.

Problems with conservationism

There are some ways in which this approach can be problematic, especially as we desire to advance technologically. Nuclear power is possibly the solution for our energy needs in the future, yet disasters such as the Chernobyl meltdown of 1986 had an immense impact on the surrounding environment and people. If we support this shallow ecology approach, the impact on the non-human entities could conceivably have an important impact on human prosperity in the future. This is one of the claims made by the climate change environmental lobby, who are seeking to redress the imbalance that currently exists by ensuring that people become more environmentally aware and responsible.

Libertarianism

This approach, also known as **deep ecology**, seeks to recognise all life forms as having value and rejects any form of anthropocentric arguments as **speciesist**.

Aldo Leopold (1887–1948) believed that it was time for humanity to stop being so fixated upon itself and that it should once again focus on the relationship that humans have with the land, the animals and the plants. He believed that the social conscience of humans must extend to the soil, to mountains and to non-human animals and that, rather than viewing ourselves as the 'dominators' of the land, we ought to view our existence as part of a moral community that includes the land and its other inhabitants.

> *A thing is right when it ends to preserve the integrity, stability and beauty of the biotic community. It is wrong when it tends otherwise.*
>
> Round River, 1949

The philosopher Arne Naess (1912–) was the first person to use the phrase deep ecology to describe deep ecological awareness. He argues that inherent worth and intrinsic value should be attributed to the environment and referred to this approach as **ecosophy** – the idea that all living things, whether humans, animals or plants, have rights. Naess argues that this approach tries to 'preserve the integrity of the biosphere for its own sake' and not for any benefits to humans. All aspects of the environment are interconnected and interdependent and no specific species has the right to claim dominance due to possession of a soul, consciousness or the ability to make reasoned decisions. It is for this reason that Naess is very critical of the Christian ideas of stewardship and he opposes this as an 'unnecessary arrogance.'

Naess' solution for the planet to avoid any future environmental crisis is very simple and is still quite revolutionary. He suggests that humans should:

- significantly reduce the population of the planet
- abandon any goals for economic growth
- preserve and conserve diversity of species
- live in small, self-reliant communities
- 'touch the earth lightly'.

These ideas are quite controversial and have been rejected by many other environmentalists as too radical and also too unrealistic in light of the significant growth in population.

STRETCH & CHALLENGE

Look at some environmental disasters that have been caused by anthropocentricism, e.g. Chernobyl or the *Exxon Valdez* oil spill. How could these events be justified as 'accidents' when humankind knows the impact that its progress has on other aspects of the environment?

KEY WORDS

Deep ecology/ libertarianism: the belief that all life forms have intrinsic value.

Speciesist: discrimination in favour of one species, usually the human species, over another.

Ecosophy: the idea that all living things, whether humans, animals or plants, have rights.

ACTIVITY

Look at Naess' proposals in groups of three or four. Draw up a list of changes that you believe would need to be made in the United Kingdom to fulfil these suggestions. Also discuss larger global implications as a class.

Environmental and business ethics

10.3 Ecological extension

In this topic you will learn about the approaches to the environment that believe the planet is, in some form, a living entity.

KEY WORDS

Ecological extension (eco-holism): the belief that all ecosystems and living things are interdependent.

Gaia hypothesis: the hypothesis that suggests that the world's physical properties and the biosphere join together to form a complex interacting system.

Gaia: the idea of Gaia comes from the name of the Greek goddess of the Earth, who was believed to be intrinsically part of the planet.

The belief that Earth is a living entity sounds quite bizarre. If it is, what do you think it would feel about humanity right now?

The ecological extension approach is not focused on human rights concerning the environment, but rather on the whole environment. In other words, it seeks to respect and include all aspects of ecosystems as an intrinsically valuable entity.

The ideas of **ecological extension** are also known as **eco-holism** and in the 21st century the most notable theory of this approach is called the **Gaia hypothesis**.

The Gaia hypothesis 

James Lovelock (1919–) first put forward his Gaia hypothesis in 1977 suggesting that planet Earth is a massive, ego-centric, self-regulating biological organism and is not necessarily focused on the survival or preservation of humanity. Basically, the Earth is alive!

The theory suggests that humankind is not indispensable to the Earth, therefore the idea that man is superior to other life forms is flawed.

Within Aboriginal and other indigenous cultures, there is also a strong tradition of the Earth as a living entity that will ensure survival and longevity of the planet. Lovelock developed these ideas and believes that the planet regulates itself in favour of life and has a sense of intelligence that enables life to survive in some form.

> *For me, Gaia is a religious as well as a scientific concept, and in both spheres it is manageable...God and Gaia, theology and science, even physics and biology are not separate but a single way of thought.*
>
> Lovelock, *The Ages of Gaia*

The evidence of fossils

Lovelock's understanding of this was developed by looking at fossils that showed that, even with extreme changes in weather in the past, life in some form had always survived. He saw this as evidence of organisation and intelligence in the Gaia system, rather than the randomness that Lovelock believed Darwin had proposed through his 'survival of the fittest'.

Take the example of the dinosaurs. They roamed the Earth for millennia and were successful life forms, yet a meteor hitting the planet wiped them out, and very nearly wiped out all life. Lovelock attributed the survival of life on the planet to the intelligence of Gaia, which ensured that it continued. Life cannot be destroyed if Gaia does not permit it.

There are more modern examples of life surviving or adapting in extreme conditions. The ecosystems in the areas where nuclear bombs were tested or where nuclear accidents took place (e.g. Chernobyl) are now beginning to develop living organisms again. Life returns and develops to ensure survival of the planet under the auspices of Gaia.

Humans and the Gaia system

Another of Lovelock's ideas is that, unless humankind values and treats Gaia with respect, our survival as a species is under threat, because we are a threat to the survival of the Gaia system on the planet. He believes that, unless we confront the environmental crisis that has arisen through human negligence, we are fated to become another extinct species on this planet.

Challenges to the Gaia hypothesis

Richard Dawkins (1941–) claims that Lovelock's theory that all life 'clubs together' for some sort of mutual advantage or benefit is inconceivable. He says that basic evolutionary theory disproves this almost completely. The scientific idea of the 'survival of the fittest' means that species that adapt and develop in response to altered conditions will survive.

Lynn Margulis (1938–) suggests that Dawkins' perspective and the Gaia hypothesis are compatible if ideas of a **symbiosis** are accepted. She believes that organisms will, at times, combine with other organisms in a symbiotic relationship in order to survive, whilst still remaining individual organisms. There are many examples from nature, such as pilot fish that clean the teeth of sharks in return for their protection. The idea of symbiosis suggests that living organisms will work together to ensure mutual survival, therefore bringing some of the ideas of Darwinism closer to the ideas of the Gaia hypothesis.

FOR DEBATE

'If the Earth is an "ego-centric, self-regulating biological organism", then it could become "angry or hurt" if I cut the grass or if I spray week killer in the garden.' Discuss this with reference to Lovelock's theory.

KEY WORD

Symbiosis: the mutually beneficial relationship between two things, where they are dependent on each other.

ACTIVITY

Using your knowledge of the Gaia approach, basic evolutionary development and the teachings of Margulis, produce a large mind map outlining the various approaches to this area. Don't forget to include criticisms and counter-arguments.

STRETCH & CHALLENGE

All the secular approaches to the environment generally present a good platform for ethical and moral discussion. However, what questions do you perceive are still unanswered or unaddressed?

Environmental and business ethics

10.4 Christian views of the environment

In this topic you will learn about religious approaches to the environment.

FOR DEBATE 

Then God said,
'Let us make people in our image, to be like ourselves. They will be masters over all life – the fish in the sea, the birds in the sky, and all the livestock, wild animals, and small animals.'
(Genesis 1:26)

Does believing this provide a helpful ethical approach to the environment?

Ask yourself what Christians believe about the environment. You may come up with the answer that Christians believe they are the most important species on the planet and can do what they want with the planet. Although a simplistic answer, it may be a reflection of what some Christians believe. However, it is not an accurate reflection of what is found in the Bible.

In order to understand what Christianity teaches, it is important to look at a variety of approaches.

KEY WORD

Dominion: belief that God has given humankind authority over the Earth and all its animals and plants.

Dominion

The Bible isn't always clear about what human responsibility towards the environment should be. Humankind is given **dominion** because humans are created in the image of God and have a special relationship with him.

> *let them have dominion over the fish of the sea, and the birds of the air, and over the livestock, over all the earth, and over all the creatures that move along the ground.*
>
> Genesis 1:28

FOR DEBATE 

In groups, take opposing perspectives on whether humankind has the anthropocentric right to be dominant on the Earth. What would Christian ethics and Natural Law say?

This extract suggests a very anthropocentric approach and one that has its roots in the teachings of Aristotle:

> *She (nature) has made all animals for the sake of man.*
>
> Aristotle, Politics

The idea of dominion presented here seems to have negative ideas behind it – ideas of domination and force. However, it seems that this usage is more about putting humankind at the top of the hierarchy of life on the planet.

The biblical story of creation offers a different interpretation of the word dominion. When God creates the things, he says that they are 'good', and to all of creation he says 'be fruitful and multiply'. This wording would seem to suggest that it isn't just humanity that God is concerned with, but rather that all creation has an intrinsic value. This reading of the creation story is difficult to reconcile with the traditional dominion idea.

Stewardship

The idea of **stewardship** is one that seems to bring a sense of responsibility without the idea of domination. In the second creation narrative in the book of Genesis, the emphasis is upon protecting and preserving God's creation. The analogy of being caretakers of the planet is made; it suggests that we are merely caring for the planet on behalf of the owner, God the creator.

Taking this explanation a little further it can be suggested that humankind is responsible to God for the use of his Earth. The Parable of the Talents (Matthew 25:14–30) shows that humanity may be judged according to how we have taken responsibility for the things that God has left in our care.

The responsibility that is suggested in this second creation account includes animals, as well as plants and non-breathing parts of the environment. Christians believe that they are the pinnacle of God's creation, with the ability to reason and to be moral. Therefore they have a duty to be:

> *courteous, tolerant, humble, just and in awe of the creation that God has entrusted to their care.*
>
> Adolpho Masteranti, 1667–1749, quoted in 'A Collection of Miscellanies', John Norris, 1713

Creation spirituality

The Christian Saint Francis of Assisi (1182–1226) believed that God can be seen and found in all creation. Animals and birds convey to us the understanding of God's purpose and plan; to destroy or harm them is a sin as God entrusted their well-being to us. His approach was one that is viewed as a form of **creation spirituality** similar to other Christian mystical writers, like Mother Julian of Norwich (1342–1416). The approach of those who follow this idea of Christian spirituality towards the environment has been compared to the Gaia approach outlined on page 180, as both approaches see humanity as part of the whole of creation rather than as separate to it.

Consequences of sin

Some Roman Catholics believe that the Original Sin that humans committed has had a negative effect on the relationship between God and humankind, as well as humans' attitude towards the environment. As a consequence of disobedience in the Garden of Eden, humans have neglected their responsibility and ownership of the environment and this has therefore damaged their relationship with God. In order to rectify this situation, a return to the principles of stewardship, as found in the book of Genesis, is vital to resolve the breakdown in relationship between God and humanity.

KEY WORDS

Stewardship: belief that God has given humanity responsibility to care and look after the planet.

Creation spirituality: a religious approach that emphasises that humankind is part of creation and that God can be found in all his creation.

STRETCH & CHALLENGE

Is it possible to reconcile the ideas of stewardship and dominion as outlined in the early chapters of Genesis? If so, how could it be presented so that both perspectives are satisfied and valued?

FOR DEBATE

'Christian responses to the environment are outdated and useless in the real world.' In small groups and then as a large group, discuss this issue from both perspectives. You should explore the perspectives of Natural Law and Christian ethics in your discussion.

Environmental and business ethics

10.5 The relationship between business and consumers

In this topic you will learn about how businesses and consumers work together in a mutually beneficial relationship.

FOR DEBATE

'The solution that Keith Tondeur suggests may be an ideal way to live your life ethically, but it's not practical!' Discuss this with reference to your own views about business.

FURTHER RESEARCH

Many of the multi-national companies that we find on our high street have, in the past, been accused of unethical practices, for example Gap, Nestlé, Nike, etc. Find out more about these claims. What makes these practices unethical?

KEY WORDS

Micro-ethics: this deals with the smaller details that constitute an ethical approach.

Social responsibility: a belief that businesses have a responsibility towards society as well as their own interests.

Stakeholders: those people who own the company, and also its employees, its consumers and the wider community.

Is ethical living possible?

The economist Keith Tondeur (1947–) believes that people should become more ethical in how they live their lives, especially how they relate to money and services. His suggestions for living a more ethical life are:

- model yourself on good people, e.g. Mother Teresa
- live more simply, e.g. use public transportation, recycle, grow your own produce, buy only what you need
- invest wisely and only with organisations that have ethical investment records
- find out about current affairs and the economy of the less developed world
- use your influence, e.g. writing to members of parliament about ethical issues
- choose the companies you buy from carefully – they should have good records on environmental issues and human rights (e.g. no child labour).

But, as consumers, do we always have the choice to buy only fair trade products? Can we truly find out about the background of the businesses that we deal with?

The relationship between businesses and consumers

Micro-ethics deals with the intentions, promises, obligations and individual rights that form the relationship between businesses and consumers.

In the early 1970s, the economist Milton Friedman (1912–2006) claimed that 'the **social responsibility** of business is to increase its profits'. He claimed that social responsibility in business was a delusion; for him the only responsibility for corporations was to their stockholders.

It is only relatively recently that businesses have moved from focusing on their stockholders towards an emphasis on its **stakeholders**. Social responsibility is central to an understanding of this relationship between businesses and consumers. The actions of businesses affect not only the stockholders but also the wider stakeholders. For example, if a business has to downsize due to a recession, stockholders will lose some money, whilst stakeholders lose jobs and local economic input.

Legal requirements

Businesses have a requirement to ensure that their products are safe and that they contain appropriate guidance for their use. If a product is not appropriately labelled and someone gets injured or hurt, it will be the responsibility of the business. If a company advertises that one of its products will cure baldness, then it must cure baldness to satisfy advertising laws. If it doesn't cure this problem, then it cannot advertise that it does.

The trust that consumers place in a business is vital. A consumer must be able to trust that a product is safe, labelled correctly (i.e. not misleading) and usable; if this is not the case, then the trust has been betrayed. The trust that a business places in the consumer must also be maintained, as goodwill is required when dealing with dissatisfaction and return of goods.

The power of the consumer

If consumers don't buy a business' products, then it will not make a profit. Therefore it is within the best interests of the company to listen to its consumers. But what role should profit play in this relationship? If we take Friedman's view, profit is paramount and must come first, regardless of anything else.

Consumers may find that it is harder to make a difference against large multi-nationals than if they were making a stand against the ethical practices of the local butcher or farmer.

The Nestlé Corporation has been criticised over a period of 30 years concerning its policy of providing powdered milk for sale in less developed countries where water is not usually clean enough to drink. The controversy in this situation was mostly to do with Nestlé giving the milk for free and then, once the babies were on the milk and breast milk had dried up, Nestlé started charging for it – therefore forcing a situation where mothers might not be able to feed their children due to poverty. Is it ethical to boycott a company? Can our ethical stand make a difference?

ACTIVITY

Look at Friedman's theory on stockholders and compare it to the theory on stakeholders. Outline the arguments for how each could be beneficial to the business and to its consumers. Which theory would be the more ethical?

FOR DEBATE

'Companies need to advertise and promote their product so they can sell the most. It doesn't matter how they do it!' Discuss this in light of the ideas above and also using some of the ethical theories that you have studied previously.

ACTIVITY

Investigate the success of The Body Shop's ethical policy.

FURTHER RESEARCH

Investigate what became known as the 'McLibel trial' – a court action taken by McDonalds against a factsheet that criticised its practices. Find out about the criticisms and use the information to expand your knowledge of the topic.

10 Environmental and business ethics

10.6 Employers and employees

In this topic you will learn about the relationship between organisations and their employees.

KEY WORDS

Bourgeoisie: the middle-class industrial owners who have the proletariat working for them.

Proletariat: the workers and lower wage earners who depend on the bourgeoisie for employment.

ACTIVITY

Smith's idea of the symbiotic relationship between employer and employee would appear to be true, yet the scepticism of Marx's approach can also be seen as true in the light of Friedman's focus on stockholder profits alone. Write a newspaper article outlining the different approaches and draw some conclusions about which approach seems more likely and socially appealing.

FOR DEBATE 

Friedman says that corporations cannot meaningfully be 'persons with responsibilities'. Does this then mean that profit comes before principle in dealing with employees?

The nature of the relationship

For many people in the 21st century, this is how they feel about their employers: they are working to fill the pockets of the 'fat cat' boss.

The relationship between the employer and employee is one that has existed for millennia and one that is vital for the success of our society.

Adam Smith's (*c.*1723–90) theory of free market competition explored the way that employers could best serve the interests of their employees, i.e. by employing them according to supply and demand. The community would prosper as employment would be high and people could live well on their wages. Smith saw the employer as having a responsibility to employ people fairly and justly and avoid selfishness. This relationship was based upon the need of the employer for labourers and the need of the employee for work.

Karl Marx (1818–83) disputed that the role was as equivocal; he believed that the employer (**bourgeoisie**) could find almost anyone to do the work, but unless the worker (**proletariat**) agreed to work on the employer's terms then he would go without. Therefore the bourgeoisie control the market and the proletariat have no bargaining tools except their labour, which must be given if they are to live and survive.

Do employers have an obligation to their employees?

In the stakeholder theory, it is generally accepted that the most undervalued member of the circle is the employee. An employee is, to a certain extent, only another commodity of the business that is linked to supply and demand and to profit, therefore other stakeholders usually overlook their perspective.

In the UK, there are certain legal requirements and guidelines that govern the relationship between employers and employees. An employee has the right to be safe at work and to be warned about potential risks; it is the responsibility of the employer to ensure that health and safety regulations are met.

There are several large companies in the United Kingdom that have ethical business approaches to their employees. Two of the best known are the John Lewis Group, which owns the food supermarket chain Waitrose, and the Cooperative group. These organisations provide ownership of the company to their employees on a rising scale that provides financial dividends each year.

Psychologists suggest that investing in and valuing employees has a positive effect on their well-being and also on the well-being of the company.

Profit or principle?

If a business believes that it can make more profit by employing someone who is younger, most of us would say that this is unacceptable because it is ageist. Yet it can be perfectly legal and possible to do it.

In this age of large multi-national companies it is possible to close a call centre in Reading and transfer it all to a city in India, where costs for offices, staffing and telecommunications is much lower. This is beneficial for the company in terms of cost and increases their overall profit. However, one of the negative sides to this apparent good for the company is the number of employees that they have to make redundant in Reading. It could be argued that multi-national businesses don't have a sense of responsibility or true concern for the impact on communities and families.

Ted Snyder (1953–) supports Friedman and believes that profit is more important than general matters of principle. However, he believes that businesses do have an element of social responsibility towards their employees and stakeholders, but that this responsibility is secondary to the requirements to make profit. His research into emerging markets suggests that profiting by moving business outlets to less developed countries benefits the workers in those countries even more than it would have benefited those left behind in the western nations.

Whistleblowing

Whistleblowing can require an employee to make a choice, either to speak up about wrongdoing in the business, or to remain loyal to the company that pays their wages.

It is a difficult decision to make and one that, ethically, many people struggle with. Should they report malpractice, injustices and criminal activity? Should there not be a sense of loyalty that an employee should have to exhibit towards an employer?

Either way, this area is likely to put a strain on the employer and employee relationship, especially as it relates to the key concept of trust.

FOR DEBATE

Do you think that companies should offer share or profit options to their long-serving employees? What are the arguments for and against this approach? Is it ethical?

FURTHER RESEARCH

Investigate the contribution of Robert Solomon in *Ethics and Excellence* to the issues on these pages, specifically in the area of ethics concerning profit, and contrast them with Friedman's ideas.

KEY WORD

Whistleblowing: revealing to the public some sort of corruption or wrongdoing in business.

FOR DEBATE

If your boss, who is also your best friend, broke or exploited the law at work, then it is your responsibility to inform the appropriate authorities!

ACTIVITY

Research a case of whistleblowing (typing it into Google usually works). What were the difficulties that the whistleblower faced? Write up a summary of the case and comment on the ethics of it.

10 Environmental and business ethics

10.7 Business and the environment

In this topic you will learn about the responsibilities that businesses have towards the environment.

FOR DEBATE 

'If aeroplanes cause air pollution, then it's not the fault of the airline providers. It is down to the supply and demand of consumers. Therefore consumers are to blame! Or perhaps the increase in pollution is due to the higher number of cheap flights and, therefore, more people are choosing to fly!'

Many businesses impact our environment through their use of natural resources to provide a product, whilst others do it through manufacturing of a product and contributing to pollution. Most people today will have travelled on an aeroplane at some stage in their life, and the companies that own the aeroplanes contribute to pollution in the air. Is there an ethical responsibility for businesses to consider the impact on the environment?

Kyoto Conference 

In 1997 the Kyoto Conference on Climate Change committed to reduce pollution and fight the impact of global warming. Many nations committed to do this, however the USA has refused to accept and to follow the Kyoto Protocol. Peter Singer believes that if the largest polluter in the world will not try to reduce pollution and the progression of global warming that 'the prospect of finding solutions to global problems are dimmed'.

Cynics have suggested that George W. Bush has consistently refused to accept the Kyoto Protocol because of the financial backing that he received in his election campaign from the oil, gas and car industries, as they would be some of the primary industries that would suffer if Kyoto was accepted.

A sustainable future?

Unless businesses take responsibility for their impact on the environment, there is a risk to the sustainable future of the planet. James Lovelock pioneered the Gaia approach. He believes that if individuals and corporations don't respect the earth, then human survival is in jeopardy because we are a threat to the survival of the Gaia system on the planet.

Do big corporations really care?

Corporations will soon need to take responsibility for the effects that their company has upon the environment. It is only recently that travel companies have given consumers the opportunity to 'offset' their carbon emissions by paying an ecology tax on their trip. Some ecologists view this as a responsible start to redressing the balance caused by emissions from planes and trains. However, is this not just another way to 'fool' people that big corporations care? Perhaps if they did care, the company would foot the bill instead of the passengers.

Should the company have been held responsible for this big environmental disaster? What if it was caused completely accidentally?

The Napoli disaster

There are major concerns about major environmental disasters that involve large corporations, especially oil spillages that kill animals and organisms in the local ecosystems. For example, the ship 'Napoli' that was grounded off the Devon coastline in January 2007 caused many animals to die and a stretch of historic coastline to be polluted.

ACTIVITY

Read the newspaper articles on this page and provide ethical responses to the various issues raised. Use the ethical theories and approaches that you have studied elsewhere in the course to discuss these issues.

FURTHER RESEARCH

Look at several environmental disasters that have been caused by businesses over the last 20 years, e.g. the *Exxon Valdez* disaster, Bhopal disaster, Chernobyl disaster. Look at the arguments that these were caused by the businesses, but also at the approach that says they were 'just' accidents.

The economist Milton Friedman said that companies should only be focused on stockholders and their profit margins rather than on the stakeholders, which could include the living and non-living environment.

Environmental and business ethics

10.8 Business and globalisation

In this topic you will learn about the ideas of globalisation and how ethical considerations play a part in it.

What is globalisation?

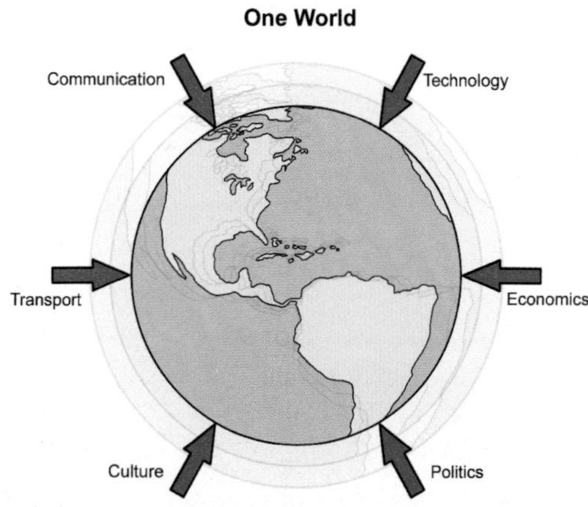

Globalisation is defined by Jagdish Bhagwati as '…integration of national economies into the international economy through trade, foreign direct investment, capital flows, migration, and spread of technology'. Does this mean the world is getting smaller?

FOR DEBATE

'Globalisation is inevitable, therefore, every business must push their needs so they can please their shareholders.' Discuss.

KEY WORD

Globalisation: the integration of economies, cultures, governmental policies and political movements around the world.

ACTIVITY

Investigate how many countries the following companies have outlets in:

- McDonald's.
- Boots.
- Pizza Hut.

Write down your opinion about why globalisation has helped their expansion.

In many ways we talk about the world getting smaller because it is easier than it ever has been to travel to most places in the world. It is also true in the business world due to transportation developments, technological developments and international trade agreements.

It is now much easier to run a business and source raw materials in foreign countries where trade is cheaper and so are labourers. Importing and exporting goods from abroad makes it easier to run a business that is profitable and also one that supports the economy of other countries.

The impact of globalisation on international markets

The value of global trade has increased astronomically in the last 60 years: between 1958 and 1998 it was believed to have increased by a factor of over 80. There is big money to be made if you are a transnational corporation, as they seem to control approximately two-thirds of all global products and the international trade that sells them (Philippe Hugon, 1999).

These large corporations control a significant amount of worldwide trade and the competition in the manufacturing industries is immense. This **globalisation** has provided opportunities for countries to develop economically and become more involved in international trade.

Most goods can now be made and bought in most places around the world, so in effect a country's individuality is diminishing as this giant called globalisation moves in.

The effects on less economically developed countries (LEDCs)

As the cheap production of goods is so much easier to obtain now from **LEDCs**, it would seem likely that the local economies would benefit and they would become more prosperous. The local community benefits through employment, technological advances, investment in the community and trade development.

This seems very admirable for these large globalised companies, yet they still increase their profits through possible exploitation of this cheaper labour, lower overheads and general gratitude of the local people.

Perhaps the LEDCs don't benefit as much as may first seem apparent. The Uruguayan journalist, Eduardo Galeano in an interview on Venezuelan television in 2005 said that:

> *...the exploitation of the resources of the labourer nations will only benefit the global traders. They push them down so they can't stand by themselves.*

If the LEDCs were to trade their own products, they could conceivably exploit their own economic potential, rather than doing it through the generosity of these transnational corporations.

The ethics of globalisation

The United Nations Development Project (UNDP) aims to make the ideals of globalisation a reality, aiming to ensure that it is just and fair.

> *Globalisation has fundamentally altered the world economy, creating winners and losers. Reducing inequalities both within and between countries, and building a more inclusive globalisation is the most important development challenge of our time.*
>
> Kemal Derviş, UNDP Report, 2007

However, one ethical criticism is that globalisation discriminates against those workers in LEDCs who work at a wage that is a pittance compared to workers in more economically developed countries (**MEDCs**). Yet this charge of injustice is answered by claiming that the cost of living is much lower in these countries and that the wage they receive is many times higher than the average wage in the country (sometimes up to five times).

Globalisation has a tendency to provide greater unemployment in areas where the manufacturing industry was more prevalent. If a company can move a clothing factory from Luton to Thailand and increase its profits, then it is prudent for it to do so. However, these people in Luton are now unemployed through no fault of their own, but are discriminated against because they live in a MEDC.

KEY WORDS

LEDC: less economically developed country.

MEDC: more economically developed country.

FOR DEBATE

'Fair trade is just a way for large companies to claim that they are ethical to get more money for their products!'

FOR DEBATE

'Globalisation is the best approach for all stakeholders in multi-national businesses.'

STRETCH & CHALLENGE

If international trade continues to develop in the way it has over the last 60 years, ethical practices will have to develop and become more explicit. In what ways could this start to be achieved now? Is there a limit to how much profit that these corporations make?

Environmental and business ethics

10.9 Evaluating ethical responses to the environment

In this topic you will examine how the ethical theories you have studied respond to the issues concerning the environment.

ACTIVITY

Kant's ethics are too anthropomorphic to really be of any use when making decisions regarding the environment. How could this be argued as true and as false? You should refer to the work you have previously done on Kant.

What do Kantian ethics say?

Kantian ethics are generally seen to only be applicable to humans, as only humanity is capable of morality. This is quite an anthropocentric approach and would seem to suggest that Kant would permit humankind to exploit the planet for their use and benefit.

The idea of universalisability is that we should only do something that we believe everyone else should be morally obliged to do as well, therefore it is not in the best interests of humanity for humans to exploit the environment as this would suggest that everyone has an obligation to do so.

Kant's beliefs that morality only applies to rational beings seems to contradict this approach, however he believes that if we mistreat and exploit animals then we are likely to do the same things to other humans, who are rational beings. Therefore Kant suggests that we ought to treat non-rational beings with respect, as this ensures that we treat other rational beings with respect too. It is important to note that Kant didn't believe that animals had any moral significance in themselves and therefore cruelty towards them was only wrong because of the impact that it would have on human attitudes to other people.

Kant's ethics would suggest that humans have a moral responsibility to protect the environment and not to destroy it, as this could lead to exploiting other rational beings in a similar way.

Paul Taylor suggests that animals and plants should not be afforded moral rights as they aren't rational beings, but instead ought to be given legal rights so that they are protected and preserved. This approach would seem to be one that would satisfy the requirements of Kantian ethics.

STRETCH & CHALLENGE

How could a Utilitarian approach provide a solid basis for governmental policy on the environment? Consider act, rule, preference and motive Utilitarianism. Also look at some of the writings of Peter Singer, as he provides some good approaches.

Utilitarian perspectives

The Utilitarian idea of the 'greatest happiness for the greatest number' is good to bear in mind when dealing with the environment. Many people today propose the idea of 'live for today' – however this approach when applied to environmental issues can have dire effects. The needs of future generations may be jeopardised by our exploitation and abuse of the environment today, for example the burning of fossil fuels.

Mill's Utilitarianism is based on qualitative pleasures and the distinction between higher and lower pleasures. The preservation of the environment would therefore be a higher pleasure and one that has a higher quality of pleasure as it ensures the well-being and enjoyment of future generations.

Peter Singer (1946–) encourages humankind to look at the world that we admire now and to think of future generations where these places may no longer exist because of humankind's attitude to the environment.

Long-term harm to the planet is a major concern that Utilitarians try to address. They would suggest that gaining something in the short term by abusing the environment could potentially have disastrous effect in the future, for example removing a rainforest for housing can kill an entire ecosystem.

FOR DEBATE 

'Ethical theories don't really help when it comes to the environment; they only confuse the issues.' Discuss this with reference to all the approaches that you have looked at in this chapter.

Is this World Heritage Site important intrinsically or just instrumentally?

STRETCH & CHALLENGE

How can the needs of this World Heritage Site (Mount Kilimanjaro) really be helped by philosophical discussions? Is it true that if we don't value and protect it, we'll lose it?

Utilitarianism would not see the environment as having intrinsic value in itself, but rather only instrumental value in its use for humanity. Whilst Utilitarianism is not strictly anthropocentric, it is consequentialist and therefore looks at the consequences of actions for humanity and its survival. A Utilitarian would not value Mount Kilimanjaro or the Grand Canyon as anything more than something that humans take pleasure from and therefore is only of instrumental value.

What is the response of virtue ethics?

Virtue ethics as a theory encourages human flourishing and human development. If humanity is to flourish, it must survive, therefore virtue ethics would suggest an approach that is not anthropocentric. It would suggest a more holistic approach that focuses not on what is important for humanity to survive, but instead on what would make an environmentally good person who can survive.

This approach moves away from the ideas that responsibility to the environment is based upon duties or upon consequences. In order to make ourselves more virtuous and to achieve the ideal of eudaimonia, we must objectively develop virtuous understanding of our place in the environment.

Virtue ethics also encourages the idea of modelling the virtuous behaviour of people we see exhibiting the virtues, perhaps by looking at the example of St Francis of Assisi and the work of James Lovelock and aiming to develop the virtues of compassion and pragmatism that they showed.

STRETCH & CHALLENGE

Lovelock's Gaia hypothesis may seem unbelievable, however in what ways would it provide a practical theory of environmental practice without having to have the same environmental beliefs regarding spirituality?

Environmental and business ethics

10.10 Evaluating ethical responses to business ethics

In this topic you will examine how the ethical theories you have studied respond to the issues concerning business ethics.

ACTIVITY

Look at Kant's teachings that you have studied and apply them to the issues outlined in this chapter. List ways that Kantian ethics may provide definitive answers and also discuss areas that are less concrete and perhaps ambiguous.

FOR DEBATE

'It is perfectly acceptable to have a call centre moved to India for financial reasons.' Discuss this with reference to the categorical imperative and other Kantian teachings.

What would Kant say?

In approaching business ethics from Kant's perspective it would be vital to only follow a course of action that everyone should have to follow. For example, if a business fielded its call centre to Jaipur in India to reduce costs and increase profits, then Kantian ethics would say that this should be universalisable and other companies should in fact do this also.

In most cases the financial gain for the company would be one of self-interest and relying on a good profitable outcome for their stockholders. Therefore what about the other shareholders; including the workers in Jaipur and the customers in the United Kingdom? What would be the benefit for them? Are they being used as a means to an end to facilitate the increase in profit for the company? It would seem that the requirements of business to make profits would be in conflict with this ideal and therefore fall foul of a Kantian approach.

It is difficult to approach most areas of business from a Kantian perspective, as universalising actions and ensuring that people are valued are not necessarily profitable or even desirable. However, using the principles of Kant and his teachings on duty and good will can provide an excellent platform for exploring and possibly resolving some of the potential problems of globalisation. If all stakeholders are intrinsically valued in themselves, it is possible to provide a good basis to ensure that equality and trust are central to moral and ethical business approaches.

Utilitarian approach

If happiness is maximised, then theoretically more people will benefit. However, it is important to distinguish between the ideas of quantity of pleasure and the quality of the pleasure provided.

It would be possible to suggest that thousands of children making trainers in Indonesia will maximise the happiness of consumers in western nations who desire the latest designs. Yet the conditions and pay of the children in Indonesia may not be considered as they are the minority and their happiness is secondary to the pleasure of the consumers and stockholders elsewhere.

A qualitative approach would consider the quality of pleasure gained by the material pleasure experienced by the multi-national companies as a lower pleasure compared to the higher pleasure being deprived from the young workers.

The consequentialist approach may try to justify the scenario by claiming that the pay received by the children in Indonesia is generous compared to other jobs they may end up doing instead. Preference Utilitarians would say that a fair-trade approach would be more Utilitarian and bring more qualitative happiness to all stakeholders, rather than just those gaining material and financial pleasure.

If business practices were fairer to the local economies, then all stakeholders would benefit and a more ethical way of dealing with globalisation would emerge.

If fair-trade ethics were applied, then the Indonesians would have more say in their country's resources (including the raw materials and workforce) and the profit to their economy could be reinforced by the multi-national company's investment in more just and Utilitarian practices.

Virtue ethics

Virtue ethics requires moral agents to develop themselves to become more moral. If business practices were measured along the lines of Aristotle's requirement to pursue and to achieve eudaimonia, then many business techniques could be seen to be more in-line with the vices of deficiency or of excess rather than the virtues.

Profit is always central to business ethics, yet in the 21st century the idea of responsibility to employees, to the environment and to consumers has become a pressing issue for businesses to deal with. Taking an approach that focuses on the agent's own morality, either individual or corporate, is perhaps a unique and relatively novel one in the business world.

The traditional virtues of compassion, courage or pragmatism are not necessarily at the forefront of most business practices, yet implementation of these ideas could provide a good moral basis for ethical business.

If a business venture was planned with the intention of being compassionate and pragmatic towards its workers and other stakeholders, then it would be possible to claim that it was an ethical approach to the project. The idea of sustainable development alongside social and economic considerations could ensure that employees were treated with respect and with an interest in what they do or what they produce.

FOR DEBATE

'Utilitarianism is the perfect way to deal with ethics concerning business practices.' Discuss this referring to act, rule and preference Utilitarianism.

STRETCH & CHALLENGE

If Utilitarianism is applied to all business ethics, there may be a danger of becoming detached from current realities and focusing on long-term business goals. In what ways would it be possible to amalgamate aspects of Kantian approaches with those of Utilitarianism to give a more practical approach to business ethics?

STRETCH & CHALLENGE

Business ethics will have to develop and change in the future, due to the increased rate of globalisation and increasing concern regarding the environment. How could the ideas of virtue ethicists, like MacIntyre or Anscombe, provide a basis for business ethics for the next ten years?

Exam Café

Relax, refresh, result!

Relax and prepare

Hot tips

Rachel

Environmental ethics asks what should be protected? Nothing? Only what benefits humans? Humans and non-human animals? Or everything? The problem is not what answer do you pick, but how do you justify your answer? What has value?

Danielle

I think religion has a huge role to play in both environmental and business ethics. In both areas difficult questions can be answered and the answers justified by looking at what Jesus and the prophets taught.

Will

Business ethics is about how businesses should act towards employees, consumers, shareholders and the environment. It is difficult to see how normative ethics can be applied to this debate, because the purpose of business has to include profit and this seems to produce an unhealthy slant towards unethical actions being justified in the name of money. Either that or I have read too much Marx!!

Refresh your memory

Revision checklist for environmental and business ethics

You should be able to demonstrate knowledge and understanding of:

- The issue of how humans should relate to the environment, its resources and species.
- Secular approaches – the Gaia hypothesis.
- Issues in business ethics: the relationship between business and consumers; the relationship between employers and employees.
- The relationship between business and the environment; business and globalisation.
- The application and the different approaches of the ethical theories (Natural Law, Kantian ethics, Utilitarianism, religious ethics and virtue ethics) to environmental and business ethics.

You should be able to discuss each of these areas critically.

Get the result!

Exam question

'Doing the right thing by stakeholders also benefits stockholders.' Discuss. (35 marks)

Examiner says

This is a good start from Lisa, a clear introduction which defines some of the terms in the question and lays down a simple plan for her argument.

Lisa's answer

In business ethics the debate exists between looking after the interests of the consumers or stakeholders and by doing so improving the company image and increasing profit which benefits the stockholders, or concentrating solely on maximising profits.

Adam Smith (1776) believed that strong competition, limited regulation and a free market economy would encourage entrepreneurs and lead to a stable society with high employment, as long as it was balanced by the natural human feeling of sympathy towards others within their community. He is therefore advocating looking after the interests of both stakeholders and stockholders. However, this does seem to be a rather fictitious view of humans. Do businesses and individuals really have this feeling of sympathy towards each other? Wouldn't a laissez-faire economic system encourage more individualism and less community spirit?

Examiner says

This is a good section from Lisa on Adam Smith. However, it's not clear that she understands all of the terms she has used. Ideally, Lisa needs to answer some of the questions she asks.

Milton Friedman (1970) took most of Adam Smith's ideas but chose to ignore stakeholders in favour of maximising profit. He suggested that supporting the community is not the skill or even desired aims of business, profit was. This view heavily influenced the economic policies of both Reagan and Thatcher in the 1980s despite having its critics. Solomon (1993) suggested that Friedman had an over-simplified view of the aims of business. He suggested that this view would lead to unethical conclusions and advocated aiming for encouraging and rewarding hard work and investment, building better business and serving society. But this falls into the same trap as Smith's view that profit for shareholders overrides the needs of stakeholders.

Examiner says

This section shows a really wide range of knowledge and understanding. It is an excellent example of describing a view point and showing criticisms of it in a single paragraph. What a pity Lisa didn't discuss the more recent ideas of Anthony Weston in order to demonstrate a really good knowledge of this subject.

11

Sexual ethics

If it feels good, then I should just go ahead and do it, right?

In this chapter you will learn about:

- the issues surrounding sexual ethics – premarital and extramarital sex, contraception, homosexuality
- the application and the different approaches of ethical theories to sexual ethics.

Sexual ethics

11.1 Introduction to sexual ethics

In this topic you will learn about the areas that sexual ethics deals with.

Sex is one of those topics that most people have an opinion on, whether it be a liberal approach or a more conservative approach. Words that stimulate positive or negative reactions include controversial topics such as homosexuality, bestiality, masturbation or **trans-sexuality**.

Sexual ethics explores and tackles these issues and more, including marriage, divorce, adultery, cohabitation and contraception. This area of practical ethics seeks to understand what is morally correct and acceptable.

Attitudes towards all of the sexual ethics topics mentioned above have changed a great deal in western societies over the last 50 years. It is now generally acceptable in mainstream western society to be homosexual or to cohabit with someone who you are not married to. However, there are practices that are still viewed as taboo (e.g. trans-sexuality or partner swapping), so perhaps in the future they will become as acceptable as issues such as homosexuality or cohabitation?

Cultural differences play a significant role in understanding about sex and even within societies there are differences of opinion. Religion plays a significant role in our understanding of what the purpose of sex is and also of what is morally acceptable for people to participate in.

Why is there a need for sexual ethics?

It is believed that sexual ethics is important because it involves a natural behaviour that we all display in some way in our lives, whether it be how we relate to our partners, our close friends, our own sexual identities or how we approach issues of sex and relationships.

Reproduction is essential to the continuation of the human race, i.e. if we don't have sex and reproduce, then humanity dies out. We also all have a need for acceptance, love, trust and tenderness. This is generally expressed in a sexual relationship, where two people develop and become 'one flesh'.

There needs to be a morality that seeks to ensure that all people who are involved in areas of sex and relationships are protected and that their rights are ensured. For example, there needs to be an agreement about consent or about protection of minors.

Sexual ethics attempts to look at the areas surrounding sex and relationships and to provide moral discussion about which practices are ethically acceptable and which are not.

KEY WORD

Trans-sexual: someone who was born one gender, but has had surgery to become the opposite sex due to feeling that they were born in the body of the wrong gender.

ACTIVITY

In groups, explore the changes in society's attitudes towards sexual behaviour that have taken place since the 1960s. You could look at these events:

- Abortion Act 1967.
- Sexual Offences Act 1967.
- Sex Discrimination Act 1975.
- Sexual Offences (Amendment) Act 2000.

How have these events affected our rights in society and our perspectives on sexual morality?

STRETCH & CHALLENGE

Why is there a real need for sexual ethics in society? Should it not be left to individuals to make their own decisions? What would be the problems with this approach?

Sexual ethics

11.2 Pre-Christian ideas about sexual ethics

In this topic you will learn about the understanding of sex and relationships in ancient Greece and in the Old Testament.

Sex in the Old Testament

Ancient perspectives on sex are very different in focus to those we experience in this society today. Ancient Greek sexual ethics, for example, clash with modern perspectives, especially in regard to relationships between adults and adolescents. But Greek views on sexuality were not uniform. As in other areas of philosophy, some groups celebrated physical pleasure, such as the Cyrenaics (c. 5th century BCE), and some rejected physical pleasure as a distraction from or obstacle to spiritual or philosophical progress. This separation between the pure pleasures of the mind and the corrupting pleasures of the body was influential, as we will see.

In all ancient societies, fertility was a big concern both in agriculture and in continuation of the species. A man's position and power was measured in the amount of land or property he possessed, and also in the number of offspring that he had. This is a theme seen throughout the Old Testament. Fidelity and monogamy were not valued that highly for men, as their responsibility was to maintain their power and authority. It was not unknown for men in the Ancient Near East to have two or three wives as well as several concubines and probably to have fathered children from all of them. A famous example of this in the Bible is the patriarch Jacob, with his two wives, Leah and Rachel, and his two concubines, Bilbah and Zilpah, who produced a large number of children (only the 12 males are listed).

STRETCH & CHALLENGE

Outline what you believe are the pre-Christian and religious attitudes towards sexual ethics. Would the ideas outlined here and the culture we live in today be compatible? In what ways could our culture today be changed to be more tolerant?

FOR DEBATE

Would polygamy (as outlined opposite for the patriarch Jacob) be an acceptable way to live in the 21st century? Why might it be problematic?

▪ Why do you think that our understanding of sexual ethics is so caught up in our interpretation of the story of Adam and Eve?

The teaching in Genesis is that God created Adam and Eve in his image and part of their purpose was to have sexual relations and to reproduce. It is believed that, prior to the Fall, Adam and Eve had sexual intercourse because it was good in itself; not solely because of sexual desire but because God created them to have sex and to enjoy it.

It is suggested by biblical scholars that the Genesis story provides a basis for good sexual relationships. It is interesting that prior to the Fall Adam and Eve 'walked' with God in the Garden of Eden and that he was part of their life. It is suggested that the relationship between Adam and Eve was one that included God as part of its foundation – this is why in Christian marriage ceremonies God is invited to be the third part of the marriage.

After the emergence of sin into the world the relationship between humanity and God changes in the Genesis story, as does the place of sexual relations between Adam and Eve. The third chapter of Genesis says:

> *To the woman he said 'I will greatly multiply your pain in childbearing; in pain you shall bring forth children, yet your desire shall be for your husband, and he shall rule over you.'*

In this chapter we will explore both positive and negative aspects of sex and relationships. The Genesis account does put forward some downsides:

- Pain of childbirth – consequence of sex.
- Sexual desire – lust and obsession.
- Husband ruling over his wife – sexual dominance.

After the Fall, sex can no longer be intrinsically good in itself, but rather must now have an alternative purpose for humanity to pursue: reproduction. In Genesis, the woman must suffer the consequences for her part in the **Original Sin** and through the curse of childbirth she will make amends, yet still achieve her purpose as a woman to produce children.

The teachings in the Old Testament are not necessarily consistent and seem to be very male-biased and relative to the situation. It would seem that it is acceptable for a man to control or dominate his wife and to insist that she be a virgin prior to their marriage, yet it seems that a man does not necessarily need to be a virgin. These ideas may seem very antiquated in our society, yet in certain circumstances many people would still subconsciously hold them.

There are occasions in the Old Testament where sex is used in ways we now consider to be inappropriate, for example the incestuous relationship between Lot and his daughters (Genesis 19) or the adulterous relationship between King David and Bathsheba which led to the death of her husband, Uriah. This example of adultery is one that David is punished for, yet it provides the path from which the birth of Jesus will eventually come.

One area of sexual ethics that the Old Testament has much to say about – homosexuality – will be explored later in the chapter.

KEY WORDS

Original Sin: the condition that causes all people to be sinful due to the actions of Adam and Eve.

Concordance: an alphabetical index of the principal words in the Bible, with references as to where they can be found in the book.

ACTIVITY

Explore references in the Old Testament that refer to sex. (You may wish to use a **concordance**, follow the link on www.heinemann.co.uk/hotlinks. Enter the express code 3587P.) List them in your folder so that you can refer to some of them in your examination.

FOR DEBATE

'The Old Testament contradicts itself when it comes to sexual morality, therefore its teachings are wrong.' Discuss.

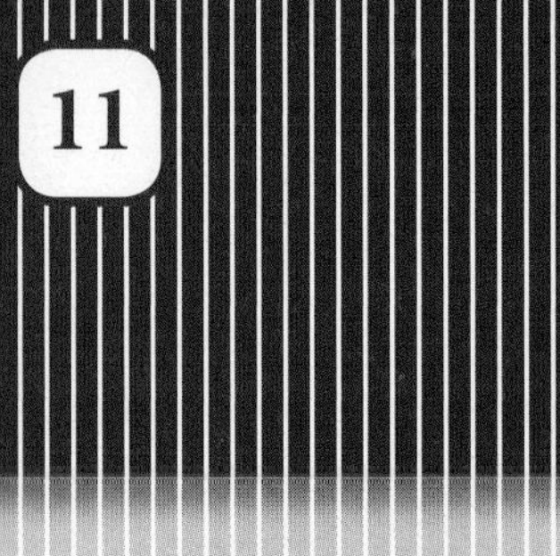

11 Sexual ethics

11.3 New Testament teachings on sex

In this topic you will learn about the teachings in the Christian New Testament referring to sex.

The New Testament

The teachings of Jesus actually say very little about sexual ethics. The principal teaching of Jesus in this area revolves around marriage, divorce and adultery. The Jewish law had very specific guidelines regarding divorce and adultery, mainly that divorce could be instigated only by the husband and that an adulterous woman should be taken out of the city and stoned to death.

Jesus' teachings on the topic of divorce are not entirely clear and are interpreted differently by biblical scholars. It can be read that Jesus allows divorce in certain circumstances and that it is permissible, whilst it can also be interpreted that it is wrong and falls short of the ideal relationship that God intended.

The passage in particular that causes differences in interpretation is Mark 10:11:

> *Whoever divorces his wife and marries another commits adultery against her...*

The interpretation of the word 'and' can also mean 'in order to', therefore we have a difference in how theologians understand Jesus' teaching on divorce. So does Jesus permit remarriage after divorce or is it a definite admonition that adultery occurs if a divorcee remarries and that it is wrong?

ACTIVITY

Look at the biblical story of the adulterous woman in John 8:1–11.

What is Jesus saying here about adultery – is he condoning it?

In groups, write down what you believe Jesus is saying. Then discuss it as a class deciding whether Jesus is saying that adultery should not be condemned or whether he is making a more generalised statement about sin.

How does it relate to Jesus' teaching on divorce?

The principal message of Jesus was one of equality and for all people to be treated in the same way. He also focused on human relationships being centred around their relationship with God, as he explained when he 'summarised' the Ten

Jesus focused on human relationships being centred on their relationship with God. How would this affect a relationship between this couple?

Commandments into the 'Greatest Commandment' – 'Love God with all your heart and love your neighbour as yourself.'

The apostle Paul provides some more perspectives on Christian biblical perspectives on sexual ethics; however, it is important to be aware of the culture in which the text was written. Paul, like most other 1st-century Christians, believed that the second coming of Jesus was sooner rather than later and therefore Christians ought to be more focused on spiritual matters rather than physical matters such as sex.

Now to the unmarried and the widows I say: It is good for them to stay unmarried, as I am. But if they cannot control themselves, they should marry, for it is better to marry than to burn with passion.

1 Corinthians 7:8–9

Paul's appeal that Christians should remain **celibate** unless their desires were too much to resist, at which point they must marry, is now generally believed to be an appeal to wait for Jesus' imminent return rather than a blanket admonition that celibacy is better.

Paul's other principal contribution to the ethics of relationships concerns the role of women within society, the family and more importantly the Church. Many Christians believe that Paul's teachings are very sexist in their treatment of women. He insists that women should be obedient and subject to their husbands and also must not speak in church. Christian feminism has much to say about this and the Christian feminist Jocelyn Burrowes (1941–) believes that Paul's teachings have provided the basis for womankind's oppression within the Christian Church for 2000 years. She even goes as far as claiming his theology is misogynistic and based in fear of equality.

However, some of Paul's other teachings emphasise the same equality that Jesus taught.

There is no longer Jew nor Greek, slave nor free, male nor female; for all are one in Christ Jesus.

Galatians 3:28

For this reason a man leaves his father and mother and is joined to his wife, and the two become one flesh.

Ephesians 5:31

Paul seems to have believed in the equality of men and woman, yet perhaps the cultural and social setting in which he lived, expecting the return of the Messiah, in some way necessitated the more extreme teachings regarding women. It is suggested that Paul was a 'child of his time' and one that struggled with the concept of equality that Jesus taught.

STRETCH & CHALLENGE

If Jesus' teaching about equality were to be followed in relation to sexual ethics, what would be the implications and effects for us in the 21st century?

KEY WORD

Celibate: the state of not being married and not having sexual relations.

FOR DEBATE

'The apostle Paul was a sexist who struggled with Jesus' teaching of equality for women.' Discuss.

STRETCH & CHALLENGE

Look at the teachings of Paul concerning sex, marriage and divorce (many of these are found in 1 Corinthians 7). How would following these guidelines absolutely affect society today in the 21st century?

11

Sexual ethics

11.4 Christian teachings on sex

In this topic you will learn about the beliefs of the Christian Church concerning sex and relationships.

FOR DEBATE

'Celibacy is a better idea for religious people.' Discuss this with reference to the ethical theories that you have studied.

The early Church

The emerging Christian Church emphasised the status and importance of celibacy as a spiritual ideal. This idea of celibacy is still important within parts of the Christian Church: Roman Catholic priests are to be celibate, for example. This idea of celibacy is an ideal for spiritual communion and closeness with God, as modelled by the life of Jesus himself.

St Augustine saw sex as a sin for anything other than reproduction as it removes the focus on spiritual obligations and puts it on to the 'immoral, negative desires of the flesh'. For Augustine, it was a 'necessary evil' that must be pursued to fulfil the commandment in Genesis 'to go forth and multiply', however it was not to be enjoyed. Thomas Aquinas' approach was less negative and appreciated the enjoyment found in the sexual act, yet he still believed that its purpose and intention was to be for reproduction as that was the intrinsic 'telos' (purpose or outcome) of the act.

Roman Catholicism

Although actual pastoral practice may vary, Roman Catholic teachings follow very closely the approach of Aquinas' Natural Law theory. The purpose of sex is purely for reproduction within a committed married relationship and for nothing else. It is for this reason that Roman Catholicism would teach the moral wrongness and inappropriateness of the following acts:

Having sex before marriage is believed to be morally wrong for most Christians, yet many Christians do have sex outside of marriage. Should only married couples have sex? Should sex only be to produce children?

- Premarital and extramarital sex.
- Sex for pleasure.
- Homosexual acts.
- Use of contraception.
- Abortion.
- Masturbation.

MAKING LINKS

Using your notes on Natural Law, and other work that you have done on religious ethics, produce a Roman Catholic approach to the six issues listed opposite.

Roman Catholicism teaches three purposes for marriage: Fides (faithfulness), Proles (reproduction) and Sacramentum (the two becoming one flesh). If an act goes against any of these, then it has no moral basis; the list above illustrates this.

Roman Catholicism also has very stringent teachings on divorce and is more absolutist than other Christian denominations. It follows the principle that divorce is never acceptable because:

- the two have become one flesh in marriage
- the couple have made sacred vows in front of God that cannot be broken.

However, the marriage may be annulled (deemed to have never existed) if the marriage satisfies certain criteria, such as the vows having been made under duress.

Liberal Protestantism

Liberal Protestantism is much more relaxed when it comes to matters of sexual ethics. This interpretation of the biblical teachings is much more allegorical and sees the passages in the Bible providing a basis for good living and giving moral guidance that is not always literal. Liberal Protestants would also take the approach that culture has changed, as have attitudes towards areas of sexuality since the Bible was written. Therefore, Christian teaching must reflect our culture and our times.

For some Christian denominations, being a homosexual Christian is not a moral problem, neither is cohabitation if it is based within a committed secure relationship. During the 20th century Christian attitudes towards sex became more focused on the idea of love being central to its purpose. This move has provided the impetus for changes in liberal Christian approaches to issues of sex and relationships. Rather than requiring marriage for sex, attitudes now hold that if a couple love each other, are committed to the success of the relationship and wish to be together, then it is acceptable to cohabit or to enjoy sexual relations outside of marriage. They would also encourage the enjoyment of sex for pleasure rather than just for reproduction.

Liberal Christians have also accepted the changes in divorce laws. They would generally accept that relationships break down and therefore, in the best interests of all parties, would agree with the concept of divorce.

Evangelical Protestantism

Evangelical Protestants have views that have similarities with both the Roman Catholic approaches and aspects of the Liberal Protestant teachings. They would accept the sanctity of marriage and the permanence of the marriage relationship, however they would appreciate that sometimes divorce is a 'necessary evil' due to irreconcilable differences, for example domestic abuse or adultery. Their approaches are generally more relativist than those of Roman Catholicism, yet stricter than more Liberal Protestants.

Evangelicals teach that sexual intercourse is reserved for within a marriage and not for outside. This is for a number of reasons:

- The Bible teaches that within marriage is where sex should take place.
- Having sex should be for reproducing (although not solely) and children should be born and brought up within a married relationship.
- The two partners become 'one flesh' through sex and marriage.

It is important to note that Evangelicals would be opposed to homosexual sexual relationships as they are not within the confines of marriage and cannot end in the conception of children.

ACTIVITY

Using the list of acts on page 206, write out a list of reasons why Roman Catholicism would believe that each of them is wrong. Then, looking at the religious ethical theories of Natural Law or situation ethics, try to counter some of these reasons.

FOR DEBATE

'Liberal Protestants provide an approach more in-line with Jesus' teachings of equality than Evangelical Protestants.' Discuss this and record arguments for and against the statement.

STRETCH & CHALLENGE

What would be the impact upon society if the Liberal Protestant approach was to be adopted by all Christians?

11

Sexual ethics

11.5 Libertarian attitudes to sex and relationships

In this topic you will learn about secular approaches towards issues surrounding sex and relationships.

It is suggested that, in the 21st century, humans live their lives according to the idea of 'if it feels good, then do it!' Is this necessarily true when we look at the morality of the society that we are living in?

The idea that sex permeates all of our society is based upon a libertarian idea rather than a religious or moralistic one.

Secular morality doesn't insist on marriage, sex for reproduction or heterosexuality. It bases itself on a more **contractarian** approach where, if consent from all those involved is given, then it can be morally acceptable – for example two consenting 17-year-old men entering into a same-sex relationship or two adult couples agreeing to swap partners for sexual intercourse. Within this approach the most important principles are the ability to be **autonomous** and to be free to choose.

The more extreme sexual acts that deny consent from one or more participants (rape or sexual abuse) are not acceptable to libertarian thinkers. Libertarians believe that a child cannot make an informed decision as it is not fully aware of its free will or capable of being autonomous, therefore any sexual act involving children is also morally wrong.

These principles provide a secular ethic that ensures a good, well-reasoned approach to sexual ethics. The actions that all consenting participants take part in can be acceptable as long as free will and autonomy are maintained. John Stuart Mill developed the idea of the **harm principle** – the idea that no harm must come to others. He said that if an action only directly affects the persons involved in doing the action, then society has no right to intervene, even if it is believed that those involved are harming themselves. Therefore I am free to take part in any sexual activity as long as it doesn't cause harm to anyone involved or to a third party. This harm principle is important if two consenting adults wish to begin a sexual relationship, but at least one of them is married. In this case a third party will be hurt and the libertarian approach would say that this is wrong.

For the libertarian, the idea of sexual desire is not intrinsically selfish or sinful, but is a way of bonding two people's desires and providing a positive psychological connection. Sigmund Freud believed that if people have a healthy sexual relationship that benefits both parties, then they are more likely to be better adjusted to their place in society and therefore more balanced psychologically.

KEY WORDS

Contractarian: in relation to sex something is allowed if all concerned parties are in agreement.

Autonomous: not controlled by others or by outside forces.

Harm principle: the idea that the purpose of law should be to stop people from harming others.

FOR DEBATE

Does internet pornography harm anyone? Discuss with reference to libertarian approaches and religious perspectives.

Evaluation of a libertarian approach

The focus on the contractarian approach towards sex is very positive, as it permits consenting adults to practise what they wish to do (in-line with free will, autonomy and the harm principle). It deals with issues such as homosexuality, bisexuality, contraception, divorce, cohabitation, marriage, etc. in a very rational way that permits each situation to be based upon its own merits or demerits. The individuals involved deal with the rightness or wrongness of moral acts and they are morally responsible for their own actions. This tolerant approach values each person as an end in themselves – each participant is involved as an agent in themselves with rights and autonomy.

One of the main criticisms levelled at the libertarian approach is that the balance of power in relationships is not always equal. If one participant is not equal in the relationship, then, even though they choose freely to participate in the sexual act, they may only be limited in their choices because of the imbalance in the relationship.

Feminism and sexual ethics

FOR DEBATE

If a woman is a good moral and honest person and struggles to support her family, one solution could be to turn to prostitution. She chooses to be a prostitute because of circumstances and still maintains her autonomy. Where is the balance in her relationship with her clients? Is it a morally acceptable one?

Feminists would disagree with both traditional religious approaches and libertarian ideas, as they believe that they are fundamentally flawed.

For feminists, religious roles of women as submissive, stay-at-home, child-bearing wives are wrong. Male dominance has caused women to be mistreated, abused, repressed and subservient, therefore women are perceived in this socially constructed role even by themselves. If a woman is a man's property (as sections of the Bible seem to suggest), then he can conceivably do what he likes with her. This role of woman has been reinforced through the centuries and according to feminists like Martha Nussbaum (1947–) is still reinforced by 'our archaic laws and socially inept interpretations of them'.

The libertarian approach displeases many feminists as it presupposes a level playing field for both partners; according to them this is naïve and untrue. They believe that the contractarian idea is worthless due to the social conditioning of women that limits their role in society and culture and, therefore, also affects their sexual 'contracts'.

FOR DEBATE 

'Feminist approaches towards sexual ethics are too reactionary and sexist.' Discuss.

The traditionally believed virtues of women, like intuition, selflessness, gentleness, etc., are according to Nussbaum the reason why women have been suppressed and restricted. She says that these 'virtues' are male-constructed and imposed by men upon women and, as such, many women are unaware that men have disempowered them.

Sexual ethics

11.6 Homosexuality  

In this topic you will explore the ethical issues surrounding homosexuality and Christian perspectives on homosexuality.

KEY WORDS

Queer: a term used to refer to sexual practices that are not heterosexual. It can also include bisexuality (someone who has sexual relations with both males and females), transvesticism (someone who dresses up like a member of the opposite sex) or asexuality (someone who is not sexually interested or active).

Homosexual: a person who has sexual relations with someone of the same sex.

Should people who are gay be afforded the same rights that straight people are given, for example adopting children, sex education or inheritance rights? Many conservative people would say 'no' whilst many liberals would say 'yes'. There are still people who believe that same-sex relationships are unnatural; a famous quip being 'If God had wanted us to be gay, then he would have created Adam and Steve, rather than Adam and Eve'.

Until the late 1960s, in the United Kingdom homosexuality was a criminal offence punishable by time in prison (although this wasn't enforced after 1957) and, until 1992, the United Nations Health Organisation still classed it as a mental/psychiatric disorder. The stigma that still goes with being orientated to same-sex or **queer** relationships remains into the 21st century in most social orders within society.

Why would this image be so uncomfortable for some people? Is it because of the naked bodies? Or is it our own innate prejudices, discomforts or insecurities?

FOR DEBATE 

'Homosexuals are okay – as long as they don't show affection or intimacy in public.' Discuss.

Christianity and homosexuality

Most traditional Christian teachings are against the **homosexual** act, as they interpret extracts from the Bible as forbidding it. For example, 'You shall not lie with a man as with a woman: that is an abomination' (Leviticus 18:22). The apostle Paul also condemns 'unnatural relations…men committing shameless acts with men' (Romans 1:27). Using these examples of biblical passages and others, Christian teaching has been to condemn same-sex relations as wrong and as sinful. As mentioned earlier, psychology in the past had diagnosed it as a mental disorder that needed curing and, in the same way, traditional Christian teaching has attempted to 'cure' people of this disorder.

Protestant approaches

The working principle within many of the Protestant churches has been 'to love the sinner and hate the sin' – they would see the practice of the homosexual acts to be wrong and sinful, but that the people who are homosexual are still 'individuals of sacred worth' (United Methodist Church, 1996). The belief is that unnatural relations, like homosexual sex, are incompatible with the teachings of the Bible.

Roman Catholic perspectives

Roman Catholicism says that there is no sin in having a sexual inclination towards someone who is the same sex, however, to then act upon this inclination would be wrong. They would see that the inclination towards homosexuality as a trial that was not freely chosen, however the person involved must not act upon these desires but instead commit themselves to **chastity** and celibacy.

The principal reasons why the act is considered immoral for the Roman Catholics is that the Bible prohibits it and also that it does not enable a child to be produced by the act (remember the purpose of sex for Catholics is to reproduce).

Liberal approach

Other more liberal approaches within Christianity would say that homosexuality is not a major moral issue. If it is a committed, monogamous and high-quality relationship, then it is to be valued as highly as a **heterosexual** partnership. If the Bible teaches that all humans were 'made in the likeness of God', then God created people as straight or as gay. Therefore they must be good, as all that God created is good.

Evaluation of Christian approaches to homosexuality

Christian approaches to homosexuality are varied and also contradictory to each other. If the Bible is interpreted literally, then homosexuality is completely wrong as it goes against specific teachings that say that it is 'unnatural' or an 'abomination'. However, by taking this approach, it would also then be essential that other verses of the Bible be taken as literally, e.g. adulterers should be stoned, wearing two different types of material is wrong, and so on.

It is definitely an issue that must be dealt with by the 21st-century Church if it is to be an organisation that aims to be relevant to all people. The liberal approach may seem the most appealing to non-religious groups, however, does it satisfy the moral imperatives that are found elsewhere in the Bible? Clergy from various denominations, liberal and evangelical, believe that this is the issue that will be the focus of great debate and possibly even split the Christian Church within the next ten years. If the teachings of Jesus to 'love your neighbour as yourself' or 'do to others as you would like done to you' are followed, then possibly the Christian churches will need to revaluate their approach and their position on homosexuality.

KEY WORDS

Chastity: being virtuous in relation to sex and celibacy.

Heterosexual: someone who has sexual relations with a person of the opposite sex.

FOR DEBATE

Cardinal Glemp's (1929–) claim that homosexuals are 'backyard mongrels' and the belief of Pope Benedict XVI (1927–) that their practices can seriously threaten the well-being of others are strongly controversial. However, from a biblical perspective, are they not just voicing what the religious teachings suggest?

STRETCH & CHALLENGE

If Christian homosexuals were permitted to have sex, adopt children and be in Church leadership, would this undermine the basis and integrity of the Christian faith and Church?

Sexual ethics

11.7 Premarital and extramarital sex  

In this topic you will explore ethical perspectives on sexual intercourse before marriage and also issues surrounding adultery.

For philosophers, it is very difficult to give a precise perspective of what morally is correct or incorrect without approaching it from either a relative or absolutist perspective. These two issues need to be explored from both perspectives and placed in a proper context.

STRETCH & CHALLENGE

What are the potential cultural, psychological and sociological outcomes if premarital sex is universalised?

Premarital sex

For many people, this subject is one that has become blurred in recent years, due mostly to the changes in social and cultural attitudes in the last 30 or 40 years. Phrases such as 'living in sin' don't have the same impact or meaning for western societies that they did in the latter part of the 20th century, yet they still provide an insight into religious attitudes and more conservative perspectives on sexual ethics.

The crux of the issue would seem to rest on whether sex should only take place within a marriage relationship or whether there are other factors that are more pertinent. It is important to look at the differing approaches to this topic:

- Traditional Christian approaches.
- Liberal Christian approaches.
- Secular approaches.

Traditional Christian perspectives

The principle teachings of the Bible suggest that sex is for married couples only and also reserved solely for heterosexual relationships. Paul's teachings in Corinthians do not mention the possibility of same-sex marriage relationships but emphasise the role of men and women as complimentary.

Roman Catholicism teaches that the joy and purpose of sex is to be found within the bonds of marriage and not outside of them. Having sexual intercourse is part of the promise and commandment of God as found in Genesis.

FOR DEBATE 

'Sex before marriage will only ruin the intimacy and bond that occurs after marriage.' Discuss.

Conservative Protestants have similar beliefs to Roman Catholics and emphasise the security that marriage brings in ensuring that the consequences of sex (pleasure or procreation) are morally acceptable.

Liberal Christian perspectives

More liberal Christians would encourage people to marry before having sex; however, they realise that emotions and desires sometimes get the better of us. If the relationship is committed and strong, then some Christians

wouldn't condemn premarital sex if the intent is not to be promiscuous or to undermine the unity that sex can provide. This approach is not one that is explicitly supported by biblical teaching; however, it is one that ensures that the principles of a sexual relationship as outlined by the Bible are met.

Secular approaches

Many secular perspectives do not see any reason why sex must be reserved for within the marriage state. They would believe that sex is an individual couple's decision that does not require an institution such as marriage to authorise or validate. To many people, marriage is no longer required for a number of reasons:

- Women are no longer reliant on men for financial security.
- Legal rights that were only given to married couples in the past are now available to cohabiting couples and to **civil partnerships**.
- There is no longer the social stigma that once attached itself to children whose parents were not married (i.e. the label 'bastard').

Extramarital sex

Extramarital sex means **adultery**. The social understanding of adultery is one that is still a taboo subject of sorts. We publicly would seem to denounce it, yet privately we are more likely to accept it as a fact of life. In legal terms, adultery is still one of the primary reasons for suing someone for divorce, under the heading of 'irreconcilable differences'. Therefore it is an issue today as much as it has been throughout history.

Biblical teachings are specific and say that adultery is wrong and can be punished by death (Old Testament), yet, in a famous encounter with an adulterous woman who was about to be stoned to death, Jesus intervened and saved her life.

One of the basic teachings of the Bible says that 'Thou shall not commit adultery', therefore there must be a moral or ethical reason why it is forbidden. Christian teaching emphasises the bond of marriage as a sacred union that has been joined together by God and within that union sex may take place and be acceptable. If someone who is married has sex with someone other than their marriage partner, then they are betraying those vows and the union of marriage.

Some Christians view people who divorce and remarry as having an adulterous relationship because they made sacred vows to their first spouse and now they are having sexual relations with another person. They see the joining of two people as a permanent arrangement that cannot be broken by anything except death.

Extramarital sex is divisive and is very much viewed in a negative light by most societies. Even by most participants in adultery it is clandestine and seen as deceitful and almost 'dangerous'. As marriage is based on trust, having sex outside of marriage betrays and makes a mockery of that trust.

KEY WORDS

Civil partnership: a legal union between two people of the same sex that has the same role as marriage.

Adultery: having sexual relations with someone other than your marriage partner.

FOR DEBATE

'Couples who don't have sex before marriage should then only have sex to have babies.' Discuss.

ACTIVITY

In groups, list reasons why adultery is morally wrong (include religious, social and psychological reasons).

Discuss why adultery may not be morally wrong, but instead have some other purpose.

Refer to teachings from religious texts and also from the laws of society.

Sexual ethics

11.8 Contraception 

In this topic you will explore religious and secular perspectives on contraception.

KEY WORDS

Contraception: methods used to prevent or reduce the chance of sexual acts leading to pregnancy.

STI: Sexually transmitted infection.

We believe that the use of any contraception is wrong because it interferes with the primary purpose of having sex, which is to reproduce. Our teachings are based on the Bible's approach, which can be found in Genesis when God told us to be fruitful and multiply. We also believe that all sex should be unprotected because the only reason to have sex is to reproduce. Some Roman Catholics allow women to have sex during their infertile time when they cannot get pregnant. They believe that this is a natural break provided by God and this is a natural form of contraception called the Rhythm Method.

We used to believe that having sex using a condom or other sort of contraception was just a way for people to be promiscuous or to be irresponsible. It also was thought that it took away the gift of sex that should be reserved for within a marriage commitment. Our perspective now is that sex can be for reproduction, but that it also unifies the couple as well, therefore contraception can be used so that unplanned children are not born. The use of contraception can help to preserve a marriage, but also, if used responsibly, it can enhance the loving intimacy between a married couple.

FOR DEBATE

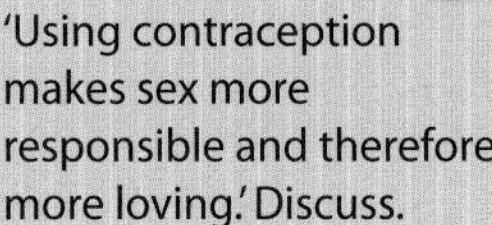

'Using contraception makes sex more responsible and therefore more loving.' Discuss.

For too long men have dominated women and one way in which they have done this was by the use of contraception. They have relied on us to stop the pregnancy through the contraceptive pill, the intra-uterine device or the diaphragm. Men must respect us as valuable in ourselves and make sex less about them and more about equality.

STRETCH & CHALLENGE

Investigate the variety of types of contraception available. Why are some more morally acceptable than others?

Contraception enables me to have control of my own life and to share it fully with my partner. I want to know that I am safe from STIs and also that we don't have an unplanned pregnancy. We both exercise our free will when we have sex and therefore we know we have the right and ability to choose.

In my country of China in 1983, I was forced to have an IUD (intra-uterine device) inserted after my first child was born so that I wouldn't add to the population here by having a second child. I wanted more children, but when I became pregnant again my baby was aborted and my husband was sterilised.

My daughter suffers from a form of mental retardation and has psychotic episodes. She became sexually active at the age of 14 and I was worried about the health of any child that she had if she became pregnant. I spoke to the local health authority and they agreed to inject her with a contraceptive drug to stop her getting pregnant. She turns 18 next month and our next step is to ensure she is sterilised to protect her from actions that would cause her and any child that was born from suffering.

ACTIVITY

Look at the four examples on this page. List reasons why they cause moral problems and controversy. How could they be resolved without people going against their religion or social responsibility? Apply ethical approaches to them.

Roman Catholic prohibition of any contraception is not helping the population crisis in Africa that has been caused by more children surviving beyond infancy due to better health care. It has also meant that many people in Africa are now dying of AIDS because they had unprotected sex or were born from parents with the disease.

ACTIVITY

Apply the ethical theories and approaches that you have studied for this course (moral relativism, Natural Law, virtue ethics, Utilitarianism, Kantian ethics, free will and determinism and conscience) to the issue of contraception.

I had sex last night with my boyfriend without contraception. If I take the morning after pill to prevent pregnancy, my church youth leader has told me that it's a form of abortion and therefore I'm murdering a human life.

FOR DEBATE

'Roman Catholic teachings on contraception are partially responsible for the high spread of HIV in Africa and Asia.' Discuss.

11.9 Ethical approaches to sexual ethics

In this topic you will explore the following ethical approaches to sexual ethics: Natural Law, Utilitarian and the approach of Kant.

Natural Law approach

The principal teachings of Thomas Aquinas' Natural Law state that everything works towards becoming good and achieving its telos. The principal teachings of Roman Catholicism are based upon Aquinas' teachings and, therefore, the perspective of Natural Law towards sex and relationships will be generally the same as Roman Catholicism.

The purpose of sex according to Natural Law is to procreate: that is what genitalia are designed for. Therefore, sex for any other reason apart from procreation is morally wrong. Aquinas does allow for enjoyment during sex, but only if the intention of the act of sex is to produce a child.

Aquinas' approach also insists upon people being married before having sex according to Christian teaching found in the Bible. If marriage is required before sexual intercourse takes place and the purpose of sex is to produce children, this raises some areas of concern within sexual ethics:

- Contraception stops a child being conceived.
- Homosexuality can never result in a child being produced and involves unmarried people having sex.
- Infertile couples should not have sex.
- Sex cannot be for pleasure alone.
- Masturbation cannot result in a child.

STRETCH & CHALLENGE

The use of contraception isn't only to stop the conception of a child. More importantly in the 21st century, it is used to stop the spread of STIs. How could the Natural Law approach be used or developed to deal with this more pertinent issue?

FOR DEBATE

'If the only reason for having sex is to reproduce, then why is it so pleasurable?' Discuss with reference to Natural Law teachings, the teachings of the Roman Catholic Church and the teachings from the Bible.

Why are two parents of the same sex not believed to be as competent as two parents of the opposite sex? Does this perspective have any basis in fact or is it solely based on forms of prejudice?

Utilitarian perspectives

Many people believe that the Utilitarian approach would provide a very good and straightforward way to look at sexual ethics, based around its principle of 'the greatest pleasure for the greatest number of people'. To a certain extent, this approach focuses on the amount of pleasure that an action can bring and, in relation to sex, this could be seen to support having sex purely for pleasure.

The Utilitarian approach to sex can be seen to be very libertarian in outlook by allowing people to do whatever they choose according to the principles of contractarianism (the idea of free will and autonomy) and also in line with the harm principle. However, it is very important to emphasise that Utilitarianism seeks to ensure the greatest utility in every choice made.

John Stuart Mill's (1806–73) development of Utilitarianism emphasised the quality of the pleasure achieved rather than just the quantity. His perspectives on sexual ethics are likely to be more just than those of Jeremy Bentham and, therefore, be more applicable to modern interpretations. Mill emphasised the idea of liberty and freedom to express yourself as you believe that you ought to, again in line within contractarianism and the harm principle. Utilitarianism would be a tolerant approach to alternative sexual expressions such as homosexuality and trans-sexuality. However, if either of these became the norm in society, it would not bring the greatest good for the greatest number, i.e. the continuation of the human race would not be possible.

ACTIVITY

Use the teachings of Mill and Bentham (and any other Utilitarian approaches that you have studied) and produce a table listing all the different issues of sexual ethics. Outline how each approach or proponent would deal with each issue.

A Kantian approach

Generally the approach of Immanuel Kant can be seen as conservative in relation to issues of sex. He would perceive all moral actions to be dictated by our duty and in-line with his categorical imperative. If we consider the first maxim of the categorical imperative, an action should only be performed if it can be universalised, e.g. have sex for pleasure only if you believe everybody else should only have sex for pleasure, or use contraception only if you believe everybody else should use contraception. In some ways this would almost seem to rule out many actions concerning sex, as they cannot be universalised and applicable to everyone in the same way.

Kant also believed that it was not permissible to use people as a means to an end. So, if you desire and lust after someone, you are using that person as a means for your satisfaction rather than as an end in themselves. Kant would seem to be saying that sexual acts are wrong if they involve using another person for one's own pleasure.

Kant would believe that marriage is the only circumstance in which sex should take place, as theoretically neither party would be using or abusing the other in a relationship based on common trust. Within marriage this approach would say that enjoyment of sex is permissible as long as both partners are treated as equals and no coercion takes place.

Kant proposes a contractual approach towards sexual ethics; that is, if both parties are consenting, then it can be acceptable as long as it doesn't go against the categorical imperative. From the principles of Kant, it is also possible to suggest that prostitution could be morally acceptable as long as both sides have fully consented and are not used as a means to an end. However, Kant would say that the use of pornography is morally unacceptable because you are using people as a means for your own sexual gratification.

FOR DEBATE

'Kant's approach to sexual ethics provides a good basis for ensuring the protection and rights of all those involved.' Discuss.

Sexual ethics

11.10 Ethical approaches to sexual ethics (2)

In this topic you will explore the following ethical approaches to sexual ethics: relativist, situation and virtue ethics and the approach of Christianity.

Relativist approaches

Cultural relativism would suggest that we ought to conform to the expectations of the culture in which we find ourselves. This can produce problems if we have a moral objection to some of the practices that we believe may undermine human freedom: e.g. arranged marriages and female circumcision for some, promiscuous lifestyles and public displays of sexuality for others.

Arranged marriages are standard in some cultures, but not in all. What are the principal concerns of western thinkers about them?

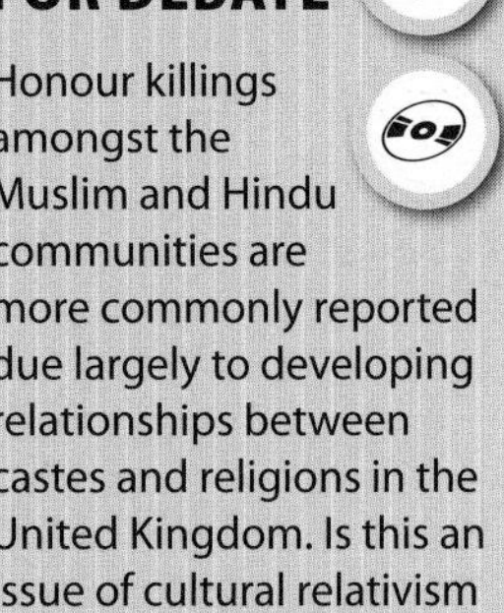

FOR DEBATE

Honour killings amongst the Muslim and Hindu communities are more commonly reported due largely to developing relationships between castes and religions in the United Kingdom. Is this an issue of cultural relativism or something that is absolutely morally wrong?

Situation ethics

Joseph Fletcher's situation ethics is based around the principle of agape and doing what is the most loving thing in moral situations. Agape is not an emotional type of love, but a love that seeks to put what is best for other people first and, therefore, provides a good approach to understanding the ethics surrounding sex.

Fletcher's ideas are not traditional Christian teachings based on absolute rules, but rather that each situation is individual and must serve the purpose of love (agape). This approach to ethics seeks to value people as important in themselves and to fulfil their purpose.

As situation ethics encourages people to act out of love, it would seem that the only thing that it would not want to condone is sex merely for enjoyment without a loving commitment. Therefore, casual sex would be seen as morally wrong as it is based on lust rather than love.

Absolute laws for Fletcher can be set aside in order to show the most love, even if it means ignoring the law. For example, if a promiscuous 12-year-old girl becomes pregnant, for some the most loving thing might be for her parents to arrange an abortion and to provide her with contraception to prevent the situation arising again.

This ethical approach is teleological, relativist and Christian and provides an alternative religious approach to that of Natural Law, which is mostly deontological, Christian and absolutist.

STRETCH & CHALLENGE

For many people, situation ethics seems like the most useful and practically applicable ethical approach to sexual ethics. What are the dangers of adopting this theory in relation to sexual ethics?

Christian ethics

The Christian ethical approach to issues of sex and relationships is primarily based upon the teachings of the Bible and of the Church.

Roman Catholics would value the authority of the Bible and the interpretation of it by the Church fathers, including the Pope. The principle behind not allowing the use of contraception is that it goes against one of Thomas Aquinas' primary precepts, to reproduce. Catholicism teaches that every sperm and every egg is sacred and a potential life. Therefore, to prevent it achieving its telos is morally wrong. This has proved controversial in sub-Saharan Africa where AIDS is at epidemic levels, spread rapidly via unprotected sex.

Evangelical Christians value the Bible as the ultimate authority in moral matters and use the teachings of the Church and their interpretation of the Bible as a means to understand what they ought to do. Many Christians would believe that sex should be reserved for marriage and that it is only possible to have a proper relationship within it. Sex is a unifying act that brings two people together in the eyes of God and that children should only be born into this secure setting.

Liberal Christians value the Bible as a guide in moral matters and would interpret teachings in the context of modern life. For example, the Bible's prohibition of homosexuality may be seen as specific to the time it was written and not as applicable to modern society, as many same-sex relationships can be just as committed as heterosexual ones. Fletcher's situation ethics would consider a same-sex relationship as morally acceptable if love and commitment are evidenced.

Some Christians would rely on the guidance of their consciences in making decisions concerning sexual issues, believing that their consciences are given to them by God to enable them to make moral and ethical decisions.

ACTIVITY

Look back at the work you did on conscience and apply the principles of conscience to the issues raised by the ethics of sex and relationships. Remember to include religious as well as secular and psychological approaches to conscience.

STRETCH & CHALLENGE

Using the teachings of Christian ethics, situation ethics and Natural Law, explore the differences in morality between differing Christian approaches to the issues listed on page 206. Do any of them provide an adequate approach to the issues?

Virtue ethics

Virtue ethics does not focus on what the right or wrong action in a situation might be, but rather will focus on the moral development of a person through their actions.

In relation to sexual ethics, this theory would seek to find out how a person can develop virtuously through sex. Central issues in virtue ethics include ideas of love, friendship, companionship, faithfulness, commitment and trust. Therefore, by developing sexual intimacy and investing in another person, we are in fact becoming more virtuous. Being generous with the gift of oneself rather than using a partner as a means of sexual gratification could be seen as virtuous, for example.

It would seem that a virtue ethics approach towards issues of sex and relationships is likely to be more tolerant towards some alternate sexual activities, due largely to its basis on self-development through the ideals of virtue listed above, e.g. love and trust. If people develop virtuously, then it can be acceptable and not necessarily involve prohibiting certain acts or approaches.

FOR DEBATE

Why might a virtue ethics approach to sex and relationships be seen as controversial and dangerous?

Exam**Café**

Relax, refresh, result!

Relax and prepare

Hot tips

Lisa

I found it really difficult discussing the ethics of homosexuality because I found that I brought too many of my own prejudices into my arguments. I could not find evidence to support my arguments unless I looked in the Bible, and those views seemed to be so out of date. I also started to consider the idea of human freedom and autonomy in a different way. If wanted the freedom to choose my sexual partners, why should I stop others from having the same freedom!!?

Will

Premarital sex does not seem like a contemporary issue but it starts you thinking about what sex is and what it's for. It makes you think about how sex is used in the media and how this media is targeted towards teenagers, and then it opens up a whole range of issues I had not even considered, not least of which was the whole marriage thing.

Danielle

Contraception is such a huge issue for teenagers today, I am glad we studied it in this context because it made me think about it in a different way. I used to think only about sexually transmitted diseases, but I ended up focusing on the procreative element of sex and whether it was right to interfere with that.

Refresh your memory

Revision checklist for sexual ethics

- You will need to make sure you are able to demonstrate knowledge and understanding of the issues surrounding sexual ethics. You will need to know about premarital and extramarital sex, contraception and homosexuality.
- You will also need to be able to apply Natural Law, Kantian ethics, Utilitarianism, religious ethics and virtue ethics to the issues surrounding sexual ethics.
- You should also be able to discuss all of these areas critically.

Get the result!

Sample answers

Exam question

Critically assess the view that Natural Law is of no use when discussing sexual ethics. (35 marks)

Read the abridged essay below and decide for yourself whether it is a good answer. Is there anything you would improve or add?

Callum's answer

St Thomas Aquinas did not prove a convincing ethical theory and it is of little or no use when discussing sexual ethics.

This is because Aquinas suggests that we should use our reason to determine how to act. In this case reason would suggest that anything which is not in agreement with the observable laws of nature should not be ethically correct. Aquinas believed that everything had a purpose and that purpose could be reasoned by observing the laws of nature. For example, the sexual organs when observed in nature are for reproduction and therefore are only right if used for that purpose.

This could mean that sexual acts that do not end in reproduction would be seen to be wrong. Natural Law would therefore object to homosexuality, masturbation and anal sex as none of these sex acts would end in reproduction.

However, this creates a real problem because this would also mean that infertile couples should not have sex as they would not reproduce. It might also mean that if a woman was raped and the end result was a pregnancy, then this would be an ethically correct act.

Therefore, Natural Law is of no use when discussing sexual ethics.

Examiner says

This is the general line of argument for most candidates with a question such as this. It is quite general and fails to give, firstly, a good explanation of Natural Law and, secondly, Callum does not adequately explain the ethical wrongness of certain sex acts beyond the general comment of going against the laws of nature. Callum's comment that Natural Law would permit a rape if it resulted in pregnancy is incorrect. Natural Law would not allow any action which would harm another. Finally, Natural Law does not object to infertile couples having sexual intercourse. Although wrong, it shows that Callum has tried to apply the primary precepts to different situations he may have studied.

Glossary

Adultery: having sexual relations with someone other than your marriage partner.

Agent-centred: ethical approaches that are focused on the development of the person rather than on the morality of what they are doing.

Akhira: literally, the hereafter, everlasting life after death.

Analogy: an approach to religious language that compares the normal use of a word to its religious use. To say God is good means a similar thing as saying that John is good.

Analytic statements: statements that are true by definition, e.g. 1+1=2.

Anthropocentric: belief that humanity is central and more important.

Anthropomorphism: conception of God as having the form, personality or attributes of man.

Arbitrary: an action based on random choice.

Atman: a word used to describe the soul or 'principle of life'. All forms of life have atman.

Authoritarian conscience: conscience that is imposed by authority figures and uses guilt to control them.

Autonomous morality: when someone is less reliant on the moral authority of people around them and is able to develop their own perspectives (usually after the age of ten years old).

Autonomous: not controlled by others or by outside forces.

Beatific vision: the immediate sight and vision of God in heaven.

Blik: Hare's term for a basic belief that is not altered despite empirical evidence.

Boo-Hurrah Theory: another name for emotivism.

Bourgeoisie: the middle-class industrial owners who have the proletariat working for them.

Brahman: God or the absolute in Hinduism.

Calvinism: theological system named after John Calvin (1509–64) which emphasised grace, faith and predestination.

Celibate: the state of not being married and not having sexual relations.

Chastity: being virtuous in relation to sex and celibacy.

Civil partnership: a legal union between two people of the same sex that has the same role as marriage.

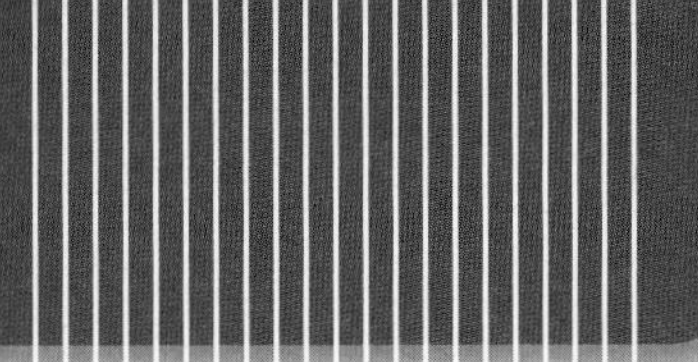

Cognitive: a statement that is subject to being either true or false. For example, 'the cat is asleep on the chair'.

Concordance: an alphabetical index of the principal words in the Bible, with references as to where they can be found in the book.

Conscientia: using the principles of synderesis, this is the ethical judgement which leads to a specific action.

Conservationism (shallow ecology): the theory that the environment's importance is related to its usefulness for humanity.

Contraception: methods used to prevent or reduce the chance of sexual acts leading to pregnancy.

Contractarian: in relation to sex something is allowed if all concerned parties are in agreement.

Convert: to change in form, character or function. To cause a person to change beliefs.

Corporate experiences: used to describe religious experiences that happen to a number of people at once in the same location.

Covenant: a binding agreement. In theology it describes the agreements made between God and humans. Jesus is seen as bringing in a new covenant.

Creation spirituality: a religious approach that emphasises that humankind is part of creation and that God can be found in all his creation.

Deep ecology/libertarianism: the belief that all life forms have intrinsic value.

Deism: the belief that God creates the world but is then separate and uninvolved in its continuing affairs.

Demythologising: the process of removing the elements of the biblical accounts that are purely 1st-century myth in order to discover the essential message of Jesus.

Determinism: the idea that all actions are governed by laws outside of our control.

Disembodied existence: literally the idea that we are able to exist in some form without our bodies.

Doctrine of the mean: the desirable middle between two extremes, one of excess and the other of deficiency.

Dominion: belief that God has given humankind authority over the Earth and all its animals and plants.

Dualism: the idea that there are two aspects to human beings, the physical and the mental. The mental may be identified with the soul.

Ecological extension (eco-holism): the belief that all ecosystems and living things are interdependent.

Ecosophy: the idea that all living things, whether humans, animals or plants, have rights.

Ego: part of the personality that experiences and reacts to the world, as well as mediating between the drives of the id and the superego.

Emotivism: the idea that the meaning of ethical language is not knowable as its use is only an expression of emotion.

Empirical evidence: information that is gained using sensory data (i.e. what we see, smell, hear, taste and touch).

Empiricism: the idea that observations via our senses lead us to understanding the world.

Equivocal: the same word is used with two completely different meanings. The word 'cricket' could describe an insect or a game.

Eschatology: literally the study of 'the last things' or end times.

Eudaimonia: a contented state of being happy, healthy and prosperous.

Everlasting: the belief that God moves through time along with creation but has no beginning or end.

Falsification principle: a principle for assessing whether statements are genuine scientific assertions by considering whether any evidence could ever disprove them.

Fideism: the belief that faith is more important than reason. Beliefs cannot be subjected to rational analysis.

Foreknowledge: the knowledge of what will happen in the future.

Form criticism: a theological movement that analysed biblical texts in order to discover what form they were originally used in.

Free will: the ability to make free, unhindered choices.

Gaia hypothesis: the hypothesis that suggests that the world's physical properties and the biosphere join together to form a complex interacting system.

Gaia: the idea of Gaia comes from the name of the Greek goddess of the Earth, who was believed to be intrinsically part of the planet.

General revelation: revelation of God available to all people at all times.

Globalisation: the integration of economies, cultures, governmental policies and political movements around the world.

Gnostic: religious groups in the 1st and 2nd centuries after Jesus who claimed to have secret knowledge of God and salvation.

Hard determinism: the teaching that denies that humanity has free will and believes that all actions have a prior cause. It removes moral responsibility for actions.

Harm principle: that idea that the purpose of law should be to stop people from harming others.

Heteronymous morality: occurs when the conscience is immature and the consequences of the actions determine whether it is right or wrong (usually between the ages of five and ten years old).

Homosexual: a person who has sexual relations with someone of the same sex.

Humanistic conscience: conscience that focuses on achieving our potential by evaluating our behaviour.

Id: part of the unconscious personality that is driven by impulses to seek pleasure and satisfaction.

Immanent: the idea that God is active and closely involved in the world.

Immutable: the idea that God cannot change.

Ineffable: the idea that an experience cannot be properly described.

Instrumental value: belief that something is only valuable because of its importance to something else.

Intrinsic value: belief that something is valuable in itself.

Intuitionism: a theory that ethical and moral truths are known and understood by our intuition.

Karma: the principle of actions, deeds and effects, that our actions in this life affect the next. Regarded as a law of the universe.

LEDC: less economically developed country.

Libertarianism (incompatibilism): this theory claims that we are morally responsible for all our actions and are free to make choices.

Logical positivism: a movement in philosophy that believed that the aim of philosophers should be the analysis of language, particularly the language of science.

Materialism: the idea that human beings consist of physical matter alone.

Maya: the illusion or the unreal world of separate consciousnesses.

MEDC: more economically developed country.

Meta-ethics: the area of ethics that seeks to explore and discover the meaning of words used in ethical statements.

Metaphysics: literally meaning 'above or beyond physics' invloves questions concerning being and ultimate reality.

Micro-ethics: this deals with the smaller details that constitute an ethical approach.

Middle knowledge: the idea that God knows all the possibilities of what would happen in different scenarios.

Moksha: literally meaning 'release' or 'liberation'. In Hinduism this refers to the final escape from the continuous cycle of death and rebirth, which is known as Samsara.

Monism: the idea that human beings are made up of one substance, the word is often used synonymously with materialism.

Monotheistic: the belief in the existence of one God, for instance in Judaism, Christianity and Islam.

Mystical experiences: used to describe experience of direct contact or oneness with God or ultimate reality.

Naturalism: the belief that suggests that all things are knowable (provable) using empirical evidence.

Naturalistic fallacy: claims that good cannot be defined and that attempting to provide ethical conclusions from natural facts is wrong.

Noetic: the idea that an experience imparts or reveals knowledge.

Non-cognitive: a statement that is not subject to truth or falsity. For example, 'hurray' or 'ouch'.

Non-naturalism: the belief that all things to do with meaning are knowable using intuition rather than empirical evidence.

Non-propositional revelation: the idea that God does not reveal facts or information during the process of revelation. God makes himself known during the experience.

Normative ethics: the area of ethics that attempts to discuss whether something is right or wrong, good or bad.

Numinous experiences: used to describe experiences of awe and wonder in the presence of God.

Original Sin: the condition that causes all people to be sinful due to the actions of Adam and Eve.

Paradox: a situation where two contradictory statements both appear true.

Partisan: a strong supporter of a certain party or group, often in times of war.

Pluralism: the idea in religion that truth is to be found in many faiths.

Pragmatism: an account of truth that states that the truth is not a fixed thing but is whatever has value or works for us.

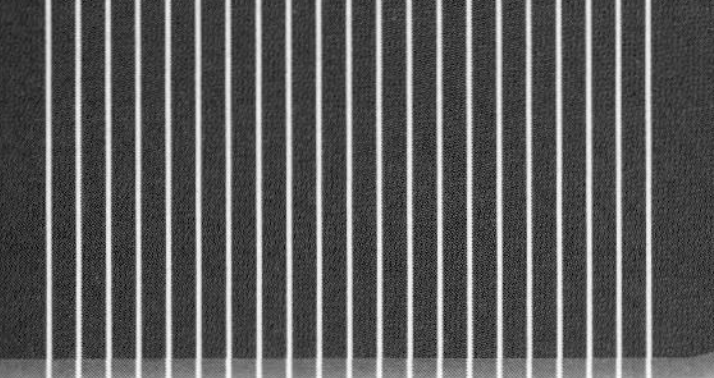

Predestination: also known as theological determinism. This is the belief that God already knew before all time began who would be 'saved' and go to heaven. Therefore there is no choice.

Prescriptivism: the idea that the meaning of ethical language is not knowable as it is a manner of prescribing a subjective belief or course of action.

Prima facie duties: this translates as 'at first appearance'. It means these duties are the primary ones.

Process theology: a reformulation of the concept of God which rejects the immutability of God and teaches that God is also in the process of becoming and change.

Proletariat: the workers and lower wage earners who depend on the bourgeoisie for employment.

Propositional revelation: the idea that the process of revelation involves God revealing facts or information.

Providence: God's goodness and continuing activity on behalf of his creation.

Purgatory: a state or place where souls are purged or purified before entering heaven.

Queer: a term used to refer to sexual practices that are not heterosexual. It can also include bisexuality (someone who has sexual relations with both males and females), transvesticism (someone who dresses up like a member of the opposite sex) or asexuality (someone who is not sexually interested or active).

Reincarnation: the belief that after death, our soul lives again in another embodied form.

Replica theory: the name given to John Hick's theory that God can recreate an exact copy of us in the Afterlife.

Resurrection: the belief in an Afterlife that involves the embodied existence of individuals.

Revelation: the act of God revealing himself or knowledge about himself and his will to human beings.

Social responsibility: a belief that businesses have a responsibility towards society as well as their own interests.

Soft determinism (compatibilism): the teaching that says we can be both determined and free, as some of our moral choices are free but aspects of our nature are determined.

Special revelation: revelation of God to specific people at specific times.

Speciesist: discrimination in favour of one species, usually the human species, over another.

Stakeholders: those people who own the company, and also its employees, its consumers and the wider community.

Stewardship: belief that God has given humanity responsibility to care and look after the planet.

STI: sexually transmitted infection.

Superego: part of the personality that seeks to censor and restrain the ego. Often associated with feelings of guilt.

Symbiosis: the mutually beneficial relationship between two things, where they are dependent on each other.

Synderesis: the innate 'right reason' that gives knowledge of the basic principles of morality.

Synthetic statements: statements in which the predicate is not a necessary part of the description, e.g. 'The mermaid has a large comb.'

Tautology: a logical statement that we can know to be truth by definition.

Timeless: the belief that God stands outside of time and that all time is equally present to him.

Traducianism: an early Christian teaching that souls were passed down from parents rather than uniquely implanted by God.

Transmigration: a word used of the soul's passage or journey to another body after death.

Trans-sexual: someone who was born one gender, but has had surgery to become the opposite sex due to feeling that they were born in the body of the wrong gender.

Universalism: the belief that all people will ultimately achieve salvation.

Univocal: the word has exactly the same meaning at all times. For example, the word 'boy' or 'girl'.

Verification principle: the belief that statements are only meaningful if they can be verified by the senses. There are strong and weak forms of the principle generally associated with the Vienna Circle and A.J. Ayer (1910–89) respectively.

Vienna Circle: the group of philosophers including Schlick (1882–1936) and Neurath (1882–1945) who gave rise to the logical positivist movement.

Virtue: a positive characteristic that suggests moral excellence or goodness.

Whistleblowing: revealing to the public some sort of corruption or wrongdoing in business.

Index